BERTRAM GROSVENOR GOODHUE

Special thanks go to Skidmore, Owings & Merrill, whose generous grant helped make possible the publication of this book.

American Monograph Series

Editor: Robert A.M. Stern

Bertram Grosvenor Goodhue, Richard Oliver. 1983
The Almighty Wall, The Architecture of Henry Vaughan,
William Morgan. 1983

Bertram Grosvenor Goodhue, ca. 1923

BERTRAM GROSVENOR GOODHUE

Richard Oliver

THE ARCHITECTURAL HISTORY FOUNDATION
NEW YORK

THE MIT PRESS, CAMBRIDGE, MASSACHUSETTS
and LONDON, ENGLAND

Library of Congress Cataloging in Publication Data
Oliver, Richard, 1942–
    Bertram Grosvenor Goodhue.
    (American monograph series)
    1. Goodhue, Bertram Grosvenor, 1869–1924.
2. Architects—United States—Biography.
I. Title.   II. Series: American monograph series
(Architectural History Foundation, New York, N.Y.)
NA737.G604   1982   720'.92'4   [B]   83–8927
ISBN 0–262–15024–7   AACR2

Richard Oliver is an architect, teacher, and author, who practices in
New York City.

Designed by Gilbert Etheredge

CONTENTS

To my parents, Arlene and Ernie

ACKNOWLEDGMENTS

My first and fundamental debt is to the distinguished San Diego architect Frank L. Hope. In the spring of 1960, Mr. Hope, together with his sons, Frank, Jr., and Charles, undertook to provide a scholarship that ensured my education in architecture at his alma mater, the University of California at Berkeley. Mr. Hope's generosity came at a critical moment in my life, and it is a pleasure to express my gratitude once again, all these years later.

The initial research into Bertram Goodhue's career was made possible by the Arnold W. Brunner Scholarship given in 1977 by the New York Chapter of the American Institute of Architects. The two chairmen of the Brunner committee with whom I worked—Der Scutt and Bartholomew Voorsanger—helped in many ways. The first results of that research came in the form of an article that appeared in *The Architectural Record* in September 1978 due to the enthusiastic support of its editor, Walter Wagner, and its then associate editor, Gerald Allen.

This book could not have been possible without the help of Bertram Goodhue's family. His son, Hugh Grosvenor Bryant Goodhue, and his daughter, Frances Goodhue Satterlee, shared their knowledge of their father. Hugh Goodhue allowed me to quote from a large body of his father's correspondence, and he subsequently gave these papers to Avery Library at Columbia University, where they joined a growing repository of Goodhue documents and drawings. I am especially grateful to Mr. Goodhue for this, and for the many pleasant occasions I have spent with him and his wife, Fanny, during the preparation of this work. John Rivers, Bertram Goodhue's great-grandson and the caretaker of many of his extant drawings, allowed me to reproduce a number of them. While I was reading the Goodhue papers in Pasadena, California, I was able to reside at the Gamble House, thanks to its curator, Randall Makinson.

The preparation of this book was facilitated by the incomparable resources of Avery Library. I am grateful for the generous assistance provided by the librarians, Adolf K. Placzek, Charling Fagan, and Angela Giral, and by the curator of drawings, Janet Parks. Special thanks are also offered to the librarians and/or staffs of the many other institutions whose archives were such important resources. It is not possible to list all these people, but the institutions they serve are cited throughout the notes and sources of illustrations of this book.

An invitation from Cecil Steward and Thomas Laging of the University of Nebraska at Lincoln to give a design studio related to Goodhue's Capitol provided a special opportunity to refine the manuscript. Gerald Allen, Moira Duggan, Hugh Hardy, and Steven Semes read drafts of the manuscript during various stages of its revision, and offered many suggestions for its improvement. In addition to doing the same, Frances Halsband and Robert Kliment offered a special incentive during the preparation of the first draft. Other individuals, including Diana Balmori, Thomas Hines, Richard Longstreth, Stefanos Polyzoides, Helen Searing, Gavin Stamp, and Douglass Shand Tucci, generously discussed their own research into late-nineteenth- and early-twentieth-century architectural theory and practice. Robert A. M. Stern offered advice and support in the early stages of this project. As the book's general editor, he continued to be a source of astute and stimulating criticism.

I am also indebted to The Henry L. Meltzer Group for generously providing access to the electronic word processor on which the manuscript was written and revised.

Finally, I am grateful to Stephen Gooch for his frequent and much appreciated encouragement during the long period of preparation.

FOREWORD

Richard Oliver's *Bertram Grosvenor Goodhue* inaugurates the Architectural History Foundation's biographical monographs on American architecture, a series of books intended as serious introductions to the subject that will meet the needs of architects, historians, and interested laymen alike.

The series will introduce Americans who worked in the late nineteenth and early twentieth centuries and who defy the established categories of traditional history. Each title in the series will provide a brief, scholarly essay on an architect—or in some cases several architects working within a similar mode—for whom no biography exists. Each volume will be richly illustrated and will include a serious analysis of essential aspects of the *oeuvre* and career within the context of both the architect's time and our own.

While the compact format inevitably requires some selecting—not every building by a given architect can be discussed in full nor every aspect of a subject's career be analyzed in depth—it is our expectation that the series will provide historians and architects with a vivid impression of the architects and their work. In this respect, our inaugural volume goes far. Its author, Richard Oliver, a practicing architect and teacher as well as a productive scholar, has delved deeply into the career of a highly complex architect, Bertram Grosvenor Goodhue, whose synthesis of modern and traditional forms and building techniques has particular relevance to current directions in architectural theory and practice.

Perhaps more than at any time since his death in 1924, the example of Goodhue's work and his refusal to adhere to any rigid dogma find a sympathetic audience among contemporary architects who struggle to recapture his confident handling of mass, his sure sense of detail realized through craft, and his faith in the capacity of the past to enrich the present.

This volume and its immediate successors—*The Almighty Wall, the Architecture of Henry Vaughan*, by William Morgan, and *On the*

Edge of the World, Four Architects in San Francisco at the Turn of the Century, by Richard Longstreth—provide provocative new ideas on the relationship between architectural invention, or the creative use of existing forms, and architectural innovation, the discovery of entirely new forms. These and future volumes in the series challenge accepted definitions of "modern architecture" as a style and ideology and encourage reconsideration of the very nature of twentieth-century architecture.

Robert A. M. Stern

BERTRAM GROSVENOR GOODHUE

CHAPTER ONE · A CONNECTICUT YANKEE

ERTRAM Grosvenor Goodhue was born on April 28, 1869, in the ancestral home of the Grosvenors in Pomfret, Windham County, Connecticut. The date is recorded in the *History and Genealogy of the Goodhue Family*[1] and on a family tree chronicling nine generations which Goodhue prepared as a gift for his two children in the years after his mother's death in 1907.[2] His father, Charles Wells Goodhue (1835–1891), born in Brattleboro, Vermont, married a widow, Mrs. Elizabeth Eldredge Larned, in 1857, and to that union one son, Wells (1859–?), was born. After the death of his wife, Charles married her cousin, Helen Grosvenor Eldredge (1838–1907). To this second marriage four sons were born: Bertram Grosvenor (1869–1924); Henry Eldredge (1873–1918), who worked as a stained-glass designer and manufacturer; Edward Eldredge (1875–?), who was a career officer in the United States Navy; and Donald Mumford (1876), who died at the age of four months.[3]

The Goodhues descended from William Goodhue, who was born in England in 1612 and emigrated to America in 1635, where he established the beginnings of a sizable estate. In the late eighteenth century, the family moved from Ipswich to Brattleboro, Vermont, where successive generations were prominent businessmen. However, Charles Wells Goodhue seems to have done little to sustain his share of the Goodhue inheritance, because when he married Helen Grosvenor Eldredge, he chose to move into her family's house at Pomfret, where he subsequently lived the life of a somewhat impoverished country gentleman.[4]

The Grosvenors descended from John Grosvenor, who was born in England in 1640, and who emigrated to Massachusetts in 1680. Grosvenor was one of twelve grantees who were given joint title to 15,100 acres of wilderness land in the Wabbaquasset Country in the Connecticut Colony. This land was transformed into the Township of Pomfret in 1686. After resolving problems with the title, Grosvenor's land was settled by his widow, Esther, in 1700. For the next two hundred years, the Grosvenors devoted themselves to their land and to town and county politics.[5]

The most distinguished member of the family was Colonel Thomas Grosvenor (1744–1825), Goodhue's great-grandfather, who served in the Revolutionary War as a lieutenant in the First Regiment Connecticut Line. He was immortalized in Trumbull's heroic battle painting which hangs in the Bunker Hill monument at Charleston, Massachusetts, and was elected a founding member of the Society of the Cincinnati.[6]

Bertram Goodhue took pride in his ancestors. The solid reputation of the Goodhues and Grosvenors, their long presence in New England, and their Anglo-American heritage all helped to shape his sense of himself. He was proud that he had five ancestors among the Mayflower party and six who had served in the Revolutionary War. He was by birth and by inclination a Connecticut Yankee, with a fierce sense of the honor, pride, and rectitude that went with his heritage.

Goodhue received little formal education. In his early years, he was tutored at home. The world of music was opened to him by his father, who sang every evening to his wife's accompaniment on the piano.[7] This early exposure to music played an important role in Goodhue's life because he came to regard music and architecture as the two greatest arts. He felt the formal constructions of music and architecture were essentially abstract, embodying human acts of pure creation; in contrast, he felt that the constructions of painting, sculpture, and literature were, perforce, an imitation of the structures found in Nature.[8]

Goodhue was introduced to history and to the visual arts by his mother. Helen Grosvenor Goodhue, an imposing and cultivated woman, was educated at the Emma Willard School at Troy, New York, and there she pursued an innovative and intellectual curriculum that introduced her to the major ideas of the time.[9] Helen Goodhue and her elder brother, Edward Eldredge, showed an interest in artistic matters that was not generally shared by other family members. She would sketch in a room in the attic of the house at Pomfret which she called her studio. At the opposite end of the attic, Goodhue arranged a room of his own when he was about ten years old. "I can see it now," recalled his brother Edward, "with the windows painted to represent stained glass and articles that [Bertram] considered artistic."[10] In his studio, Goodhue created a world of his own, fueled by an artistic vision that developed early. The cultivation of this vision usually has been attributed solely to his mother, and while it is certain that she was influential, there were other adults whom he admired. One was Frances Harriet Eldredge (1830–1899)— his beloved Aunt Hattie, a spinster sister of Helen Goodhue's who lived with the family at Pomfret.[11] An aunt and uncle, Mary Ann and Edward Eldredge, had been born in Bahia, Brazil, where their father, Edward, had been a merchant, and they introduced a degree of cosmo-

2

politanism into the small country town.[12]

The family library at Pomfret was an intriguing haven for Goodhue. Although its exact contents are not known, Goodhue fondly recalled that the volumes ranged "from Harvey's *Meditations Among the Tombs* and Burton's *Anatomy of Melancholy* down, or up, to *Roderick Random* or the *Farmer's Almanac*."[13] As a child he also read the Arthurian legends and as a young man translated *The Song of Roland* from French into English.[14] He was a voracious reader from an early age. Indeed, he read widely throughout his life and in the process created an impressive library of his own.[15]

Pomfret, while nothing more than a rural village, possessed a number of spacious houses of real architectural merit designed by Howard Hoppin. These buildings, which Goodhue looked at as a child and later sketched in 1887, were characterized by their crisply delineated massing (Fig. 1).[16]

In 1880, when Goodhue was eleven, he was sent to New Haven

1. Pen and ink sketches of buildings in Pomfret, Connecticut, 1886–1887

and enrolled in Russell's Collegiate and Military Institute. Goodhue spent three years in this preparatory school, and it was a dull and uninspired time for him.[17] He was required to wear a uniform, to engage in sports and drills, and to pursue studies which failed to capture his interest. A classmate recalled him as "a rather chubby, jolly, little chap, with a round head covered with light brown or rather yellow, curly hair, who spent most of his time, when in the school room, drawing caricatures of his school mates, and fancy pictures."[18]

Although Russell's was not a very distinguished preparatory school, it is not known if this is why Goodhue returned to Pomfret in 1883. It has been presumed that he was disgusted with formal education, but it is also possible that his parents were unable to pay the tuition fees any longer. In any case, he returned to his studies in the family library, to his artistic endeavors in his studio, and to hunting, fishing, and the other attractions of country life.[19]

Goodhue described his parents as "poor but honest"; they lived in the spacious house at Pomfret in a modest style.[20] He was raised in a household that was cultivated, moderately intellectual, and genteel, but which lacked the financial resources to allow him and his brothers to pursue the natural paths open to young men of their position. There were no funds to send him to Yale, for instance, which would have been an obvious choice for a young man from an old and distinguished Connecticut family. Colonel Thomas Grosvenor, his most admired ancestor, had graduated from Yale University in 1765, and Goodhue would have wanted the same.[21] In June 1920, shortly after having been appointed architect for the proposed Sterling Memorial Library at Yale, Goodhue wrote to an old classmate from Russell's about his experiences there, which had been less than pleasant:

> Truly time does bring its revenges. You will remember that I am a Connecticuter born and also the scorn with which we were held at Russell's by the University. It is a comfort to feel that now after nearly forty years I should have this opportunity given to me. Along with the financial reward that, of course, goes with the work, they have already indicated that they are going to make me a Yale man which I take it means a letter or two after my name.[22]

Goodhue yearned for the outward signs of academic distinction and relished the idea of a degree, in part because he lacked one. Indeed, his favorite photographs of himself were those taken upon the occasion of his receiving an honorary degree from Trinity College in Hartford in 1911, in which he is robed in full academic splendor.[23]

Goodhue possessed a somewhat inconsistent attitude toward formal education. He endorsed the idea of a general education in arts and humanities, and yet he denied the need for professional academic training

4

in architecture. Although he himself was largely self-educated, he made a not inconsiderable sacrifice to provide his own children with excellent schooling.[24] Yet Goodhue disparaged professional training in an academic setting, and he heaped special opprobrium upon the Ecole des Beaux Arts, its methods, and its graduates. In response to Dean William Boring's invitation to lecture at the Columbia University School of Architecture in 1921, for example, Goodhue wrote:

> Are you quite sure that the kind of talk or rather what I would say in general conversation with them would be quite what you or the other dons of the University would approve? My creed is so certainly different from that held by any academy; I can put it in a few words here and now—that the architect, like the poet, is born, not made; that the "made" architect, no matter how correct or how scholarly, is a failure while the "born" architect is sure to have something to him even if wholly uneducated; that the best training for the born architect is in the office of someone with whose work he is sympathetic. . . .[25]

Throughout Goodhue's career, architecture schools in America stressed the methods of the Ecole des Beaux Arts in Paris, and encouraged the almost exclusive use of the classical language of architecture. Goodhue regarded classicism as rule-bound, academic, and dry, and for him architecture schools were the bastions of training in classicism. In contrast, he regarded the apprenticeship method of professional training as less inhibiting, an opinion he based on his own personal experience.[26]

In 1884, he left Pomfret for New York City to pursue an apprenticeship in architecture.[27] At this time, there were two acceptable routes toward becoming an architect. One was the time-honored apprenticeship method popular in England and America, in which one worked and studied in the office of a great or at least a well-established man. A more modern and increasingly popular path in 1884 was to spend a period of years after completing college at the Ecole des Beaux Arts in Paris. There a student would join an *atelier* and follow a course of studies, taking the great buildings of the past as models. Design was a rational process expressed in the plans, sections, and elevations of a building. The student would be exposed to the architectural achievements of Paris, the most cosmopolitan city in the world at that time, and to those of other European capitals as well. For an American it was an opportunity to refine one's character and insights as well as one's architectural abilities.[28]

By no means all of the eminent American architects at this time received formal training in Paris—Stanford White among others did not—and in any case, a period of time in a good office was still considered important to one's training. Whatever Goodhue's true feelings about academic education may have been, apprenticeship was the only avenue

5

open to him because of his financial situation, a fact that placed him at a psychological disadvantage later in his life. During his career, architects in New York City comprised a society of graduates of the Ecole des Beaux Arts. That Goodhue did not belong to this circle reinforced his feelings of being an outsider.[29]

Goodhue applied for work in 1884 at the office of Renwick, Aspinwall & Russell and was hired. The firm was still run by James Renwick, Jr., by then an aged and venerable man. Renwick was an inspiring teacher of the apprentices in his office and took a keen interest in this educational aspect of his practice. He was, by nature, experimental, alert to the artistic fashions of his time, well traveled, and self-trained. His office was a congenial place for the fifteen-year-old Goodhue to begin work.[30]

Goodhue probably chose to apprentice with James Renwick out of sympathy and admiration for the architect's work, but it is also possible that the choice was merely lucky. Someone, very likely General W. H. Russell of New Haven, sent a letter of introduction to Renwick, Aspinwall & Russell. A letter of reply, addressed only to "my dear Billie" and signed by W. H. Russell, a partner in the firm (*not* General Russell), discusses the terms of Goodhue's employment and gives a picture of the young man's bleak financial condition:

> I received your note about Goodhue and, talking the matter over with Aspinwall we decided to give him $5.00 a month. He is a very nice boy and does very well for one who has been so short a time in an office; but we do not want to pay him more salary as the other boys would think we had not treated them well—it is not our custom to pay anything to pupils, and in many offices it is the custom to charge them . . . [but] if you consider him really in want I will be glad to help him personally.[31]

Goodhue's first position at Renwick's office was that of office boy, "not a very distinguished job to hold," he later recalled, "but I held it for two years when I first came to New York and made a better one it seems to me than any I have been able to get hold of since."[32] In such a position he would have been responsible for keeping track of drawings in the office, refiling them as necessary, and doing miscellaneous errands. Through close contact with drawings, an alert beginner could pick up a sense of architectural form and detail more or less by osmosis. He later worked at a drafting board tracing the drawings of the older members of the staff. Before the development of mechanical reproduction techniques, this task was often essential to a job as well as instructive to the beginner. After becoming familiar with the work of the office and the style of drafting, Goodhue was allowed to work more independently, for instance on minor aspects of a church, such as ornament or chancel furniture, or drawing

6

perspectives of proposed buildings.[33]

The office was a place to work and to learn. To supplement his training and to provide a more creative outlet for his energies, Goodhue sketched in the evening at his apartment—a hall bedroom at 112 Madison Avenue—and joined the Sketch Club. Charles H. Whitaker noted in retrospect that Goodhue "became a very popular member, although he was said to be 'very fond of having his own way' in an argument. He was known as one who seldom agreed with the other fellow, taking as a matter of habit as well as principle the opposite side of a discussion."[34] At its best, his outspokenness seemed a commitment to principles and ideals, and for this he was admired. At its worst, it made him appear arrogant, petulant, and uncompromising, and suggested that his manner masked a darker and more problematic personality. This outspokenness seems never to have softened with age, and during his career it occasionally created difficulties between himself and his clients.

2.   *Sketches of a house and lodge for the coast of Oregon, 1887*

Goodhue became renowned as an accomplished delineator. At a young age he was adept at arranging for the publication of his designs to promote his ideas, a talent that would prove invaluable to him in his later career. Several of his early sketches and designs were published in the magazine *Building*,[35] one of which was for a house and lodge on the Oregon seacoast (Fig. 2). The sketch was probably prepared for a local competition, one of several sponsored both by the Sketch Club in New York and the T-Square Club in Philadelphia; it shows a large, three-story gabled house with symmetrically placed semicircular bays protruding to the front, sheltering a three-arched entrance porch. The heavily rusticated yet simple masses pile up to a central cluster of chimneys, and the overall effect is not unlike buildings designed by Henry Hobson Richardson, which Goodhue would have seen in magazines.

An architectural competition was a means by which an architect, even a very young one, could obtain often sizable work. The first of

3. *Ralph Adams Cram's competitive design for the Cathedral of Saint John the Divine, New York City, 1889*

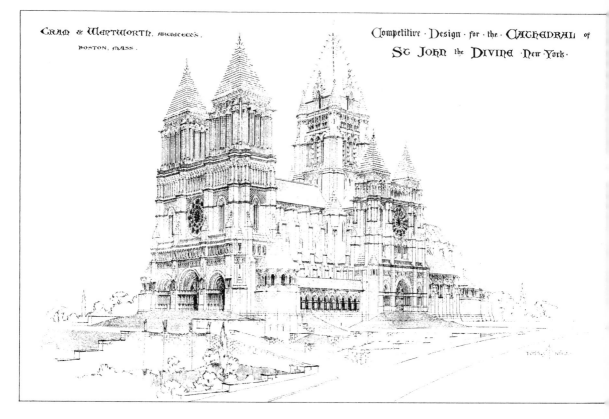

several important competitions which Goodhue entered during his career was for the Cathedral of Saint John the Divine in New York City. The competition, held in 1889 when Goodhue was only twenty, called for the design of a cathedral for the New York diocese of the Protestant Episcopal Church, on a site high above the city atop Morningside Heights. Nearly one hundred entries were received in the first stage of the competition.[36] Almost all of them reflected two major trends in American architecture at the close of the 1880s. One was the influence of Henry Hobson Richardson's Romanesque style, particularly Trinity Church in Boston; the other was what Henry-Russell Hitchcock has called the Academic Reaction against Richardson's free conceptions in favor of a more academic, "correct," historicizing design. The Academic Reaction was not necessarily synonymous with a revival of classicism, as is usually implied. On the contrary, architects felt free to use a variety of sources including

4. Bertram Grosvenor Goodhue's competitive design for the Cathedral of Saint John the Divine, New York City, 1889

9

Gothic with its myriad of spiritual and structural evocations.[37]

The mechanics of the competition were badly managed, and it was sharply criticized in the architectural press.[38] Finally, the cathedral trustees selected four schemes to be developed further. After long delay, these were received in 1891. Three were inspired by English Gothic; the winning scheme by Heins & LaFarge was not. Its plan suggested domed Byzantine spaces rather than vaulted Gothic; its crossing tower was strongly influenced by Richardson's Trinity Church; and its massing was robust and free of the strict neo-Gothicism advocated by the English Oxford Movement.[39]

Two other schemes submitted in the first stage, although not premiated, are of interest nonetheless: one by Goodhue, the other by Cram & Wentworth.[40] The designs provide a look at the work of Goodhue and Ralph Adams Cram just before their partnership was established, and suggest that they had strong, complementary talents. Cram's design is calm, ordered, and shows the influence of Richardson, especially his most academic project, the 1882 competition design for the Episcopal cathedral at Albany, New York (Fig. 3). Goodhue's design is centered on a large, cubical volume that is like a castle keep (Fig. 4). The crossing is under a bulbous dome, and the nave is a simple gabled volume with two large bays. The small-scale ancillary parish buildings cower in the shadow of the grandly scaled main body of the church and are abruptly connected by an arcade. Although awkward, Goodhue's design is imaginative in its conception and free in its attitude toward style; it is thus different from and at the same time complementary to the design by Cram & Wentworth. Cram's design is disciplined and ordered, while Goodhue's is impetuous and experimental. To a great extent, each scheme was a mirror of its designer.

As Goodhue came of age in 1890, he was already a complicated man. He was characterized by the strengths and weaknesses of his childhood, nourished by the same confidence and haunted by the same fears that marked his youth. In his years in Renwick's office his natural sense of steely independence and self-reliance had been reaffirmed, and yet his lack of European professional training made him an awed, reticent, and defensive outsider among his peers. He was devoted to architectural principles but skeptical of binding stylistic rules. If his upbringing had liberated his fertile mind to range widely and freely in the humanities, it had also constrained him with fears about the financial security of his existence and doubts about the true value of his talent, which troubled him his whole life. Even after he began to enjoy the financial rewards of a successful career, he worried about money matters and seemed to view each new commission as yet another instance of keeping the wolf from the door. As he developed a distinctive personal style in his maturity, he nonetheless remained a taciturn leader of his profession. The idealistic

view of the world opened up to him in his childhood by Helen Goodhue
and Hattie Eldredge was tempered by the practical problems of pursuing
a career in architecture, leaving him both a romantic and a pragmatic
man. The high-strung Goodhue was neurasthenic, a condition characterized by fatigue, anxiety, worry, and even localized body pains.[41] As a
result, Goodhue experienced conflicts that caused him to oscillate between periods of elation and periods of depression, alternately magnani-
mous and mean, madcap and morose, sympathetic and supercilious, cau-
tious and yet susceptible to his reckless will. In an appreciation after
Goodhue's death, his close friend Donn Barber recalled the "defensive
sharpness in his manner and speech," but noted that "underneath his
seeming severity he was sensitive, gentle, and . . . blessed with a sense
of humor."[42] In themselves, these traits are not unusual, but with Goodhue's impulsive and ebullient personality, these contradictions and oscil-
lations made him a mercurial yet engagingly attractive individual.

In 1891, Goodhue won a competition for the Cathedral of St.
Matthew to be built in Dallas, Texas. This victory signaled the moment
to conclude his apprenticeship in Renwick's office. Goodhue realized
early in his life that he wanted to be an architect, and the Texas commission provided the opportunity to establish his own practice and to begin
in earnest. Yet his strong and striving ambition was tempered by detours.
His abundant talents as a delineator had provided a means to sharpen
his architectural ideas, but they also allowed him to explore an auxiliary
career as a designer of books and typography. Seeking a challenging and
congenial milieu, Goodhue left New York for Boston, where he found an
atmosphere that nourished the two distinct but complementary directions
of his career and satisfied the intellectual as well as artistic dimensions of
his life.

CHAPTER TWO · EARLY WORKS

I N May 1891, Goodhue traveled to Boston to confer with Ralph Adams Cram and Charles Francis Wentworth about associating with them to carry out the commission for the Cathedral of St. Matthew in Dallas. It is not known why he regarded an association with them as a desirable arrangement, but as a result of their meeting, Cram & Wentworth apparently offered Goodhue a partnership in their firm. However, this offer had to be postponed when their own projects became delayed. Cram & Wentworth wrote to Goodhue in June 1891, proposing an interim arrangement:

> You shall have as much room in our three rooms as you want. You shall use our men as much as you like and in return shall give us as much of your time at the rate of $25 per week as will pay for the time our men give you at the rates we pay them. Room rent we will throw in. Of course, you would have your name on the door of the third room, and would realize all your commissions on whatever you did.
>
> We only suggest this as a temporary arrangement and simply because we want to keep hold of you. . . . We write frankly in the matter, for we feel that we ought to be able to work together, and as we said before, do not want to lose you under any circumstances. . . .
>
> Very truly,
> [signed Cram & Wentworth][1]

It has usually been thought that Goodhue began his association with Cram & Wentworth as the firm's chief draftsman, but this letter suggests that the three men regarded each other as equals. This was fitting inasmuch as Goodhue was bringing with him a potentially lucrative commission as well as his proven talents as a delineator. The letter also suggests that Goodhue was concerned with his professional image—his name on the door—from the beginning of his career. He undoubtedly

12

suspected that he would never receive credit for his artistic achievements by remaining an anonymous member of a firm. By nature competitive and individualistic, these traits surely affected his relationship with Cram. Goodhue seemed to sense that Cram was at once a colleague and a rival.

Goodhue appears to have been satisfied with the proposal, and in the fall of 1891, he moved to Boston. The relationship of the three men proved to be rewarding, and, as a result, the firm of Cram, Wentworth & Goodhue was established on January 1, 1892.[2] In 1897, Charles Wentworth died. Frank William Ferguson, an employee with engineering capabilities, was taken on as a partner, and the firm was changed to Cram, Goodhue & Ferguson on January 1, 1898.[3]

Ralph Adams Cram was born on December 16, 1863, at Hampton Falls, New Hampshire.[4] Five years older than Goodhue, he was the eldest child of William Augustine Cram, a Unitarian minister, and Sarah Elizabeth Blake. He turned to architecture after first considering a career as an artist, for which, he was advised, he was ill-suited. From 1881 to 1886, he worked for the firm of Rotch & Tilden. For the next four years he pursued an assortment of jobs: he was an art critic for the *Boston Evening Transcript;* he wrote a series of articles on home decoration for *The Decorator and Furnisher;* he designed wallpapers for George K. Birge of Buffalo, New York; and he took on private interior-design commissions. Cram traveled to Europe in 1886 and in 1887. During the second trip, he attended Christmas Eve mass in Rome and, overcome by the mysterious and splendid ritual, was struck by a vision of Roman Catholic tradition with its social, cultural, and architectural implications. He did not become a Roman Catholic but he did reject his Unitarian upbringing for the Anglo-Catholic or Oxford Movement, notably its revival of certain Roman Catholic doctrines, and rituals held within Gothic-style churches.

In 1889, Cram formed a partnership with Charles Wentworth. The firm's first commissions were small residential remodeling jobs. Wentworth married a woman of some means and social connections who helped the firm to secure commissions. For example, she introduced her husband and Cram to Edward Gale and James Ide, brothers-in-law who commissioned substantial summer residences in Williamstown, Massachusetts. The designs for these first houses are competent but unexceptional, and reflect ideas developed by other architects five to ten years earlier.[5]

The firm also looked for other kinds of commissions. Churches seemed natural because of Cram's newly kindled enthusiasm for Anglo-Catholicism. With no actual church commissions on the horizon, the firm prepared designs for hypothetical projects. One such design for a "Berkshire County Church," published in *American Architect and Building News,* shows a modest, attractive building composed of clearly articulated stone volumes based on a careful study of English precedents (Fig.

13

5. *A Berkshire church by Cram and Wentworth, 1890*

5).[6] Cram and Wentworth also hoped to secure work through competition. In 1890 they submitted an awkward and unsuccessful entry for the Church of the Messiah at Boston.[7] These two designs show that Cram & Wentworth's early work, like that of many young firms, was speculative and of uneven quality—sometimes promising and sometimes disappointing.

In the late summer of 1891, Cram & Wentworth began work on their first important ecclesiastical commission, All Saints', Ashmont, in suburban Boston; the plans were completed before the end of the year.[8] In the fall of 1891, Goodhue arrived in the office bringing with him the commission for the Dallas cathedral. The designs for these two churches formed the basis for several subsequent designs produced by the firm in the 1890s and later, and provided Cram and Goodhue with their first opportunity to collaborate.

The plan of All Saints' is linear, without transepts, composed of a west tower with vestibule, a six-bay nave, a two-bay chancel, and a one-bay sanctuary joined along a central axis. Flanking the nave are low, narrow aisles with large clerestory windows above. The nave is finished in plain, buff-colored plaster with stone columns and moldings, and roofed with a wood-trussed ceiling. The repetitive elements of the nave

14

frame the perspective view toward the chancel, marked at its portal by a polychromed rood beam, and decorated with carved oak choir stalls, a stenciled ceiling, and stained glass. The altar with its myriad accessories is sheltered by a noble reredos of Caen stone (Figs. 6–8). The massing of All Saints', Ashmont, clearly expresses the plan which itself reflects the relationships of space and of the participants in the liturgy. The massing is articulated into tower, nave, aisle, and chancel, all constructed of craggy, brown, seam-faced granite.[9]

All Saints' was intended to embody the qualities of an ideal church. Cram outlined four such qualities in his 1901 book, *Church Building*, for which Goodhue prepared the drawings. The first quality called for the

6. *Perspective of All Saints' Church, Ashmont, Massachusetts, as proposed by Cram, Wentworth & Goodhue, 1891*

15

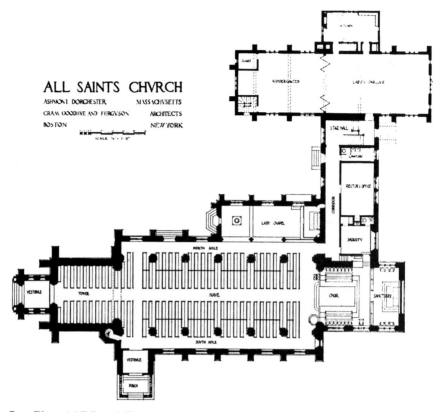

7. *Plan of All Saints' Church, Ashmont, Massachusetts,
as completed by Cram, Goodhue & Ferguson*

structure, furnishings, and accessories of a church to contribute to an all-encompassing mood, to create a "visible type of heaven." The second called for an architectural distinction between the nave and chancel, typically to be achieved by the use of more refined forms, more expensive materials, and more elaborate ornament in the chancel—particularly about the altar—in contrast to simpler treatment of the nave. The third quality called for art and symbolism to present the vast lore of Christian history, "to lift man's mind from secular things to spiritual." The fourth quality called for a nave "where a congregation may conveniently listen to the instruction of its spiritual leaders," and where every worshiper could see both the preacher and the altar.[10]

These four qualities of an ideal church create what essentially is processional architecture, dependent upon both the composition of the plan and the perceptual clarity with which the plan is expressed in space, structure, and ornament. These two vital aspects of a building are present

8.   *All Saints' Church, Ashmont, Massachusetts, looking toward the chancel*

in much of the firm's early work, especially All Saints', Ashmont.[11] In it, Cram and Goodhue created what has been described by Douglass Shand Tucci, the leading Cram scholar, as "an art where all the parts of the church's fabric worked together, organically, inconspicuously, for the larger liturgical environment it was the function of a Christian art to create."[12]

The strength of the church's design lies in its connection to the formal and philosophical intentions of the English Gothic Revival, especially the churches designed a half century earlier by A.W.N. Pugin. The typical features of a Puginian church—an asymmetrical tower, a south porch, low aisles, a deeply projecting chancel, a Sanctus bell housed in a belfry on the east gable of the nave—appear in All Saints', Ashmont. The church also reflects the admiration Cram and Goodhue felt for the buildings of John Dando Sedding, such as the Holy Trinity Church in London, and those of Henry Vaughan, especially the Perpendicular Gothic chapel at St. Paul's School in Concord, New Hampshire. Like Pugin and other subsequent Gothic Revival architects, Cram and Goodhue aspired to design buildings which began with an articulate and functional plan yielding vigorously composed, scenographic masses enriched throughout by a program of expressive liturgical symbolism and built with a craftsman's attitude to construction.[13]

This is not to say that Cram and Goodhue attempted to replicate existing churches. Formally, they eschewed the excessive spiky qualities of a Puginian church in favor of a simpler, more integrated vision of the whole, dependent upon the sculptural strength of the masses and the rugged texture of the surfaces. And ideologically, as Cram explained in a retrospective article written for *The Churchman* in 1899,

> . . . the governing idea was to build in accordance with the eternal principles of Christian and Anglican architecture as they had come to be at the highest point of their development in the fifteenth century, disregarding the details, the temporary characteristics of the time, and substituting something in their place that should be modern, local, consistent. . . . We have simply tried to preserve the spirit of the past, not its forms.[14]

In the same article, he also renounced those architectural styles the firm would not espouse:

> . . . there hardly seemed the possibility of any question as to the architectural style. Romanesque was at once ruled out as affected and artificial, while possessing no conceivable kinship either with the history or temper of the American people and the nature of the nineteenth century, or with that portion of the Catholic Church that was in question . . . the classical styles, pagan in their origin, Roman in their modern associations, were quite out of the question.[15]

18

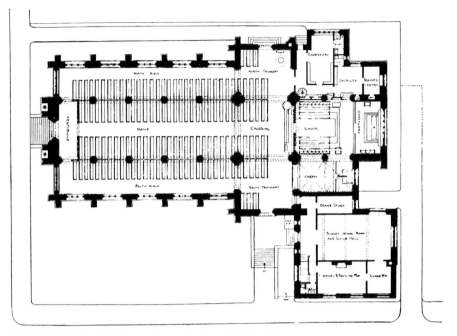

9.   Plan of the Cathedral of Saint Matthew, Dallas, Texas,
by Cram, Wentworth & Goodhue, 1892

10.   *Perspective of the Cathedral of Saint Matthew,
Dallas, Texas, by Cram, Wentworth & Goodhue, 1892*

Cram advocated a return to the pre-Reformation church architecture of fifteenth-century England. In his view, that was the last English style to embody the ritualistic Christian worship he favored. Although Cram undoubtedly believed this, his statement is unusually doctrinaire, and it implied a new propriety in the use of historical styles and a greater fidelity to their traditional models: he preferred the firm to use an appropriate style for each commission, and the one he felt was best for an Episcopal church was English Gothic.

While All Saints' was being designed, work on the Cathedral of Saint Matthew progressed, and by February 1892 plans and specifica-

11. Perspective of Cram, Wentworth & Goodhue's competitive design for the proposed City Hall, New York City, 1893

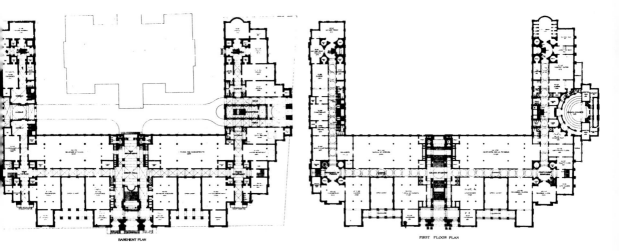

12. *Plans of Cram, Wentworth & Goodhue's competitive design
for the proposed City Hall, New York City, 1893*

tions had been completed and sent to Dallas (Figs. 9, 10).[16] Although
the cathedral was never constructed, it did offer the firm the opportunity
to design a larger church. These first two commissions represented two
different types which the firm used frequently: All Saints' was linear in
plan and massing with a west tower, and Saint Matthew's was cruciform
in plan and massing with a crossing tower. All Saints', Ashmont, provided a model that was the basis for several later churches: the First
Congregational Church, Plymouth, Massachusetts (1894); All Saints'
Church, Brookline, Massachusetts (1895); Christ Church, Waltham,
Massachusetts (1896); First Parish Meeting House, Cambridge, Massachusetts (1898); Saint Stephen's Church, Cohasset, Massachusetts
(1899); Christ Church, West Haven, Connecticut (1908); and Saint
Mark's Church, Mount Kisco, New York (1909–1920; Fig. 49). The
Cathedral of Saint Matthew provided a second model on which several
subsequent churches were based: Saint Andrew's, Detroit, Michigan
(1894); Saint Paul's Church, Rochester, New York (1896); the Church
of Our Savior, Middleborough, Massachusetts (1898); the West Point
Cadet Chapel (1903; Fig. 35); and Saint John's Church, West Hartford, Connecticut (1907; Fig. 48).[17]

The young firm did not specialize exclusively in the design of
Episcopal or even Gothic churches.[18] Cram recalled in his autobiography

21

that, "in addition to our standard 'CG&F Gothic' we began to experiment in Colonial work, both for Protestant churches and for schools."[19]
In fact, both Cram and Goodhue were pragmatic men seeking their way
in the world. Like many of their fellow architects in the 1890s, the firm
designed various building types in many styles, including Classic, Spanish, and Tudor, with an ease that belied the doctrinaire tone of its
published philosophy.[20]

A noteworthy example of the firm's classical work is its 1893
competitive design for a proposed city hall for New York City (Figs. 11,
12).[21] In style it resembled that of John Belcher's much-praised competition design for the Victoria and Albert Museum (1891) as well as
subsequent Edwardian Baroque buildings in England, like the Colchester
Town Hall (1897–1902) by John Belcher, the War Office at Whitehall,
London (1898–1906), by William Young, and the Cardiff City Hall
(1897–1906) by Lancaster, Steward & Rickards.[22] In the U-shaped
composition, four stair halls, expressed on the exterior as square lanterns,
surmounted by domes, were joined by three long galleries. The offices
were fitted into blocks of space of varied width which paralleled the
galleries. The five-story building was expressed on the exterior as two
monumental floors atop a rusticated base. Corinthian pilasters gave a
lively rhythm to the broad wall surfaces, and profuse ornament and
statuary provided an exuberant air. A tall tower, austere in the lower
stage and encrusted at the top, reared up out of the main body of the
building. Although it is impressive as a civic gesture, compared with
Goodhue's later towers, it is placed too casually in the geometric order
of the plan. Cram and Goodhue did not rail against the actual elements
of the classical language of architecture, but only against the dull use of
them according to strict formula.

The firm also designed a series of libraries in varied styles, and
three of these were built: at Fall River, Massachusetts (1896–1899), in
a form that recalled the Renaissance-style London clubs of Charles Barry
(Fig. 13);[23] at Nashua, New Hampshire (1901), in a Tudor style (Fig.
14);[24] and at Pawtucket, Rhode Island (1898–1902), in a restrained,
austere Greek style (Figs. 15, 16).[25] An Ionic-columned porch adorns
the facade of the Pawtucket Library, which is built on a strongly cross-
axial plan centered on a square, skylighted entry and delivery hall, with
twin reading rooms on either side, book stacks at the rear, and secondary
rooms fitted into the corners of the orthogonal wings. Columns separate
the delivery hall from the reading rooms and stacks, creating an open and
cohesive spatial effect. The long, blank walls of the reading rooms are
interrupted by two groups of windows. Each window is flanked by plain
pilasters and has above it a bas-relief figure panel depicting a moment in
the great ages of Western culture: Egyptian, Greek, Latin, Hebraic,
Teutonic, and Anglo-Saxon. The panels were sculpted by Lee Lawrie

22

13. *Perspective of the Public Library, Fall River, Massachusetts,*
by Cram, Goodhue & Ferguson, 1896–1899

14. *Perspective of the Public Library, Nashua, New Hampshire, by Cram, Goodhue & Ferguson, 1901*

15. *1902 view of the Deborah Cook Sayles Public Library, Pawtucket, Rhode Island, by Cram, Goodhue & Ferguson, 1898–1902*

16. *Plan of the Deborah Cook Sayles Public Library, Pawtucket, Rhode Island, by Cram, Goodhue & Ferguson, 1898–1902*

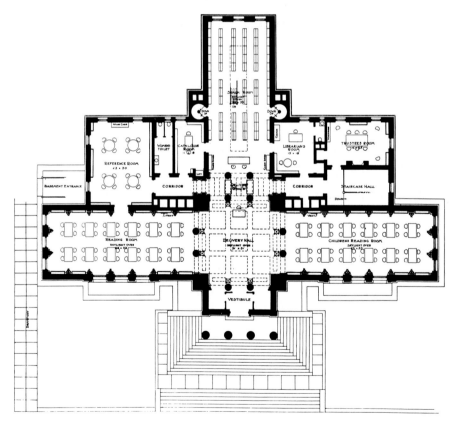

24

for what was his first commission, and the first instance of a lifelong collaboration between himself and Goodhue.

Born in 1878 in Rixdorf, Germany, Lawrie was brought to America as an infant. He began work at age fourteen in the studio of sculptor Richard Henry Park in Chicago, and subsequently worked in the studio of Augustus Saint-Gaudens in New York City. Lawrie eschewed the production of "gallery" sculpture; his work almost always was an integral part of the architecture that provided its setting. He modeled the figure sculpture for every important building designed by Goodhue, and after the latter's death emerged more clearly as an important artist in his own right, creating figure sculpture for major architectural projects across America, notably for Rockefeller Center in New York City.[26]

The firm's early Spanish-style designs were probably a result of Goodhue's keen interest in Mexican architecture. In 1892, he traveled to Mexico and upon his return wrote *Mexican Memories*.[27] In 1899, he went there again with Sylvester Baxter to measure buildings and collect impressions and data for a book. The result was Baxter's ten-volume *Spanish Colonial Architecture in Mexico*, published in 1901, for which Goodhue prepared the plan drawings and Henry Greenwood Peabody the photographic plates. As the three men roamed the countryside, they analyzed and discussed the buildings they saw. They noted "the frankly organic character of the structural work, freely confessing itself in all its functions" and "the universal concentration of ornament at a few salient points." They observed that the "portions of the building upon which, as a rule, ornament is concentrated are the facade, the towers above the roof-level, the side entrances and the dome . . . and its concentration here prevents the eye and the thoughts from wandering." The analysis that resulted from their observations amounted to a theory of architectural form:

> In structural work the main function of ornament is to enhance the interest. It justifies itself by carrying the attention from the general to the particular. It logically leads the thought from the stage in which a building first declares itself to the eye and impresses its character upon the beholder through the large effects of mass, form, outline, and proportion. It thence indicates the finer structural gradations—explanatory, elucidative, illustrating—until the function and purpose of the work has been set forth in a depictive fabric of the finest texture.[28]

Baxter and Goodhue saw in Mexican architecture an integration of craft, structure, ornament, use, and cultural purpose, and they understood that their analysis of these buildings could apply more generally to all architecture.

At first the new office did not have many architectural commissions, and so both Goodhue and Cram pursued outside literary and artistic endeavors. In Boston they were at the center of a local bohemian intelligentsia with ties to Charles Eliot Norton and Charles Herbert Moore of Harvard University. Cram recalled that it was Goodhue who seemed to be the focus of these activities "through that singular quality that drew all sorts of interesting and provocative people within the sphere of his dynamic personality."[29]

Goodhue and Cram were involved in two social groups. The first, "Pewter Mugs," was an eating and drinking group, and the second, "Visionists," consisted of about twenty people with artistic and/or literary interests.[30] Each Visionist was required to contribute a completed literary work or one prepared especially for the group. Goodhue conformed to the latter requirement: he wrote and had printed fifty copies of *The Ballad of Saint Kavin*, thirty-five stanzas of doggerel in honor of a "modern sort of saint," a "sybarite and pessimist" who when "Knowledge came to his front door" would prefer to creep "to his little attic floor where his mistress Wisdom slept." Perhaps the most revealing aspect of this amusing ballad is the way that the themes of romantic medieval literature are interwoven with the conditions and ideas of contemporary Boston.[31]

Goodhue's involvement with these two clubs, and with the Tavern Club of which he was also a member, brought him into contact with a circle of men anxious to revive the craft of fine bookmaking. Four firms were at the heart of this revival: Copeland and Day; Stone and Kimball; Small and Maynard; and the Merrymount Press. Goodhue knew the partners of all these firms, and for them he designed title pages, decorations, and initials. Goodhue's most distinguished book design is *The Altar Book of the Episcopal Church*, published in 1896 by Daniel Berkeley Updike's Merrymount Press, founded in 1893 as the American counterpart of William Morris's Kelmscott Press. In addition to the borders, initials, and cover, Goodhue designed the typeface known as Merrymount especially for this book. The Merrymount face was inspired by Morris's Golden typeface, in turn based on a late-fifteenth-century typeface designed by and called Jensen. Golden was used in an 1891 edition of *The Story of the Glittering Plain*, the first book printed by the Kelmscott Press. Over the years, Goodhue produced different elements of about twenty other books, including the famous Cheltenham typeface, designed for Ingalls Kimball, the head of the Cheltenham Press. It was first used for Cram, Goodhue & Ferguson's thesis accompanying the West Point competition drawings, and it was introduced publicly in 1904. Cheltenham was perhaps the first new typeface to be designed for setting by hand and by linotype machine. Like Merrymount, Cheltenham reflected the influence of Morris and the revival of medieval typefaces.[32] Goodhue's book designs and bookplates constituted a subsidiary career for him; it was an endeavor that he loved and abandoned reluctantly only as his architectural career assumed paramount importance at the turn of the century.[33]

Goodhue's ability at book design was used to good effect in the office. In the construction of most churches, there would be a period of time needed to raise funds, and for many of their clients the firm designed appeal booklets describing the future church in almost irresistible terms. Cram would write a stirring piece about a revitalized Christian and Gothic art, and Goodhue would prepare beautifully rendered plans and perspectives depicting the object of the fund-raising. The hand-printed booklets were at once coolly professional and passionately medieval, and the images they portrayed in word and drawing were of a contemporary church shaped at once by the traditions of the past and by the conditions of the present day.[34]

For the two young men, the 1890s were a time of impetuous revelry and earnest seeking. Perhaps nothing epitomizes this time more clearly than *The Knight-Errant*, a short-lived quarterly they produced as an opportunity to publish avant-garde essays on various topics.[35] Cram was the editor and Goodhue designed and drew the cover illustration and the decorative initials used inside (Fig. 17). The publication was patterned after the English periodical *Hobby Horse* and was intended as a model of excellent typography and book design. Both men wrote articles, as did their friends—poets like Bliss Carman, Richard Hovey, and Louise Guiney, and other acquaintances like Bernard Berenson. Cram's editorial on the purpose of the magazine evoked images from medieval literature: ". . . to assail the dragon of materialism . . . to ride for the succor of forlorn hopes and the restoration of forgotten ideals." Each man fancied himself a knight-errant—a free agent, a knight with no master—championing the cause of an art and architecture that restored the ideals and the romanticism of the medieval past.[36]

Goodhue wrote two articles for *The Knight-Errant*. A short piece in April 1892, called "A Criticism of the Methods which Obtain in Journalistic Reviewing of the Period," compares a "golden age of Art," in which no critic was necessary, with the "sordid squalor of our latter days," in which the critic plays an undeserving role as arbiter.[37]

The second article, "The Final Flowering of Age-End Art," which appeared in January 1893, lamented "the modern theory that the ideal need not enter into any art," and noted that "clever craftsmanship is everywhere accepted in lieu of idea." The essay presents one theme that recurs throughout Goodhue's career in his writings, lectures, and buildings: "a return to greater simplicity—subtler simplicity is a better term—and directness of method." This single theme meant various things to Goodhue: It implied the use of materials in a way that revealed their inherent qualities and beauty; it ruled out extraneous ornament; it railed against pretension; it endorsed a clarity of structural system in the creation of architectural space and form; and it implied a preference for hand-crafted elements and finishes in a building. By the time this article was published, Goodhue had espoused the principles of the English Arts and Crafts Movement which had infiltrated all levels of artistic and craft activity in England, and was beginning to be felt in America, especially in New England, Chicago, and California.[38]

Goodhue's connection with English theorists and practitioners was a great influence upon his career. Of chief importance was his admiration for William R. Lethaby, whom he referred to later in life as "the greatest living theorist on matters architectural," and in whose writings can be found a reinforcement of Goodhue's own intuitive feelings for architecture.[39] Although Lethaby was a practicing architect, he exerted greater influence on architects, historians, and educators through his writings and his teaching. He played an important role in the founding of the Art Workers' Guild and the Arts and Crafts Exhibition Society, two organizations which among other things supported the development of what is now known as "English Free Architecture." When the Royal College of Art was reorganized in 1900, Lethaby became the first Professor of Design.[40]

Lethaby's first book, *Architecture, Mysticism & Myth*, was published in 1891. In it, he presents his theory that architecture and symbolism are inextricably related, and sets out three "ultimate facts behind all architecture": the needs of man, the materials and methods of construction, and "the influence of the known and imagined facts of the universe on architecture, the connection between the world as a structure, and the building. . . ." This third "ultimate fact" gives a prominent place in architecture to tradition and to those symbolic forms and ornaments which explain the cultural lineage and purpose of a building, while the first two "facts" reiterate the Vitruvian prescription that all architecture has a fundamental basis in utility and in construction.[41]

Lethaby's second important book, *The Church of Sancta Sophia, Constantinople; a study of Byzantine building*, was published in 1894. In its preface, Lethaby asserted that "the necessity for finding the root of architecture once again in sound common-sense building and pleasurable craftsmanship remains as the final result of our study of Sancta Sophia." This book singlehandedly returned Byzantine architecture, with its brick constructive forms and its approach to integral ornament, to the attention of the contemporary architectural profession in England and America.[42]

In 1904, Lethaby published *Mediaeval Art, from the peace of the Church to the eve of the Renaissance, 312–1350*, which dealt with "two chief styles of mediaeval art . . . the eastward culmination, or the By-zantine school, and the western, or Gothic." In the book's introduction, Lethaby proclaimed that

28

A·QVARTER·YEARLY
REVIEW·OF·THE·LIB-
ERAL·ARTS·CALLED
THE·KNIGHT·ERRANT
BEING·A·MAGAZINE
OF·APPRECIATION

PRINTED·FOR·THE·PROPRIE-
TORS·AT·THE·ELZEVIR·PRESS
BOSTON··A·D·MDCCCXCII···

VOLVME·FIRST·   NVMBER·ONE·

17.   *Drawing for the cover of* The Knight-Errant, *1892*

the long and eventful period, the thousand years from A.D. 300 to 1300, from Roman to Renaissance art, is yet a perfectly organic one . . . [it is] a period of free experiment between the authority of Roman architecture and the renewed interest in scholarship typical of the Renaissance.[43]

Lethaby's theories were published at the height of the Beaux Arts influence in Europe and America. Their great significance to Goodhue and his peers was that they portrayed architecture as a synthesis of common-sense construction, artistic craftsmanship, and a broad romantic view of the traditions of the past.

The collaboration between Cram and Goodhue, like that between other teams of talented architects, was a complex matter. In presenting the designs and ideology of the firm's work to the public, the role of each man is relatively clear. Cram wrote and lectured extensively in an attempt to carry his ideas to a larger public, and as a result he had a firmer and more articulate grasp than Goodhue of the theoretical structure and cultural implications of the firm's ideas.[44] Goodhue's scenographic drawings portrayed buildings which embodied these principles, giving him a more confident grasp of the firm's formal intentions. Goodhue lectured only infrequently and with great reluctance, preferring to let his ideas emerge within specific works of architecture.[45]

It is more difficult, however, to ascertain exactly what each of the partners contributed to the design of a project.[46] The more familiar description of their relationship is found in Cram's autobiography, *My Life in Architecture*, which was published in 1937, when Cram was seventy-four and Goodhue had been dead thirteen years:

> What ability I had stopped short at one very definite point. I could see any architectural problem in its mass, proportion, composition, and articulation, and visualize it in three dimensions even before I set pencil to paper. I had also the faculty of planning, and I generally blocked out all our designs at quarter-scale. There my ability ceased. I had neither the power nor the patience to work out any sort of decorative detail. At this point Bertram entered the equation, to go on without a break to the completion of the work.[47]

Cram has described a linear and compartmentalized process of design and production, which might be possible in a very large and specialized office, but which is difficult to imagine in a small office with three equal partners.[48] In Cram's description, there is the implication that Goodhue had no real grasp of the larger issues of architecture—siting, planning, and massing—and that he excelled only at the decorative aspects of a building, such as ornament and interior furnishings.[49] But there is evidence that Goodhue had an early command of all aspects of architecture in the form of a set of drawings of imaginary places which is solely attributable to him.

Between 1896 and 1899, Goodhue prepared drawings of three places which exist on no map except that of his imagination: "Traumburg" (1896), "The Villa Fosca and its Garden" (1897), and the town of "Monteventoso" (1899).[50] Accompanying each set of drawings was an essay that was part fictitious memoir, part architectural description, part polemical commentary, and part travel guide. He worked on these drawings at home, and as his cousin, Constance Alexander, recalled upon the occasion of their publication in 1914:

> . . . so many of these, too, I saw grow under your pen in the living room of 7 Buckingham Place—and I have only to shut my eyes to see the dear group, you at the desk, and the blessed aunts and the rest of us gathered about.[51]

Charming in their romanticism and sly wit, these drawings confirm Goodhue's view that architecture had to be more than picturesque design and decoration. For him, architecture had to be an organic unity of siting, planning, structure, massing, materials, color, and ornament, in which an underlying abstract order was as important as the pictorial effect, and in which a purity of style gave way to a free and vigorous eclecticism. These drawings and essays embodied ideas that Goodhue was to use later in actual buildings, and they established his commitment to three major artistic concepts in his work: the modulated integration of architecture and landscape; the belief in unpretentious vernacular forms as a primary inspiration for design; and the love of tall, exuberant towers as potent symbols, standing as markers in the landscape, giving prominence and authority to the buildings below.

"Traumburg," or "Dream Town" in German, has as its most important building the Church of Saint Kavin. Saint Kavin, of course, was Goodhue's own literary invention, and his church was likewise an imaginary commission. The church was the result of three distinct building campaigns that combined various styles: Romanesque; "Gothic of different varieties, ranging from the severest Geometrical . . . to a nondescript and very debased sort of Flamboyant"; and "Renaissance, of no recognized kind, but with enough badly proportioned classical pilasters, broken pediments and the like to be roughly ranked under this head." The plan of Saint Kavin's is composed of a three-bay nave, a square crossing with transepts, and a French choir and ambulatory leading to five small chapels (Fig. 18). There are low aisles above which are large clerestory windows, a system that is used in many of Goodhue's later churches (Fig. 19). The structural expression of the aisle arcade is unknown, but at the crossing the vertical shafts are unaccented by capitals

31

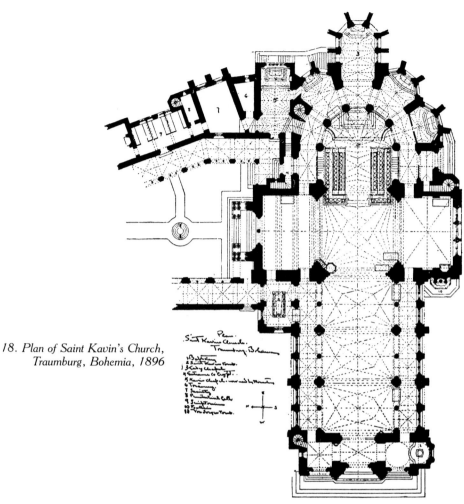

18. Plan of Saint Kavin's Church,
Traumburg, Bohemia, 1896

and flow directly into the vault ribs above. The pattern of the nave vaulting ribs is unusual and is to be found, as far as is known, only in three late-fourteenth-century north chancel aisle bays at Ely Cathedral, and in Cram, Goodhue & Ferguson's entry in the competition for the Lady Chapel of St. Patrick's Cathedral in New York in 1899.[52]

The massing of Saint Kavin's is characterized by clear structural shapes enlivened at critical points by ornament. The nave vaults are supported by massive piers which rise on the outside in stages without reliance upon flying buttresses. Goodhue described the church as built

> . . . of a very light local stone of a crystalline formation, which glistened and glowed in the sunlight like a Turner, with pinks and dove-colours, warm sienna and orange, and upon which each pro-

jection cast lovely transparent purple shadows. In the twilight,
however, it loses all these qualities and assumes in their stead a soft
gray gloom, quite as charming in its way as the brighter colouring;
while at night, the tall tower, silhouetted against the stars, seems
to tremble and waver in mysterious instability.[53]

The tower of Saint Kavin's is particularly striking for its large size in
relation to the body of the church and for the clean vertical treatment of
the shaft culminating in a richly ornate crown. In a view of the church
seen from a valley below, the august tower looms up, a stirring precursor
of Goodhue's later schemes for the chapels at West Point and at the
University of Chicago, the Baltimore cathedral, and even for the Capitol
in Lincoln, Nebraska (Fig. 20).

   "The Villa Fosca and its Garden," set upon "a forgotten islet in
the Adriatic," had escaped notice, Goodhue wrote, "in spite of the

19. Perspective of Saint Kavin's Church and the Kavinsplatz, Traumburg, Bohemia, 1896

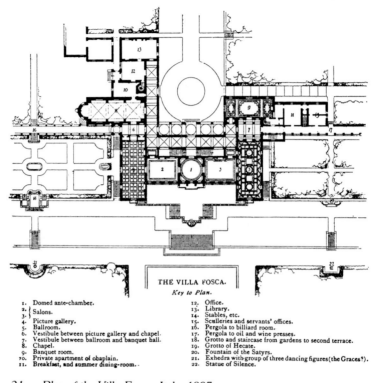

THE VILLA FOSCA.

Key to Plan.

1.	Domed ante-chamber.
2. 3.	Salons.
4.	Picture gallery.
5.	Ballroom.
6.	Vestibule between picture gallery and chapel.
7.	Vestibule between ballroom and banquet hall.
8.	Chapel.
9.	Banquet room.
10.	Private apartment of chaplain.
11.	Breakfast, and summer dining-room.
12.	Office.
13.	Library.
14.	Stables, etc.
15.	Sculleries and servants' offices.
16.	Pergola to billiard room.
17.	Pergola to oil and wine presses.
18.	Grotto and staircase from gardens to second terrace.
19.	Grotto of Hecate.
20.	Fountain of the Satyrs.
21.	Exhedra with group of three dancing figures (the Graces?).
22.	Statue of Silence.

21.   *Plan of the Villa Fosca, Italy, 1897*

hordes of Paris-prepared young prizemen who have ransacked [Italy's] every available nook and corner. . . . [It] has fallen quietly from its once high estate into a present condition of hidalgo-like decay." The essay notes that "the influence of Byzantine and Barbarian, Guelph and Ghibelline, Turk and Christian, has proved less hostile than the softer but no less sure hand of time," evoking the sense of timeworn and melancholy beauty which seemed central to Goodhue's artistic sensibilities.[54]

The plan of the Villa is centered on a dominant east-west axis: to the east is a mountainous backdrop and to the west the land falls steeply away into the sea (Fig. 21). The Villa is composed around three sides of an entry court with major rooms forming a symmetrical west garden facade facing the sea. On one side of the entry court is a five-bay, domed, columned loggia with a vaulted ceiling covered with mosaics, similar to the narthex of Saint Bartholomew's Church in New York City. The various rooms of the Villa have axially controlled vistas out onto gardens and terraces which give way to a more natural landscape effect, dotted with outbuildings, pergolas, fountains, and statuary.

The volumes of the Villa are constructed of brick covered with

22.   *Perspective of the forecourt of the Villa Fosca, Italy, 1897*

23.   *Perspective of the garden facade of the Villa Fosca, Italy, 1897*

37

24.   Perspective of the Piazza Re Umberto, Monteventoso, Italy, 1899

stucco and rendered as broad, plain surfaces relieved only by a string
course at the sill of the second-floor windows and topped with broadly
overhanging low-pitched hip roofs of tile (Fig. 22). By contrast, the
formal classical facade facing the sea was pretentious, the result, Goodhue wrote, of "the vaulting ambition of its designer, apparently some dry-
as-dust pupil of Vignola" (Fig. 23).[55] The drawings confirm Goodhue's
abilities at site planning and garden design, and suggest his later country-
house designs, especially those in California. The plan's combination of
symmetry and asymmetry characterizes many of Goodhue's secular designs, and the placement of low, solid volumes amid heavily planted
gardens forecasts the integration of architecture and landscape later achieved
at the National Academy of Sciences building and the Los Angeles
Library.

   "Monteventoso" is the fable of a town which has escaped the
vagaries of time, existing as a palimpsest with ruins dating back to the
Roman era (Figs. 24, 25). There are no buildings of architectural
distinction in Monteventoso "while about the old shadowy streets and
glittering roofs and towers is crystallized enough legendry to equip a
dozen of our States." The town is centered on the Piazza Re Umberto,
with "its musical and unmusical sounds, its clamouring people, its miser-
able bronze Umberto, and rickety iron café tables." This tale is a cele-
bration of a vernacular architecture and a small-scale urbanity dependent

38

upon strong sun and shade for effect, the sort Goodhue had admired in Mexico and later explored in the design of the company town at Tyrone, New Mexico. The architecture of Monteventoso was possessed of the dusty, worn, unsung beauty which Americans in the 1890s found so lacking at home and so appealingly abundant in Europe. One passage of the essay seems to evoke his sense of the presence of the past:

Below me in the now windless and shimmering atmosphere huddled

25. Perspective of the Church of Santa Caterina from the Public Garden, Monteventoso, Italy, 1899

the purple and red roofs of the town, the tortuous streets marked by narrow courses of liquid purple through the gold and salmon roofs and walls. From the midst of all this colour rose the campanile, clear-cut against the hazy distance, the detonation of its bells on the instant breaking the air into an invisible tempest, while its forked battlements seemed less to bring to mind "old, unhappy, far-off things, and battles long ago" than to accent the peace and stillness of today, the time and the place.[56]

These three sets of drawings and essays attest to Goodhue's independent powers of invention, but their very creation also confirms his broad and detailed knowledge of history and architecture. With such scholarly resources alone, he might have been a purely academic architect. But he was never constrained by history nor limited to academic design; on the contrary, he used his vast knowledge as the basis of imaginative works of his own.[57] Perhaps the most striking aspect of these drawings and essays is that, as embodiments of Goodhue's maverick romanticism and diligent scholarship, they established a pattern that provided direction and coherence throughout the architect's career.

The drawings of these imaginary places confirm that as early as 1896 Goodhue's architectural abilities were at least as well-developed as Cram's. The degree of order and restraint evident in them, as compared with Goodhue's 1889 scheme for the Cathedral of Saint John the Divine, also suggests that he had profited from his association with Cram. One can assume that Cram and Goodhue broadly agreed on the substance of architecture and on their firm's artistic direction. But one can easily imagine that each man, possessing a strong ego, would want to pursue a particular design in a way that the other might find objectionable. Toward the end of their partnership, it was common knowledge that the two men often did design separate schemes for the same commission. As the critic Montgomery Schuyler noted in 1911, Cram and Goodhue "have been known to submit to building committees differences of view they found irreconcilable between themselves, a procedure probably unexampled, certainly uncommercial, and as certain artistic."[58]

The drawings of imaginary places were completed before Goodhue had had much opportunity to travel. Although he had been to Mexico in 1892, the drawings described places he had never seen. In 1902, this lack of experience was in part rectified when James Waldron Gillespie, who became Goodhue's lifelong friend, commissioned him to design a house and gardens in Montecito, California, a suburb of Santa Barbara. The house, called *El Fureidis*, an Arabic term for "pleasant place," was conceived as a Mediterranean villa with white walls and red tile roofs. Gillespie took a keen interest in the design of *El Fureidis*, and especially wanted the gardens to resemble those in Persia. In order to understand

COVRT OF THE
TELEGRAPHER'S
HOVSE SHIRAZ

26.   *Perspective of the Court of the Telegrapher's House,*
Shiraz, Persia, 1902

the models he had in mind, he took his architect to see them. Riding over
four hundred miles on horseback from the Caspian Sea to the Persian
Gulf, Gillespie and Goodhue visited several Persian gardens, visiting
them by day and again in the moonlight when they took on an especially
mysterious and romantic air (Fig. 26). They traveled to Isfahan, Shiraz,
and Samarkand, and they saw the ruined gates of Persepolis adorned
with bas-relief sculptures of winged bulls. Again and again, Goodhue
recalled images seen on this journey in his designs, never more so than
toward the end of his career.[59]

27.   *Perspective of* El Fureidis, *the James Waldron Gillespie House,*
Montecito, California, by Cram, Goodhue & Ferguson, 1902

El Fureidis is composed around a central patio that is the focus of
an informal cross-axial scheme (Figs. 27–29). The principal axis con-
nects the patio and living room with a portico at the east, while it
terminates to the west in a fountain niche that shields a row of staff
rooms. The minor cross axis of the patio informally links the dining room
and a row of guest rooms to the broad southern terrace containing planted
beds and reflecting pools. The terrace is connected to generous gardens
by a long axial flight of stairs that descends a steep incline to a pavilion.
Facing this terrace is the one-story, symmetrical, south facade of the
house, columned with a bas-relief frieze depicting the Arthurian legends
sculpted by Lawrie and crowned by an entablature. The rich plasticity
of this facade, bathed in the almost constant sunshine of Southern California, creates a lively composition of light and shadow. By contrast, the
other facades of the house consist of plain stucco surfaces with only a
minimal amount of ornament around the more important openings. The
forms of the house recall those of the Villa Fosca and foreshadow the
complex eclecticism of Goodhue's mature works: a synthesis of the classical, the romantic, and the vernacular. Most of the rooms are generous
in proportion with little ornament except for the living room fireplace, the
gold-leafed "Persian" room, and the domed "Turkish" bathing room with
sunken tub.
    Upon completion of *El Fureidis* in 1903, the *Architectural Review*

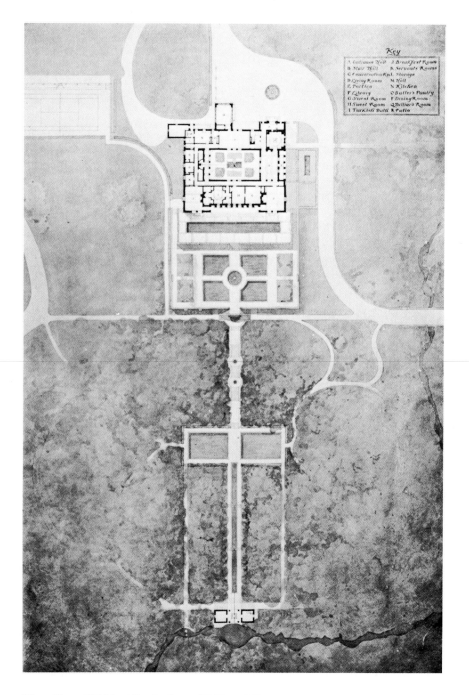

28. *Plan of* El Fureidis, *the James Waldron Gillespie House, Montecito,*
California, by Cram, Goodhue & Ferguson, 1902

29. *View of* El Fureidis, *the James Waldron Gillespie House, Montecito, California, by Cram, Goodhue & Ferguson, 1902*

asserted that "this [house] is in every way charming, simple and does not descend to the mass of accessory details so frequent in similar work."[60]

Immediately upon his return to Boston from Persia, Goodhue married Lydia Thompson Bryant (1877–1949) of Boston and Covington, Kentucky, on April 8, 1902. The daughter of James and Helen Bryant, Lydia Goodhue was an attractive companion and wife, although she was, like her husband, high-strung and impulsive. She showed great pride in her husband's endeavors, but she seems not to have had a command of the architectural ideas and ideals which formed the core of Goodhue's career.[61]

After a honeymoon trip to Spain and Tangier, Goodhue returned to Boston to complete a set of plans and perspectives for Sweet Briar College in Virginia. The will of Indiana Fletcher Williams, mistress of Sweet Briar Plantation in western Virginia, called for the establishment of a women's college on the property. The innovative curriculum combined the vocational training of western and southern schools with the intellectual pursuits of northern schools. Mrs. Williams was an Episcopalian and so were the organizers of the new college, who met in the summer of 1901. The first president, Dr. John M. McBryde, learned of Cram, Goodhue & Ferguson through an article written by Cram in the *New Churchman*. Cram was invited to Sweet Briar to look over the site and discuss the program for what would become a small town to house five hundred students, faculty, and staff. Goodhue prepared drawings of the proposed college and these were placed on exhibit in Lynchburg in the late spring of 1902.[62]

The scheme for Sweet Briar, set among rolling hills, consisted of a group of brick buildings arranged along the edges of a series of terraced gardens. The plan seems to have benefited from Goodhue's trip to Persia. His grasp of garden design and site planning contributed to this and to several subsequent commissions, including the initial plan for Rice University (1909) and the Panama-California Exposition (1911–1915). A rational order based on strong axiality and softened by picturesquely placed elements is a characteristic feature of all these designs; and it is also apparent in the firm's first really important commission—the United States Military Academy at West Point.

On June 28, 1902, $5,500,000 was appropriated by the Congress to bring about improvements to the physical plant at the United States Military Academy at West Point, New York. These included the construction of new buildings, the remodeling of existing buildings, and attention to the landscaping of the spacious, picturesque grounds overlooking the Hudson River.[63] Although there had been a fort on the site since 1779, the academic buildings date from the mid-nineteenth century (Fig. 30). The chapel (1836) was in a classical style, as was Cullam Memorial Hall (1898) by McKim, Mead & White, but the library (1841) and the cadet barracks (1851) were in a castellated Gothic by Major Richard Delafield, and they set the direction for the gymnasium (1893), academic building (1895), and guardhouse (1897), all by Richard Morris Hunt in a brusque style that has come to be called Military Gothic.[64] A report on the needs of the expanding institution prepared by Colonel Charles W. Larned, Professor of Drawing and Dean of the Faculty, was the basis of the new project of reconstruction and enlargement. He declared:

> It is not desirable that any scheme should attempt to sweep the field clean and destroy architectural associations made honorable by generations of great men, while it is of the highest importance to preserve intact the structural sentiment which gives character and individuality to the Academy. It would be a very great pity to make such an institution the subject of an architectural thesis in which the heritage of the past plays no part.[65]

45

30.   View of the Chapel (1836) and the Library (1841) of the United States
Military Academy at West Point, New York

   Nine firms accepted an invitation to compete for the commission
and eight schemes were submitted, which were reviewed by a jury composed of Lieutenant-General J. M. Schofield, Colonel A. L. Mills, and
architects George B. Post, Walter Cook, and Cass Gilbert.[66] Four of
the schemes were classical and four Gothic in style. Although invited,
McKim, Mead & White did not submit a scheme, feeling that the jury
was unduly prejudiced in favor of a Gothic solution.[67] In fact, the jury
narrowed the selection from eight to the four Gothic schemes. The critic,
Montgomery Schuyler, criticized the competition for including classicists
in an event that clearly called for some version of Gothic, but he also
noted that a publicly funded competition probably could not appear to be
so exclusive.[68]
   Of the eight schemes submitted, those by Daniel Burnham and by
Cram, Goodhue & Ferguson offered the greatest contrast. Burnham's
was the most radically idealistic as he noted in his report:

46

It . . . becomes a question whether one should adopt any compromise offering an inferior solution to the problem; and it would be a compromise to attempt to retain many of the buildings already erected, when an ideal design is plainly possible for both the practical and beautiful sides of the problem. And because this work is to be for all time, we have, after much hesitation, come to the conclusion that we should present that scheme which will ultimately bring about the noblest results.[69]

Burnham's monumental scheme was organized about a main axis connecting the river with a prominent pinnacle of land, allowing the buildings to be terraced symmetrically. It required the demolition of the Gothic buildings and even the relocation of Cullam Hall. This audacious scheme did not escape a scathing review by Schuyler, who dismissed it as a *projet* based upon "an entirely abstract and academic programme, the iridescent dream of a military academy to be erected in No-Man's-Land . . . undisturbed by the consideration of the actual problem." In Schuyler's view, Burnham's scheme had three serious flaws: It ignored the picturesque landscape; it rejected the Gothic traditions of the Academy; and it lacked a clear sense of how it could be built without suspending the educational operations of the Academy during the process.[70]

In contrast, Cram, Goodhue & Ferguson's intention was to "make the architectural style harmonize with the majority of the existing buildings"; to "prolong rather than revolutionize the spirit of the place"; to "emphasize rather than antagonize the picturesque natural surroundings"; and to be "capable of execution at the smallest cost consistent with the monumental importance of the work."[71] Organized around major east-west and north-south axes, the winning scheme integrated the existing mid-nineteenth-century buildings with several new structures, while introducing a new and monumental scale to the whole ensemble (Figs. 31, 32). A north-south axis formed the main avenue of approach and culminated at the far side of an enlarged parade field in a pair of monuments, one existing and one contemplated. An east-west axis linked the academic buildings on the plain by means of a steep set of stairs with a new observatory on top of the precipitous hill. The most monumental new building, the chapel, was located on this east-west axis. The largest building in the scheme was the riding hall at the eastern edge of the flat plateau, where the land falls away to the river, and it was designed to appear as a continuation of the rocky cliffs upon which it was placed. Schuyler was pleased with Cram, Goodhue & Ferguson's scheme and he became an ardent advocate of both the scheme and its designers:

With all its bold picturesqueness, and with its aspect of even wilful freedom and originality, one is apt to overlook what a success it is of careful and deferential conformity . . . for it does effectively

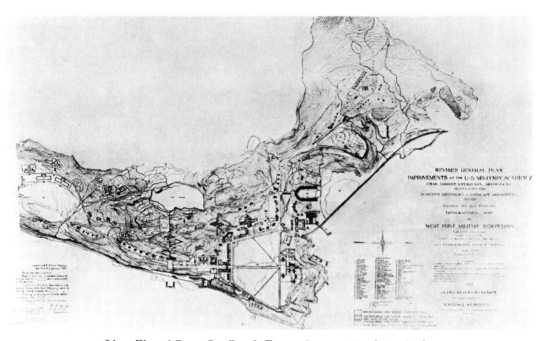

31. Plan of Cram, Goodhue & Ferguson's competitive design for the United States Military Academy at West Point, New York, 1903

mediate between the existing buildings . . . [and goes] far toward harmonizing the discrepancies.[72]

The West Point competition provides an opportunity to look at American architecture and its underlying values at the turn of the century. Burnham's scheme was a reflection of the predominant thrust in American architecture—the City Beautiful movement and the American Renaissance—which in schemes for urban centers across the continent sought not so much to reshape but to impose upon the city a grander vision.[73] In contrast, and practically alone among the important planning schemes of the turn of the century, Cram, Goodhue & Ferguson's conception for West Point created a monumental effect with a composition that embraced the idiosyncracies of the Academy's past and the more expansive demands of its future.

The Government required the firm to open a local field office to prepare the working drawings and to supervise the construction. It allowed the office to be located in New York City rather than at West Point, and Goodhue returned to New York to head the new branch of the firm. The Government also required that all working drawings for all buildings be approved before construction began on any, which led to some careless haste in their preparation.[74]

When the buildings were completed in 1910, they received great acclaim. A review in the *American Institute of Architects' Journal* stressed the importance of the site plan and noted the excellence of a few of the buildings, notably the chapel, the post headquarters, and the riding hall, but regretted the lack of thought displayed in other minor buildings.[75] Montgomery Schuyler praised the bold scale and rugged forms of the new buildings and their dramatic composition in the picturesque site:

I have spoken of Mont St. Michel as seeming to grow out of its

32.   *Perspective from the Hudson River of Cram, Goodhue & Ferguson's design for the United States Military Academy at West Point, New York, 1903*

rock, and I know of no modern structure which emulates the particular impressiveness of the fortified abbey as successfully as the new work at West Point.[76]

Winning this competition was a momentous occasion for Cram, Goodhue & Ferguson. It was a highly publicized and major commission which secured a national reputation for the firm outside ecclesiastical circles, and it bolstered the confidence of the partners in the quality of their work. But completing the commission also created changes in the structure of the firm that ultimately proved fatal to its existence. When Goodhue opened the branch office of the firm, he was very much in charge of its operation, and he began to acquire an individual identity within the architectural world of New York City. After 1903 until the dissolution of the firm in 1913, the two offices—in Boston headed by Cram and Ferguson and in New York headed by Goodhue—functioned with increasing artistic and professional independence.

CHAPTER THREE · TRADITION AND INNOVATION: ECCLESIASTICAL WORKS

T the beginning of the twentieth century, American and European architecture was seeking a new formal order, coherence, and consistency in building and planning as well as an historically accurate application of past forms. These two parallel ideas were synthesized in the work of America's leading architects, the partnership of Charles Follen McKim, William Rutherford Mead, and Stanford White.[1]

In his 1924 monograph, the English classical architect, Charles Herbert Reilly, felt the firm's great achievement was to create "for the first time an architecture of conscious eclecticism"; an architecture recognized not by a distinctive style but "by its greater breadth of treatment, its finer scale, its nobler and more reticent manner than that of its neighbors"; an architecture less personal and more appropriate to "the new scale, new requirements, and new problems in building with which America is faced."[2]

McKim, Mead & White's preeminence was assured first by its design for the Boston Public Library (1887–1895) and later by its participation in the design of the 1893 World's Columbian Exposition in Chicago. The ensemble of buildings at the "White City" was composed in such a way that the individual elements were subservient to the comprehension of the whole from one point in space in the Court of Honor. The two images seen at the fair—of classical grandeur and of formal order—were completely different from the actual environment of the nineteenth-century American city. They represented at once a link with ancient tradition, a sharp break with the immediate past, and an innovative approach to present circumstances that did much to transform the American environment in the years up until 1930.[3]

If the achievement of McKim, Mead & White's generation had been to reintroduce architectural discipline into buildings and planning through stylistic means, it was the particular challenge of Goodhue's generation to retain that sense of discipline but to move forward toward

51

a greater freedom of expression, one less dependent upon the strict repli-
cation of historical form. In both Europe and America at the turn of the
century, the dominant academic mode was being challenged by various
alternative directions. Chief among these was the Anglo-American Arts
and Crafts Movement, which advocated a search for beauty in a return
to craftsmanship and which was embodied most vividly in domestic architecture. In England, under the leadership of Richard Norman Shaw
and Philip Webb, the individual house was reinstated as the subject of
serious intellectual and artistic endeavor.[4]

A second alternative was an extension of the nineteenth-century
Anglo-American Gothic Revival, which focused primarily on ecclesiastical and collegiate commissions and, like the Arts and Crafts Movement,
upon a revival of the building and decorative crafts. In England, George
Frederick Bodley and John Dando Sedding were leaders of this movement. In America, it was led first by Henry Vaughan, Bodley's student
who had emigrated to America in 1881, and then later by Cram and
Goodhue.[5]

A third alternative was embodied in the more experimental and
personal work of a number of younger individuals, many of whom were
contemporaries of Goodhue's. In Chicago and elsewhere, Louis Sullivan
had designed skyscrapers characterized by a clear expression of the steel
frame and enriched by vivid naturalistic ornament. Frank Lloyd Wright
was designing suburban houses which combined a fluid spatial organization, expressive use of materials, and an abstract composition of form
and ornament. In California, Irving Gill, Charles and Henry Greene,
and Bernard Maybeck led a stylistically varied movement in domestic
architecture characterized by new materials, simplified forms, and attention to craftsmanship. A number of Goodhue's European contemporaries
also tried to go beyond academic design, men such as Edwin Lutyens in
England, Josef Hoffman in Austria, Peter Behrens in Germany, Auguste Perret in France, and Eliel Saarinen in Finland.[6]

These different alternatives, together with the dominant academic
mode, have common characteristics, comprising what Henry-Russell
Hitchcock described in 1929 as the New Tradition: They all combine
"the [new] methods of engineering and the revived craft of building with
an architecture which summarized the aesthetic effects of the past." In
Hitchcock's view, the New Tradition was a period of transition between
the stylistic revivalism of the nineteenth century, when architecture was
estranged from craft and engineering, and the twentieth-century work of
the European modernists who eschewed historical form in favor of the
aesthetic effects of engineering and technology alone. Although the New
Tradition began with the buildings of Richardson, the most characteristic
work was accomplished by younger men—among them the best of Goodhue's generation—who shared fundamental goals despite stylistic diversity.[7]

The New Tradition was characterized by a broad eclecticism with regard to composition and style. Freed of the narrow associational strictures that characterized the "literary" styles of the nineteenth century and the "technological" styles of the twentieth century, its architects sought to express artistic ideas intrinsic to architecture, whether by the more literal use of Roman models in some of Lutyens's monumental works, or by the more abstract representation of hearth and enclosure in Wright's suburban houses.[8] While Goodhue's generation shared such goals, it was divided by a debate over tradition and innovation that centered on questions of formal expression. It is possible to imagine a spectrum of opinion, occupied at one end by those architects who adhered to historically accurate form, and at the other by those who favored the free abstraction and simplification of form.

Cram and Goodhue were at the more conservative end of this spectrum, traditionalists who regarded Gothic as a valid style in the twentieth century. They were attracted by the balance of freedom and discipline inherent in the Gothic style, its lack of strict rules for the proportioning and relationship of parts, its emphasis on dramatic effects, its accommodation of idiosyncracies, and its Puginian mandate for "honest" structure. Similarly, Cram and Goodhue felt at ease with freer historical styles like Spanish Colonial and Tudor. By contrast, both men had an enduring professional abhorrence for the "rulebound" classicism of McKim, Mead & White, or what Goodhue denounced as "the modern French Beaux Arts sort of thing."[9]

After 1903 the attitude of each man toward tradition and innovation became more distinct, and the work of the two offices of the firm reflected this. In 1904, Cram toured the ruined abbeys of Great Britain in search of material for a book on that subject.[10] He was captivated by the romantic, archaic aura of the abbeys, with their rough stone walls. As a result of that visit, he seems to have abandoned his earlier attitudes, adhering with greater and greater fidelity to English models. His smaller buildings subsequently recalled the chaste austerity of early English parish churches, while his larger buildings became increasingly dependent upon grandiose English precedents. Like the strict nineteenth-century Ecclesiologists, Cram saw strong links between art and morality, and this had implications for his view of society as a whole. In the years after 1903, Cram evolved into what Henry-Russell Hitchcock described as a "romantic Medievalist," interested in reviving not only medieval art but the related structures of society, politics, engineering, and craft as well.[11]

Goodhue, on the other hand, was less concerned about any but purely aesthetic issues and took a more skeptical view of tradition. He was first and foremost a designer, not an historian, and while he looked to tradition for inspiration, he increasingly relied upon his own intuitive and artistic abilities.

In an article on "Some English Parish Churches," written for *The Architectural Review,* Goodhue expressed his thoughts on the value of tradition to the designer. He felt that the strength of a tradition lay in its range of possible variations and its capacity for a new organic unity of program, structure, and craft. Rather than merely reproducing the buildings of the past, Goodhue felt the modern designer should attempt only to

> . . . seize the spirit that seems to animate their every stone . . . but to laboriously search that we may strive to give, word for word, the letter of the law that governed their building; to painfully duplicate each littlest molding, each trifling crocket and buttress-weathering—this we may not do, if our own art is to be a living one. [12]

Goodhue felt that one could best recapture the "spirit" of Gothic architecture by expressing that "spirit" with contemporary materials and methods of construction. Thus, he resisted both the antiquarians who argued that the "honest" expression of traditional forms was achieved only with the materials and methods of construction used in the past, and the modernists who claimed that the "honest" expression of *new* materials and methods required the abandonment of traditional imagery. In his buildings, Goodhue tended to rely upon time-honored masonry systems or hybrid systems of masonry and concrete for the vertical parts of the structure, and upon innovative systems like Guastavino tile vaults, concrete beams and slabs, and steel trusses or more traditional wood trusses for horizontal spans. He preferred not to use a steel frame for structure, and did so in the tower of the Nebraska State Capitol only when his engineers convinced him it could not be built solely of stone.

The use of both traditional and innovative materials and methods had, for Goodhue, its counterpart in the proper balance of machine-made and handcrafted elements. Craftsmanship was so important to him that he even ruminated about a totally craft-oriented architectural practice, and he shared his thoughts on this in a letter of March 10, 1910, sent to Percy Erskine Nobbs, an architect in Montreal:

> One of my favorite theories now is this, to have . . . ten men all work together to build a building. The first done in this fashion should preferably be a small one, and the architect would be no more than a humble director of the others. He even might, like my Aztec friend Zafirino in San Miguel de Allende in Mexico, smooth off a place in the ground and draw on it with his cane, then when the workmen had built to the point so drawn, rub it out and draw the section immediately above, etc.
>
> The ten men should of course each be the best and perhaps

only ideal one of his kind, and I can come surprisingly near filling the list, i.e., I have a joiner, a wood carver, a sculptor, a tile man, a hardware man, a glass man, etc. etc., to none of whom would I venture to do more than suggest, and each of whom could be trusted to do the right thing out of his own head without any detail. The only man I do lack . . . is a plain everyday stone mason, the breed seeming to have passed away in the United States. But where shall I find a client?[13]

Although this arrangement was idyllic, Goodhue was portraying his preferred manner of working. As the architect of a project, he was the controlling figure from initial design through inspection of construction. But he realized that many of the elements which gave great distinction to his completed buildings—like the sculpture, stained glass, woodwork, and hardware—were the result of close collaboration with other artists.[14]

Goodhue tried to incorporate some handcrafted elements into every project. In Saint Thomas's Church in New York City, for example, a generous budget enabled him to specify the surfacing of the stone "to be done by hand, as many different hands as possible, though the tool used by each should be of the same kind, and that no two blocks should be made consciously alike." When a budget was small, he was "content to use the more economical, though still perfectly honest modern materials to wit, ribs built up of concrete blocks . . . and webs of Guastavino tile." But whatever the budget, Goodhue sought to use the best possible craftsmanship and materials because he was aware of how crucial these elements are in the final assessment of any building.[15]

During the decade of 1903–1913, working out of the New York office, Goodhue designed a series of churches which form a distinctive corpus. They were of such vitality and superior artistry that he came to be known primarily as a "church architect." These commissions were of aesthetic interest to him, rather than religious (he was an agnostic), and in each one, architectural precedent became a springboard for a personal form of expression. Six of these churches illustrate the variety of expression he could achieve within the limits of a well-defined, traditional building type.[16] All have in common a main ceremonial space disciplined by a repetitive structural order and enlivened by an inventive vitality in the details.

The cadet chapel at West Point (1903–1910) was the first church designed by Goodhue in this period and it was among the best. Unfettered by Episcopal liturgy in the nondenominational chapel, Goodhue was able to develop a generalized religious form modeled on the English Gothic collegiate chapel, especially Kings' College Chapel. Upon its completion, the West Point chapel was widely published and received almost universal praise.[17]

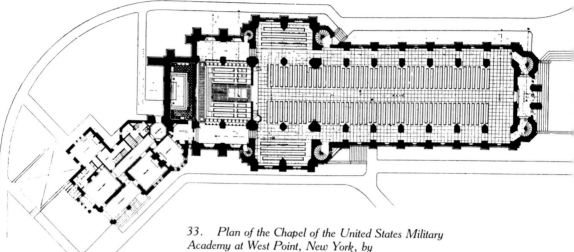

33. Plan of the Chapel of the United States Military
Academy at West Point, New York, by
Cram, Goodhue & Ferguson, 1903–1910

The plan is divided into twelve equal bays: a seven-bay nave, two-bay crossing flanked by shallow transepts, two-bay chancel, and one-bay sanctuary, yielding a hall 200 feet long by 33 feet wide by 55 feet high (Figs. 33, 34). The crossing tower is not acknowledged on the interior by any spatial or structural effects except by a slight thickening of two transverse vault ribs. The twelve repetitive quadripartite vaults, ribs, and shafts create a linear space which contradicts the transeptal plan and massing.

For the structural fabric of the chapel, Goodhue developed what became something of a signature scheme. It included a long, broad nave; aisles that are simply low passages burrowing laterally through the nave piers; and large clerestory windows above the aisle arcade, which emphasize the structure.

To roof the interior, Goodhue used Guastavino tile vaults, a system widely used by architects to span large public spaces.[18] The Guastavino vaults are essentially of a thin, monolithic shell-like construction which creates very little horizontal thrust, and therefore they are fundamentally different from the stone vaults used in medieval churches. The remarkable structural properties of the tile vaults reduce the amount of mass required in the structural piers and thus eliminate the need for flying buttresses. This resolved a number of constructional problems resulting from the harsh North American winter and also allowed a new formal expression of Gothic architecture to develop in which the gossamer complexity of a French Gothic cathedral was replaced by a crisp appearance of mass,

34.   Interior view looking toward the entry door of the Chapel of the United States
Military Academy at West Point, New York, by Cram, Goodhue & Ferguson, 1903–1910

but without the heavy bulk of an English cathedral.

The West Point chapel was the first completely mature example of Goodhue's general approach to form. Rising from its precipitous site, the base of the building is simple and solid. Two octagonal towers flank the large north window and main door, and a crossing tower, rising 145 feet above the ground, dominates the nave and transepts. As the forms of roughly textured granite rise into the sky they become set back in profile, elaborated in shape, and more refined in surface treatment. At the top of the crossing tower, the forms of the crown create a vibrant texture of light and shadow at the skyline of the building. This treatment of a simple base shading upward to a sculptural crown appears in all of Goodhue's monumental freestanding buildings, but nowhere is it expressed with such clarity as in the West Point chapel (Figs. 35, 36).

35. View of the Chapel of the United States Military Academy at West Point, New York, by Cram, Goodhue & Ferguson, 1903–1910

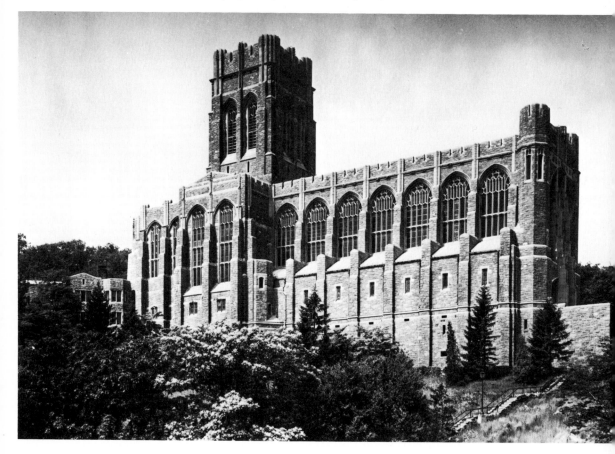

36.   Detail view of the Chapel of the United States Military Academy
at West Point, New York, by Cram, Goodhue & Ferguson, 1903–1910

While the exterior form resulted from the use of a new vaulting system, the interior was orthodox in its structural expression. The usual three-part division of aisle arcade, triforium gallery, and clerestory is employed. Each pier has a cluster of three tall, thin, engaged shafts, accented with capitals, which return to the floor and support the vault ribs. This traditional expression of the wall system seems somewhat coarse in execution, especially when compared with later examples of Goodhue's work.

37. *Cross and sword over main entry door of the Chapel of the United States Military Academy at West Point, New York, by Cram, Goodhue & Ferguson, 1903–1910*

Every public building designed by Goodhue has symbolic ornament, and none more so than his churches. The program of symbolism
for the nondenominational chapel at West Point embodies military lore.
Along the parapets above the nave clerestory windows is a row of bosses
by Lawrie, depicting episodes from the Arthurian legends, including the
Quest of the Holy Grail. Joan of Arc, Richard the Lionhearted, and
Sir Lancelot are depicted on the northwest turret of the entrance facade,

and Saint George slaying the dragon is shown on the northeast tower. Between them, the arms of the patron of warriors, Saint Michael the Archangel, are emblazoned on the apex of the front gable. Above the main door, a cross is incised with a battle sword recalling *Durendal*, the mighty two-handed sword carried into battle by the hero of *The Song of Roland* (Fig. 37).

The interior, too, is enriched with symbolic ornament. Sculptures supporting the transverse ribs of the crossing depict the four Christian Evangelists in traditional form: St. Matthew is portrayed as a winged man; St. Mark as a winged lion; St. Luke as a winged ox; and St. John as an eagle. The stained-glass nave windows depict scenes and personages from the Old and New Testaments, while the sanctuary window behind the altar depicts a series of military events interwoven into a rich texture. The Academy's collection of old military flags is hung in the nave.[19]

The symbolic elements were designed to be representational rather than abstract, and their incorporation serves a double purpose: while remaining subordinate, they enrich the composition of masses; and they clarify the purpose of the building by celebrating the history and lore which it embodies. By doing both at once, the iconographic elements become integral to the architectural composition.

On August 8, 1905, Saint Thomas's Church in New York, built in 1870, was destroyed by fire. The Vestry immediately decided to build a temporary wooden church within the lines of the outer walls of the old structure, and then approached architect George B. Post for advice on whether to rebuild the old church or to seek a new design. Post regarded the old church as the "least satisfactory and interesting of all the designs of the late Richard Upjohn, who was a very great architect," irregular in plan and massing and not easily reconstructed without interfering with the newly erected temporary church.[20] He argued that a new and less complex plan could significantly increase the seating capacity, and could be built at a scale more appropriate for Fifth Avenue as it was evolving.[21] The Vestry seized the opportunity to create a splendid new church in the heart of the metropolis, and sought the best possible architect through a competition held between November 1905 and March 1906.[22] Ten architects were invited to compete, and the program dictated that "the style of architecture for the church and adjoining buildings shall be Gothic."[23] The jury was composed of architects William Martin Aiken of New York, Frank Miles Day of Philadelphia, and R. Clipston Sturgis of Boston, all "recognized as authorities on Gothic architecture." All ten entries were rejected; none recognized "the dignity and importance of the opportunity" and all were "lacking in inspiration and a broad and comprehensive grasp of the greatness of the scheme." Nevertheless, mindful of the goal of selecting an architect rather than a particular design, the

61

Vestry hired Cram, Goodhue & Ferguson because of the firm's "thorough appreciation and understanding of the truest form and expression of Gothic art as applied to Church architecture."[24]

From March 1906 until May 1907, the firm designed a number of alternative schemes. Some were designed by Goodhue and others by Cram in a process that brought out the intensely competitive nature of each man. Goodhue recalled in a letter to D. B. Updike that

> . . . the office system kept track of this process and each new plan was lettered. Beginning at "A," the finally accepted plan was lettered "O." The day the final decision was reached, two plans were submitted, one by me (lettered "M") and one by Cram (lettered "O").[25]

Cram's plan was approved (although in the Vestry minutes it is known as "Plan R"), and it formed the basis for the completed building. In February 1908, working drawings were begun in the New York office under Goodhue's supervision, and the cornerstone was laid on November 21, 1911. The new building was built around and over the temporary wooden church. Services were held in the new church on October 4, 1913.[26] After the completion of the structural fabric, Goodhue completed the interior ornamentation, notably the reredos and the chancel furniture.[27]

38. *Plan of the completed Saint Thomas's Church, New York City, by Cram, Goodhue & Ferguson, 1905–1913*

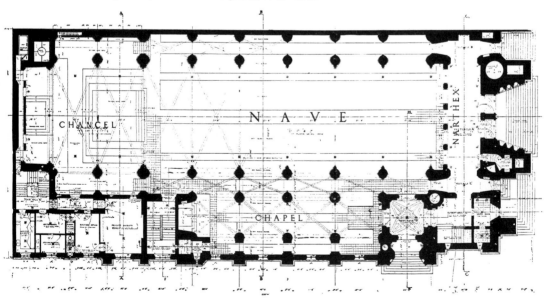

Credit for the design of Saint Thomas's Church has been and remains a controversial subject, in part because its completion coincided with the dissolution of Cram, Goodhue & Ferguson, and in part because Cram and Goodhue were so competitive over its design and construction. In his article on the church, the critic H. L. Bottomley asserted that "Mr. Cram is responsible for the general plan, Mr. Goodhue for the carrying out of it."[28] Harold Grove's guidebook to the church notes that "as senior partner, Dr. Cram was largely responsible for the overall plan and Mr. Goodhue for the interior decoration, including entire responsibility for the magnificent reredos, or altar screen."[29] Goodhue described

39.   Section of the completed Saint Thomas's Church, New York City, by Cram, Goodhue & Ferguson, 1905–1913

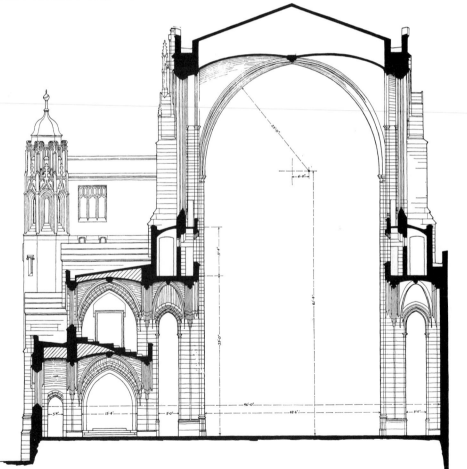

his own view of the matter in a letter of January 23, 1914, to E. M. Camp, editor of the *Church News Association:*

> The design . . . should be credited to the now defunct firm of Cram, Goodhue & Ferguson, in that its design is undoubtedly based upon a sketch plan of Mr. Cram's, which sketch I used in preparing all the building's working drawings and details.
>
> It must clearly be understood that this sketch plan was not in any sense a finished or final affair. It was, however, sufficiently clear for me to readily assume its more definite characteristics, and no doubt forms the plan (using the word "plan" in its strict architectural sense) upon which the whole design for Saint Thomas' was based, but that such a plan should be regarded as governing much beside itself, in other words, the occurrence of solids on the flat is, I think, absurd. What the public sees, the architectural mass, that is, its composition, proportion, its ornament and the placing thereof, and the working out of all the minute details of this church is, I am certain, my own work.
>
> I must refuse to comment on the statement that appeared over the signature of Cram, Goodhue & Ferguson, Boston, Mass. in which it was claimed that Mr. Cram "determined the plan, the composition, proportion, interior order and the entire organism of the church" further than to point out that the widely circulated letter that has been generally regarded as an official pronunciamento was written without my knowledge and issued during my absence from the country quite without my consent.[30]

This statement was written upon the occasion of the dissolution of Cram, Goodhue & Ferguson. The acrimony between Cram and Goodhue over Saint Thomas's undoubtedly contributed to the dissolution, but it did not deter them from creating a distinguished masterpiece. Cram's plan and consequent section, designed in the Boston office, ensured the generous proportions and the spatial complexity that are so important to this church, while Goodhue's development of the initial sketches in the New York office resulted in a building of exceptional clarity, coherence, and plasticity.

The task of designing Saint Thomas's was difficult. The architects were required to fit a complex program and an unusually large number of seats onto a site barely able to contain them, in an urban setting undergoing significant change. The church as constructed consists of a hall, 214 feet long, 43 feet wide, and 95 feet to the crown of the quadripartite Guastavino vaults. The demarcation between the seven-bay nave and the two-bay chancel, and between the latter and the sanctuary, is indicated only by a thickening of the transverse rib and a change in floor level, creating the effect of one immense and grandiose room. The nave is placed close to the north edge of the site, and on this side there is a high, narrow ambulatory. On the south side the ambulatory is duplicated: beyond it is the south porch and a chantry, or morning chapel, 18 feet wide and 20 feet high, above which is a lateral gallery. A transverse gallery in the easternmost bay of the nave covers the narthex, to the south of which sits the massive corner tower. The auxiliary parish facilities are housed in a tall block on the south side of the chancel (Figs. 38, 39).

The nave is expressed on the interior as a symmetrical space, even though it is placed off center on the property. The illusion of unencumbered centrality was accomplished by avoiding the use of transepts, which would have required too much lateral space.[31] The side walls of the nave, which have no ornament save that which enriches the structural pattern, are divided into arcade, triforium, and clerestory, and the equal bays repeat without apparent variation from the narthex to the altar. The side walls reinforce the linearity of the space and act as foils for the dramatic splendor of the large rose window over the narthex and the immense reredos wall behind the altar. While somber, the side walls are not lifeless; on the contrary, they embody a blend of traditional and inventive details. The ceiling vaults rest quite conventionally on a cluster of three engaged shafts accented with capitals, which return uninterrupted to the floor; the moldings on the aisle arcade do not return to the floor but instead feather out into the main piers, which are round in plan. This feathering out of ornamental or sculptural elements into solid masses of masonry is a personal device that Goodhue used more and more in subsequent buildings, one that introduces a vivid contrast of intricate shapes against plain surfaces (Fig. 40).

In the vaulting for Saint Thomas's Church, Goodhue used a new product which improved the acoustical qualities of the space. Called Rumford tile, it was the result of collaboration between Raphael Guastavino and Wallace C. Sabine, the pioneering acoustician.[32]

The west (or liturgical east) wall of Saint Thomas's is on a property line; thus a large stained-glass window like that at West Point could not be included. To compensate, Goodhue designed a reredos larger than any Gothic example in history, taking his inspiration from the reredos in the chapel of All Souls College, Oxford, from the wall-sized retablos common in Mexico, and from the baroque reredos he had designed for the Church of SS. Peter and Paul (1895–1900) in Fall River, Massachusetts, and for *La Santisima Trinidad* (1905) in Havana (Figs. 41, 42). The reredos was worked out by Goodhue and his assistant, Ernest Jago, and together they established the position and attributes of each figure. Lawrie modeled the sixty figures which inhabit the entire wall, and the actual carving was completed by Edward Ardolino. The subject of the reredos is the vast lore of Christianity, and includes both ancient and modern figures. At its summit, three windows are glazed with the

65

40.   *Interior view of the chantry of Saint Thomas's Church,*
New York City, by Cram, Goodhue & Ferguson, 1905–1913

41. *1913 interior view of the nave looking toward the altar prior to the completion of the reredos, Saint Thomas's Church, New York City, by Cram, Goodhue & Ferguson, 1905–1913*

42. *View of the reredos wall, chancel, and organ case of Saint
Thomas's Church, New York City, by Bertram Goodhue, 1914–1920*

deep blue found at Chartres Cathedral. In the profusion of sculpture, Ernest Peixotto saw a "wonderful impression of richness combined with order, of dignity combined with grace." One also sees a roaming imagination combined with rigorous discipline. Although the vast wall is picturesque, the strong horizontal and vertical lines of its composition maintain a majestic scale and a clear order.[33]

The chancel furniture is a group of three-dimensional wooden objects placed within and as foils to the stone structure of the main space. The organ case, carved by Irving & Casson of Boston, is set on the north wall of the chancel and projects boldly into the space; the pulpit is an intricate aedicular object placed forward of the marble and tile chancel rail; and the richly carved choir stalls are run along both sides of the chancel, reinforcing the perspective focused on the altar.

At Saint Thomas's, Goodhue had the opportunity to develop an extensive program of symbolism. In addition to the reredos, there is symbolic ornament on the organ case, choir stalls, chancel rail, baptismal font, various pieces of furniture and hardware, in the seventeen stained glass windows of the nave and chancel, and on the main entrance portal of the church itself (Fig. 43). Goodhue included both Biblical and contemporary examples. For instance, the generals of World War I, an

43. View of decorative hardware designed for Saint Thomas's Church, New York City, by Cram, Goodhue & Ferguson, 1905–1913

airplane, an automobile, and the sinking of the *Lusitania* are worked into the choir furniture along with more obvious Biblical figures; there are even caricatures of "the passing show in Fifth Avenue" represented on the facade and a dollar sign worked into the ornament over the small door at the base of the tower, known as the bride's door. When the latter were discovered in 1921, there was a minor scandal. Some observers saw in the inclusion of modern secular images a desecration of a sacred place, but Goodhue was defended in editorials in *The New York Times*. One observed that

> The architect who placed the dollar mark and a hundred or more other indisputable modernisms in Saint Thomas' was following a time-honored precedent . . . [and] what really would have been more startling, in the light of the history of ecclesiastical architecture, would have been the omission by the designers of some sort of accurate twentieth-century symbolism.[34]

Another observed that Goodhue

> . . . would scarcely have been false to the spirit of Gothic if he had shown us modern flappers fox-trotting through the Pearly Gates. Perhaps the greatest of Mr. Goodhue's services is that his pleasantries recall the robust simplicity of medieval piety and its sense of the goodness of living.[35]

The exterior of Saint Thomas's has an irregular and apparently eccentric mass, built of Kentucky limestone that turns white with age (Figs. 44, 45). The architects anticipated that the church would be surrounded by commercial buildings, and that these would rise far above any towers or spires like those on Saint Patrick's Cathedral two blocks away. They were counting on the scale and sculptural force of the exterior elements to give the church a strong presence among its neighbors.[36] The Fifth Avenue facade has a virtually equal division between the commanding but truncated corner tower and the cavernous portal and rose window which express the nave. The solid, chunky masses of the Fifth Avenue front are enriched by sculptural iconography around the portal and the rose window, and as they rise they yield to greater refinement of shape culminating in decorative turrets atop the church which reinforce the dynamic asymmetry of the whole facade. On the 53rd Street elevation, the nave, chantry and gallery, the chantry aisle, and the parish house are expressed as distinct volumes, as are the major structural piers. The picturesque, octagonal parish house stair, with its lead roof, relieves the rigorous expression of plan, structure, and mass (Fig. 46). Montgomery Schuyler observed that "the enforced peculiarity of the plan is still more clearly responsible for all the questionable points of the architecture." He acknowledged that the exterior volumes were a clear expression of the

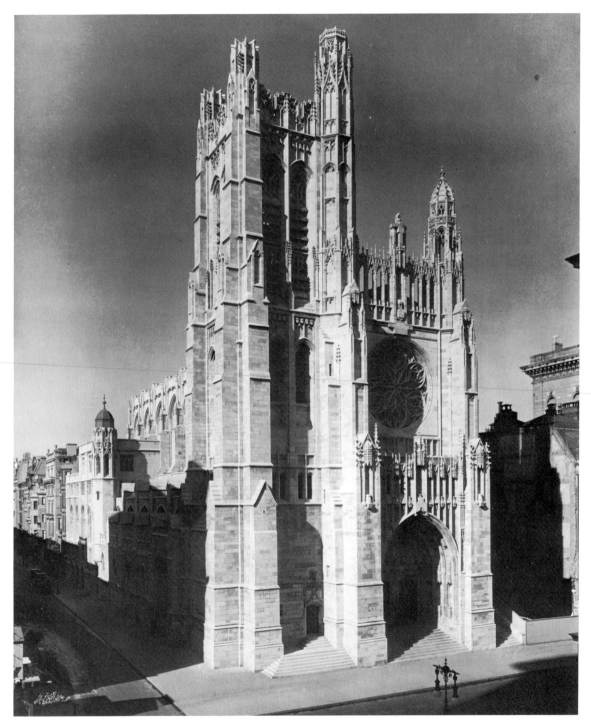

*44. 1913 view from the southeast of Saint Thomas's Church,
New York City, by Cram, Goodhue & Ferguson, 1905–1913*

45.   Elevation drawing of the completed Saint Thomas's Church,
New York City, by Cram, Goodhue & Ferguson, 1905–1913

*46. 1913 view of the parish house of Saint Thomas's Church,
New York City, by Cram, Goodhue & Ferguson, 1905–1913*

47. *Perspective of a preliminary design for Saint Thomas's Church,*
New York City, by Cram, Goodhue & Ferguson (New York), 1905–1913

interior spaces, noted that even the tiny doors that flank the main portal
were an expression of the lateral ambulatories, was "astonished at the
amplitude of space that has accrued from an arrangement enforced in the
first instance by an exiguity of space," and praised the "highly ingenious
planning."[37]

Since the interior spaces filled the entire lot, the architects realized
that the church, with two party walls, could achieve only the illusion of
standing free. The principal view of it is from the southeast, and the
design was studied from this vantage point (Fig. 47). Almost flaunting
the virtual one-sidedness of this building, the bald, north-facing structural
piers, designed to be unseen, are shorn of the decorative crockets and
other carved ornaments that enrich the south-facing piers.

Saint Thomas's was not a progenitor of Goodhue's subsequent
work, as was the West Point chapel. It stands as a singular achievement
in his career, and an important monument in American church architec-

74

ture. Its true equal, paradoxically, is not any of the so-called traditional churches of the period, but Wright's Unity Temple, designed one year earlier, in 1905. Unity Temple—itself a unique achievement in Wright's career—is undoubtedly more advanced toward nonrepresentational abstraction of form than is Saint Thomas's. But despite stylistic differences, both buildings embody a fundamental intention of Wright's and Goodhue's generation: in each, material and structural discipline, its expression enhanced by ornament, is the basis for a complex and dramatic spatial order.[38]

Saint Thomas's Church and the West Point chapel are each specific to a unique site and to a monumental program. When faced with a more ordinary site and more modest program, Goodhue tended to develop a quite orthodox variation of the traditional English parish church. He did so in a trio of Episcopal churches: Christ Church in West Haven, Connecticut (1908); Saint John's Church in West Hartford, Connecticut (1907–1909; Fig. 48); and Saint Mark's Church in Mount Kisco, New

48. Perspective of Saint John's Church, West Hartford, Connecticut, by Cram, Goodhue & Ferguson (New York), 1907–1909

York (1909–1920). In these three, he composed all the required liturgical features of the Episcopal church into a clear and coherent plan; he developed the three-dimensional qualities of interior space to create a reverent atmosphere for worship, achieving the necessary architectural contrast between nave and chancel; and he gave a fresh architectural expression to the structure, furnishings, and ornament of each church, which in turn gave each a distinctive image. Schuyler saw in each one "that homebred and vernacular air, as of some inspired mason who had never heard of 'architecture,' but put stones and timber together of his untutored best" and felt that "that is about the best impression a country church can make."[39]

The most fully traditional of the three was Saint Mark's Church in Mount Kisco, a building distinguished by superior artistry rather than by innovative features (Figs. 49–51). Goodhue was proud of this church, as he wrote to Montgomery Schuyler in 1910:

49.   Plan of Saint Mark's Church, Mount Kisco, New York, by Cram, Goodhue & Ferguson (New York), 1909–1920

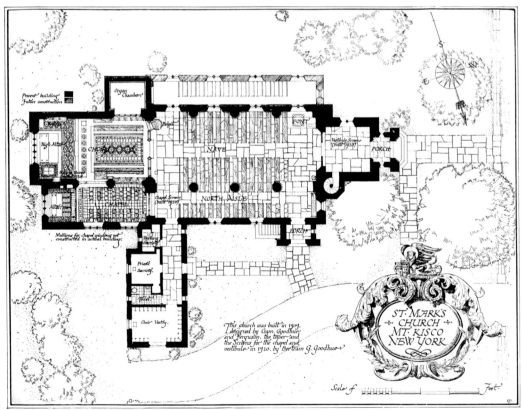

50.　*1957 exterior view of Saint Mark's Church, Mount Kisco, New York,*
by Cram, Goodhue & Ferguson (New York), 1909–1920

At Mount Kisco, we have almost completed the best . . . church
I have so far done; and though the tower isn't on, the various
details have been so carefully carried out and the atmosphere is so
much that of an English church of the "right" period, that it would
give you a better idea of my dreams and my gods (architecturally
speaking) than anything else.[40]

The church was widely admired. Ernest Peixotto regarded it as "an
edifice that . . . might well serve as a model for our smaller parish
churches in America," and he seemed especially pleased that "viewed

51.   *1957 interior view of nave looking toward the rood-screen and chancel of Saint Mark's Church, Mount Kisco, New York, by Cram, Goodhue & Ferguson (New York), 1909–1920*

from the northwest, the composition piles up in a very picturesque way." The massing does have a romantic air about it, but it is the outgrowth of a rational plan.[41]

Entrance to the church is through a west porch into a paneled vestibule at the base of a tall, square-topped tower. The figure of Saint Mark, sculpted by Lawrie, occupies a niche above the west door and is its sole ornamental detail. The four-bay nave leads to a three-bay chancel, on the north side of which is a chantry. There is a north wing containing the sacristies and choir room. The exterior material is rough-laid stone of varied tones, and the roof is of gray and purplish slate.

The main walls of the nave are of buff-colored plaster over rough stone and dressed with a hand-finished, cream-colored stone. The aisle arcades are supported by six massive columns, varied in shape: four are round, one is octagonal, and the sixth is round and ribbed with perpendicular lines to give it the effect of an octagon. The chancel is elaborately treated. An intricately detailed oak rood-screen separates it from the nave; there is a small, sculptural organ case; the ends of the choir stalls are handcarved into figures representing Music; and the bishop's throne is emblazoned with a scene representing the consecration of the first American bishop. In contrast to the nave floor of old flagstones, the floor of the chancel is paved with the then-popular, handmade, polychromed tiles produced by Henry Mercer. These tiles were widely used in Arts and Crafts buildings in America, especially houses. Goodhue's frequent use of them in his churches—like Saint Mark's or even monumental ones like Saint Thomas's—testifies to his abiding interest in an architecture that was essentially simple, unpretentious, and craftsmanlike.

If Goodhue could be true to Gothic precedent, he could also recast traditional forms to create something quite fresh. He did so in the First Baptist Church in Pittsburgh (1909–1912), which remains one of his most important buildings.[42] In 1909, the First Baptist Church was forced to find new property on which to build, and it decided to secure plans through competition.[43] The jury was composed of Professor Warren Laird of the University of Pennsylvania, Cass Gilbert of New York, and Charles D. Maginnis of Boston. Five architects, including Goodhue, were invited to compete and sixty other entries also were received.[44] *The Architectural Review* published eight of the schemes, including Goodhue's winning entry, and pointed to

> . . . the very considerable progress in an appreciation for the right use of Gothic forms, and the development of a taste in church architecture such as has within a few years brought about a tremendous and marked advance in this branch of architectural practice in America.[45]

The magazine was drawing an explicit connection between historical

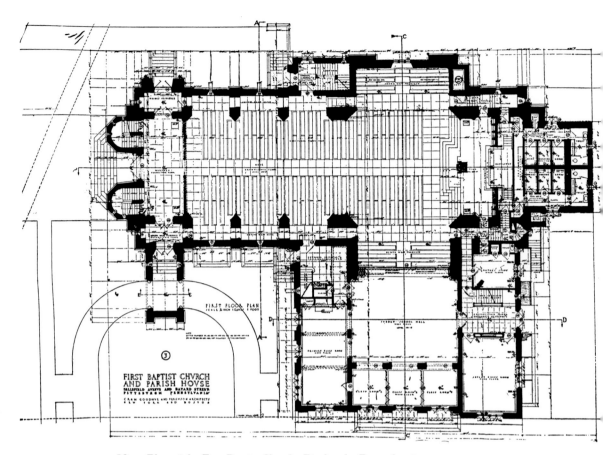

52. *Plan of the First Baptist Church, Pittsburgh, Pennsylvania,*
by Cram, Goodhue & Ferguson (New York), 1909–1912

scholarship and architectural progress in church design, a theme that
naturally applied to other building types as well.

When Goodhue's winning entry was constructed, it seemed to the
architect and critic, Arthur Byne, to be "an intelligent digest of English
and Continental Gothic" and to possess

> . . . a certain mellowness of conception which would have been
> impossible to the builders of the very period itself, since only a
> generous retrospect could produce . . . all the structural beauty
> and composition of Continental, along with the undecorated sever-
> ity and economical design of the Insular Gothic.[46]

Byne was correctly observing that the very act of retrospection could and
did lead to the creation of new forms.

The cruciform plan has a wide nave of four short bays flanked by
narrow aisles, a generous crossing with shallow transepts, and a one-bay
chancel (Fig. 52). In this church, the crossing, roofed with a most

80

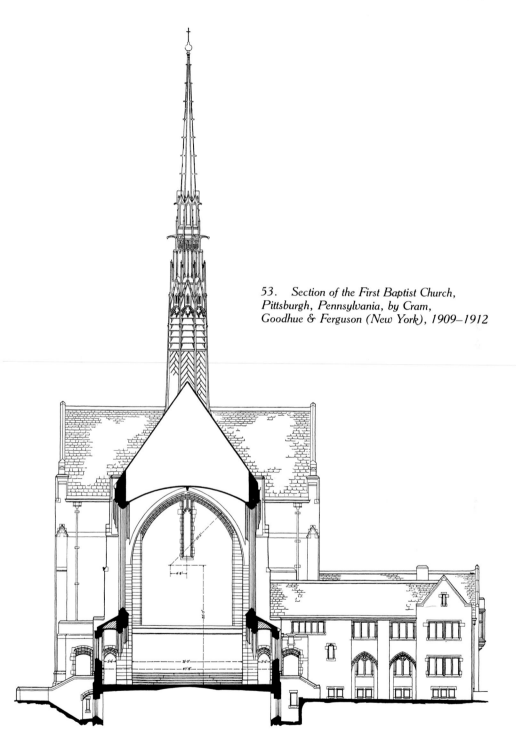

53.   *Section of the First Baptist Church,*
Pittsburgh, Pennsylvania, by Cram,
Goodhue & Ferguson (New York), 1909–1912

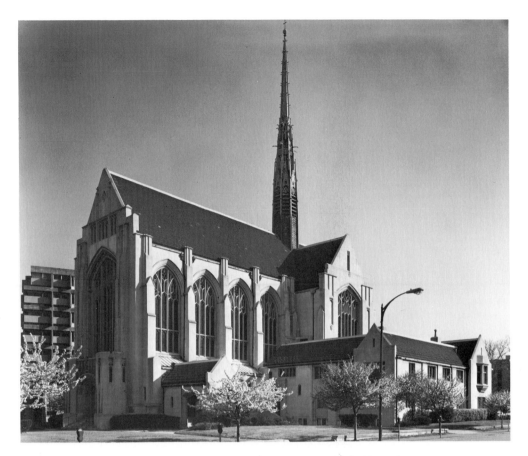

54. Exterior view of the First Baptist Church, Pittsburgh, Pennsylvania, by Cram, Goodhue & Ferguson (New York), 1909–1912

intricate vaulting pattern, assumed a more important role in the spatial composition than in any previous example, and the arrangement antici- pated the central rotundas of Goodhue's mature works. The wall system is composed of a low aisle arcade and a high, large clerestory (Fig. 53). The program required that the Sunday school be so arranged that it could become part of the body of the church with a view of the pulpit. This requirement, so troubling to the other competitors, was deftly resolved by Goodhue. He simply lengthened the south transept to create a two-story hall like an enclosed cloister-garth surrounded on two levels by class- rooms. The Sunday-school wing was treated in the massing as though it were a conventional cluster of auxiliary buildings, kept low to enhance the vertical proportions of the church itself. A traditional and even pic- turesque image was used to resolve a contemporary, functional require- ment. The exterior volumes of the church, centered on the green copper *flèche* rising 182 feet, are made of smooth, pale limestone. Their clarity is not diluted by richly textured surfaces (Fig. 54).

82

A second troubling aspect of the program was the baptistery requirement of a Baptist church, which called for the placement of a baptismal tank, together with dressing stalls, right behind the communion table. This usually interfered with the design of what was the most visible wall in any church. Goodhue placed the choir loft above the baptismal tank, and behind the loft placed a free-standing, polychromed and gilt organ case. Behind the organ in the back wall, he inserted a single small window filled with deep blue glass yielding a dramatic effect of depth (Fig. 55).

On the interior of the nave, the supports for the quadripartite vaults rise as solid simplified piers, and these blossom out into intricately molded vault ribs (Fig. 56). This expression of pier, shaft, and rib is a departure from tradition, and Goodhue defended this approach in his review of *The Medieval Church Architecture of England*, written in 1912 by the renowned historian, Charles Herbert Moore. Goodhue observed:

> One of the author's most insistent contentions is that a pier supporting a number of vaulting ribs must, in its contour, take each of these ribs upon a separate vaulting shaft. If, as is usual, there are five ribs to be caught, the transverse, the two diagonals and the two wall ribs . . . then he holds no pier is perfect whose contour fails to provide for each rib its projecting shaft. . . . Must ribs be carried down on shafts? Cannot they die away into any sort of plane or other surface? It seems to me that they can, and that in this age of costly labor they should.[47]

Labor costs were certainly important to Goodhue, but they were not his only objective. He wanted to create that contrast of bare simplicity relieved by concentrated ornament that often appears in his buildings, and he desired most of all to keep Gothic tradition free from orthodoxy and from clichés:

> No one can, or does, for an instant disagree with Professor Moore's dictum that Gothic attained its noblest and most logical development in and about the Ile de France; but . . . I venture to believe a building could be built that would be beautiful in character and thoroughly Gothic in principle, lacking almost every one of the features so cherished by Professor Moore.[48]

Moore was a scholar and historian and Goodhue was a practicing architect; therein lies much of their disagreement. Goodhue especially lamented the lack of criticism of a modern church, "one in the designing of which the architect rightly assumed the possibility of obtaining no more than the spirit—not the letter—of the Gothic style."[49]

Not all of Goodhue's church commissions called for a version of the English Gothic style. A notable exception was the pro-cathedral of

55.   *Interior view looking at the choir loft and organ of the First Baptist*
Church, Pittsburgh, Pennsylvania, by Cram, Goodhue & Ferguson (New York), 1909–1912

56.   Interior view of the nave of the First Baptist Church, Pittsburgh,
Pennsylvania, by Cram, Goodhue & Ferguson (New York), 1909–1912

Havana, Cuba, *La Santisima Trinidad*, designed in an Hispanic style in 1905 (Figs. 57, 58). The commission may have come to Goodhue through his friendship with Gillespie, who owned a house in Mariel, Cuba. The plan of the church is composed of a four-bay nave, two-bay chancel, and one-bay sanctuary, with narrow aisles. There are no windows in the aisles, and only moderate-sized clerestory windows to shield the interior against the bright southern sun. The volumes of the church are clearly delineated and the plain plaster walls of the nave are interrupted only by the structural piers, while the clerestory windows above have panelized surrounds which reiterate the structural bays. The florid Churrigueresque ornament is concentrated on the front facade, on the altar wall, and on the upper stages of the tower. Goodhue designed two other churches for Cuba which remained projects: *Los Todos Santos*, a modest church at Guantanamo; and a full-fledged cathedral at Havana. In all three Cuban designs, Goodhue combined a liturgically correct scheme with an appropriate regional stylistic expression.[50]

57. *Plan of* La Santisima Trinidad *pro-cathedral, Havana, Cuba, by Cram, Goodhue & Ferguson (New York), 1905*

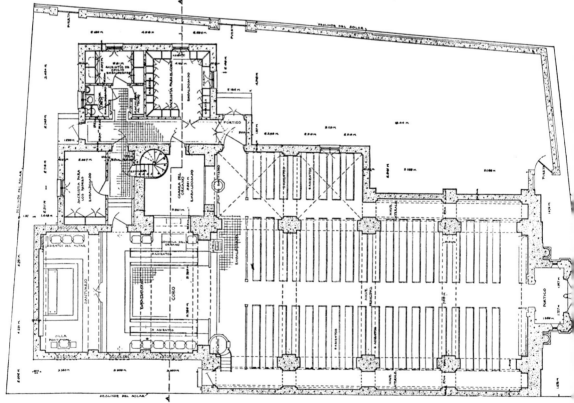

58.   Perspective of La Santisima Trinidad *pro-cathedral, Havana,*
Cuba, by Cram, Goodhue & Ferguson (New York), 1905

In May 1910, Goodhue was asked to design a new building for
the Chapel of the Intercession in Trinity Cemetery on upper Broadway
in New York, and by March 1911 the plans had been accepted. The
groundbreaking was the following September, and the new building was
first used on January 4, 1914.[51]

Trinity Cemetery was an ideal setting for the romantic Goodhue.
The site, with its mature trees and venerable gravesites, allowed the new
building to acquire an instant patina of age. This is Goodhue's most
complete ecclesiastical grouping, and its plan is deftly composed (Fig.
59). The church itself is a linear hall expressed on the exterior as a large
gabled volume. The parish hall and vicarage are housed in a cluster of
buildings of a lower and more varied profile with diverse fenestration,
composed around an open cloister garth. Thrusting up out of the center
of this picturesque composition of stone and slated volumes is a tall tower
that rises to a crenellated top, above which a decorative *flèche* rises higher
still. This tower is positioned somewhat unusually on the north side of the
chancel, allowing it to become the anchor for the whole ensemble (Figs.
60, 61).

The major element of the interior of the church is a trussed wooden
ceiling, profusely polychromed and gilded (Fig. 62). Its inspiration came

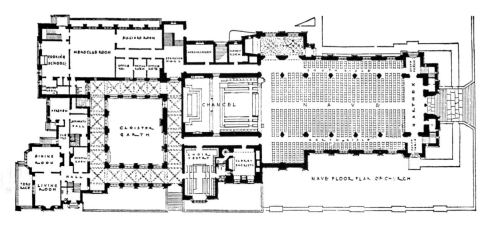

59. *Plan of the Chapel of the Intercession, New York City, by Cram, Goodhue & Ferguson (New York), 1910–1914*

60. *1914 exterior view from the northwest of the Chapel of the Intercession, New York City, by Cram, Goodhue & Ferguson (New York), 1910–1914*

61. *1914 exterior view from the northeast of the Chapel of the Intercession,
New York City, by Cram, Goodhue & Ferguson (New York), 1910–1914*

from the ceilings of parish churches in Norfolkshire which Goodhue had
seen on his travels in England, although it was more vivid in its coloring
than the originals, as he explained in a letter:

> I only wish I could have regarded it as legitimate to sand blast off
> some of the colour, which is now naturally much brighter than any
> of the beautiful old ones. The patterns are none of them traditional
> Gothic but have enough of the Gothic character to be in harmony.[52]

To emphasize the ceiling, the walls are finished in a subdued, buff-
colored, rough-textured plaster, with stone trim—a solution Goodhue
would apply later to secular works.

The space flows without structural demarcation from the narthex
through the nave and chancel to the altar. The chancel furniture and

62.   1914 interior view looking toward the altar of the Chapel of the
Intercession, New York City, by Cram, Goodhue & Ferguson (New York), 1910–1914

63.   1914 interior view of the chancel of the Chapel of the Intercession,
New York City, by Cram, Goodhue & Ferguson (New York), 1910–1914

64. *View of the sedilia and piscina of the Chapel of the Intercession,
New York City, by Cram, Goodhue & Ferguson (New York), 1910–1914*

ornament are developed integrally with the surfaces, rather than as a series
of three-dimensional objects within the chancel, as at Saint Thomas's.
The organ case is kept flush with the wall surfaces; appurtenances like
the piscina and sedilia are built into the wall; the polychromed floor is of
smooth marble instead of the more typical textured tilework, and even
the angels on the chancel parapet seem to grow up out of the stone (Fig.
63). The altar is a simple rectangular block with no bas-relief work at

92

all. Instead, bits of stone that the rector, Dr. Milo Gates, had collected from sacred sites around the world were worked into a flat design held together by a gold vine reminiscent of a Jesse Tree, a symbol of Christian lineage (Figs. 64, 65). This approach to integral rather than applied ornament anticipates all of Goodhue's later works.

The Chapel of the Intercession is the quintessential Goodhue church: the whole has an air of mellow simplicity, more gentle than heroic, while the parts have an imaginative vitality. It was Goodhue's favorite church, and in part for that reason he is entombed in its north transept (Fig. 160). The critic C. Matlack Price thought it embodied "a sort of Gothic at once rugged and refined; virile and massive without being heavy, and delicate without being trivial—and essentially scholarly without being archeological" and thought that in its design, Goodhue had "worked *in* the Gothic style, not *with* it . . . using it freely yet reverently, and simply because it was of all the styles the most adapted to the expression of the ideas and ideals which he wished to symbolize."[53]

65. *View of the altar of the Chapel of the Intercession, New York City,*
by Cram, Goodhue & Ferguson (New York), 1910–1914

Goodhue's churches were distinctly his own, and were generally recognized and admired as such. Although they all share architectural traditions that extend back into the past, they are not antiquarian and, indeed, embody many original features which attest to the unique talent of their designer. They are the result of a complex creative process combining retrospection and innovation. As buildings per se they display a strength of conception, a clearness of expression, a fitness of craft and iconography, and a lushness of effect which cause them to stand out sharply from other contemporary work. Their greater significance, however, rests in the synthesis they embody of Goodhue's free and romantic imagination as an artist and his rectitudinous discipline as a builder. The ecclesiastical commissions allowed him to develop a mastery of monumental form, ceremonial space, and iconographic ornament, which proved of great value to him in his later secular projects. Yet by a familiar irony, his very success at designing churches circumscribed the possibilities open to him. Even at the end of his career, when he had distinguished himself in the design of other building types, the clients who came most frequently to his office, almost as a matter of course, were those bearing ecclesiastical commissions.

CHAPTER FOUR · TRADITION AND INNOVATION: SECULAR WORKS

THE greater part of Goodhue's practice was devoted to ecclesiastical commissions and his reputation was accordingly that of a "church architect." But he also designed a number of secular buildings in the decade of 1903–1913, both individual structures and building ensembles. While the churches were an extension into the present of a particular building tradition, the secular projects usually required the transformation of an historical model to fit contemporary circumstances, including totally new kinds of programs. There is a consistent approach in Goodhue's secular works in which vernacular shapes composed in seemingly random patterns are ordered by means of axes, orthogonal geometry, and hierarchical arrangement.[1]

Among the first of the secular designs to be built during this period was that for the Taft School (1908–1913) at Watertown, Connecticut. Complete living, educational, and recreational facilities for a small private school are provided in a rambling group of gabled wings composed around a massive tower which dominates the silhouette of the building from most vantage points. The material is brick with precast concrete trimmings. The more important rooms have oak paneling and ornamental plasterwork, but most spaces are finished in a rough-and-ready fashion. The main entrance is in the base of the tower from which corridors lead out to the far-flung reaches of the various wings. Although essentially unpretentious, the gabled brick volumes are composed with a sense of their sculptural impact, and the boldness with which this is accomplished recalls the work of Edwin Lutyens (Figs. 66, 67).[2]

One advantage to the kind of planning used in this building is that additions can be made almost unnoticed. Indeed, in 1929, James Gamble Rogers designed a series of additions as large as the original portion, and the two parts blend almost indistinguishably together. The only marked distinction is between the stylish, even pretentious interiors of the additions and the plainer, craftsmanlike interiors of the original portion.

95

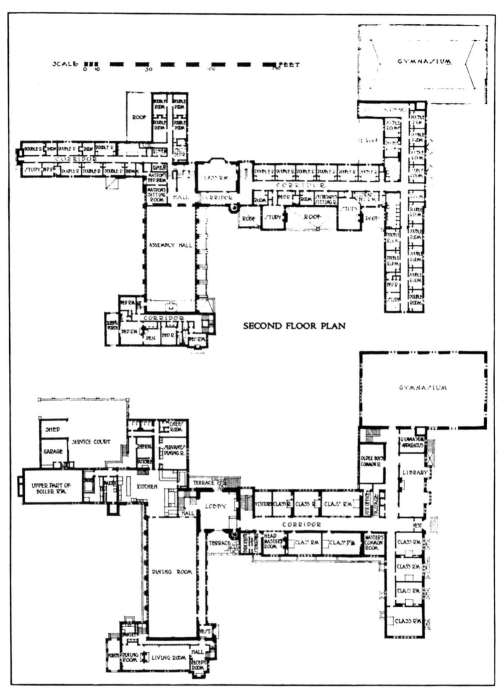

SECOND FLOOR PLAN

FIRST FLOOR PLAN

66.   Plans of the Taft School, Watertown, Connecticut,
by Cram, Goodhue & Ferguson (New York), 1908–1913

67. *Aerial view of the Taft School, Watertown, Connecticut, showing the original building by Cram, Goodhue & Ferguson (New York), 1908–1913, on the left and the later addition by James Gamble Rogers*

In 1910, Goodhue received four commissions in Duluth, Minnesota: a church, a small suburban office building, a house, and a club. The most ambitious of these, the Kitchi Gammi Club, designed to resemble a rambling Tudor house, was made of brick with stone trim, surmounted by a gabled roof of graduated slates. It combines ceremonial spaces, private guest rooms, and service facilities in a beautifully composed plan (Fig. 68). The main entrance is flanked by open loggias which face out onto a terrace and a lake view beyond. A lounge hall functions as the social and architectural heart of the building. Another lounge is at one end of the long hall; the library and newspaper room are at the other end. The dining hall is on the second floor, reached by generous stairs, and is designed to recall an English college refectory, with wood paneling, an open timber roof, and a musicians' gallery (Fig. 69). Smaller dining rooms, guest rooms, kitchen, and a separate set of public rooms for women are deployed about the major spaces with a concern for functional efficiency, privacy, and the discreet but firm separation of male and female realms.[3]

97

FIRST FLOOR PLAN

SECOND FLOOR PLAN

68.   *Plans of the Kitchi Gammi Club, Duluth, Minnesota,
by Cram, Goodhue & Ferguson (New York), 1910*

69.   *Interior view of the dining room of the Kitchi Gammi Club, Duluth,
Minnesota, by Cram, Goodhue & Ferguson (New York), 1910*

98

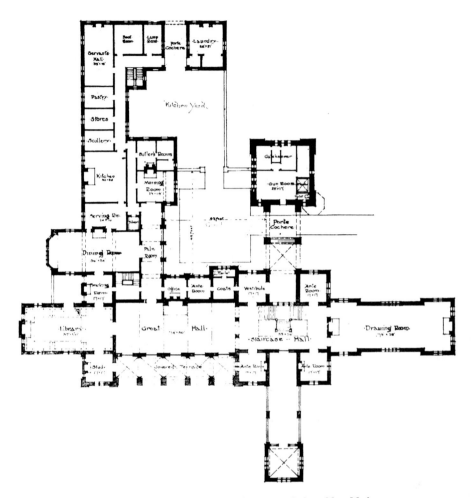

70.   *Plan of the proposed house for E. H. Harriman, Arden, New York,*
by Cram, Goodhue & Ferguson (New York), 1904

The use of English precedents in this design has given the rooms a
meaningful character, but the plan is more important to the success of the
building. There is a sense of order without rigidity, and all the major and
minor facilities are located in predictable places. The dimensions of the
various spaces and their relationship to each other suggest easy and
graceful movement throughout, and a sequence of things for the eye to see
and the mind to remember.

Among the secular commissions of the 1903–1913 period was a
palatial house proposed for E. H. Harriman in 1904 (Figs. 70, 71).[4]
This scheme seems to have been prepared for a limited competition, as
Lutyens also produced a scheme for this same commission, though the

house Harriman actually built was designed by Carrère & Hastings.[5]
Goodhue's plan is organized about cross axes: one links the tower, *porte
cochère*, and stair hall, and extends out to a templelike belvedere overlooking the garden; the other links the library, great hall, stair hall, and
drawing room, all arranged *en suite*. A minor axis off the great hall leads
to a palm room and eventually to the dining room. Secondary spaces are
placed around the major rooms in a gridlike pattern, while the staff rooms
form a large ell. The blocky masses, which pile up to the tower, are
composed to accentuate the hierarchy of major and minor rooms. The
planning of the Harriman House, with its long wings thrust along axes

into the gardens, recalls a number of Wright's houses of the period, certainly the Martin House (1904) in Buffalo, but perhaps even more the unbuilt projects for the McCormick House (1907) in Lake Forest and the Booth House (1911) in Glencoe, Illinois. Despite obvious stylistic differences, the fundamental approach to planning in Goodhue's Harriman House and in Wright's houses was similar: in each, a formal order is established by cross axes that unite the rooms of each house internally and integrate the house itself with its landscape; in each, there is a concern with partial or fragmentary symmetry balanced by the pictorial effects of asymmetrically placed elements.[6]

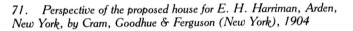

71. Perspective of the proposed house for E. H. Harriman, Arden, New York, by Cram, Goodhue & Ferguson (New York), 1904

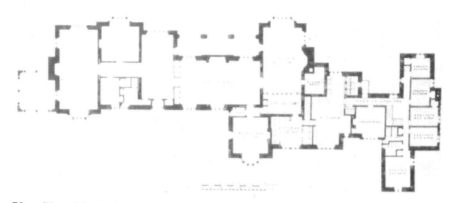

72.   *Plan of the J. E. Aldred House, Locust Valley, New York, 1913–1918*

73.   *View of the J. E. Aldred House and its gardens, Locust Valley,*
New York, 1913–1918

102

74. *Interior view of the great hall of the J. E. Aldred House,*
Locust Valley, New York, 1913–1918

In 1913, after a trip to England where Goodhue had been able to
enjoy and carefully observe English country houses for the first time, he
received a commission to design a house for J. E. Aldred in Locust
Valley, New York, that was not finished until 1918.[7] The client had
asked Goodhue to "reproduce as nearly as possible a house of the late
Tudor-Elizabethan-Jacobean Period," and the architect responded with
a design in what he called his "Anglomaniac manner" (Figs. 72–74).
He described it in a letter to the English architect Cecil Brewer:

> It's certainly big—almost as big as one of your big English country
> houses and even more English than they; but there isn't a place to
> rest your eye upon quietly, every surface is bedeviled with orna-
> mental low relief plaster or solid English oak panelling, carved to
> the utmost, or fancy electric fixtures, or historic examples and
> "Museum" pieces in the way of furniture.[8]

The Aldred House is built of fieldstone with limestone trim and a roof of graduated slates. The gabled ends of the wings are sharply delineated with stone copings and stand forward of the body of the building facing the gardens. In *The American Architecture of Today,* George H. Edgell, dean of the School of Architecture at Harvard University, took note of the gardens, which were laid out by the Olmsted Brothers, successors to Frederick Law Olmsted. Edgell saw the carefully planned asymmetry in the gardens as a reflection of the order of the entire house, "arranged to give unexpected vistas and allow the rambler frequently to come upon unexpected cozy nooks."[9]

The Harriman and Aldred houses recall the same Tudor houses that served as inspiration for Edwin Lutyens, Richard Norman Shaw, Philip Webb, and other English architects.[10] In part this can be attributed to Goodhue's ardent anglophilia. But the Tudor model was also very useful in the planning of a large modern house, an observation which influenced the work of several American architects, notably Harrie T. Lindeberg. At its most essential, a Tudor house was a collection of simple gabled volumes, and these could be composed in a variety of ways. Such a house could be fitted to an irregular site or could possess a formal facade overlooking large gardens, as does the Aldred house. But the model also was useful in resolving the typical requirements of a large domestic establishment with its need for public and private space, ceremonial rooms, and service wings. Rather than fitting all these diverse spaces into a single symmetrical form, a Tudor model allowed formality—in both rooms and facades—to occur as episodes in an otherwise rambling form. For many clients, and surely for Goodhue, such a model with its easy blend of formal and informal qualities and with its "natural" shapes was undoubtedly irresistible.

Goodhue's own house was an 18-foot-wide New York City townhouse on East 74th Street, with a major room facing the street and one facing the garden. Goodhue's remodeling of his house offered the opportunity to make a personal environment that reflected his artistic intentions. The symmetrical facade was centered on a bay of windows, at the base of which was a deep, recessed, arched opening giving onto an entrance hall. The hall had a fireplace surrounded by Moravian tiles made by Henry Mercer, and a floor of yellow marble squares and green Moravian tiles. The drawing room walls were paneled in chestnut. Its fireplace was surrounded by tiles of a Persian design handpainted by Goodhue himself, and its major piece of furniture was an upright Chickering piano with a case designed by Goodhue. At the top of the house, facing the street, was his two-story-high workroom, or studio. Its triple window had a pane of stained glass depicting a scene from *The Song of Roland,* and the musicians' gallery had newel posts carved by Kirchmayer into the shape of allegorical figures of Handicraft and Design. The effect of the

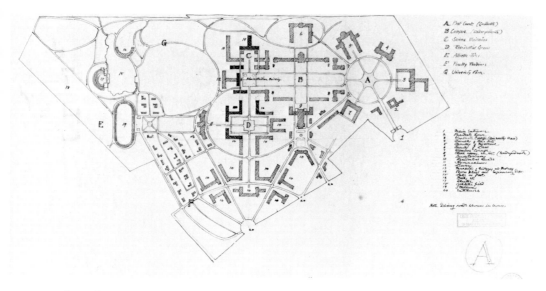

75. *Proposed plan of the Rice Institute, Houston, Texas, by the Boston office of Cram, Goodhue & Ferguson, 1909*

76. *Proposed plan of the Rice Institute, Houston, Texas, by the New York office of Cram, Goodhue & Ferguson, 1909*

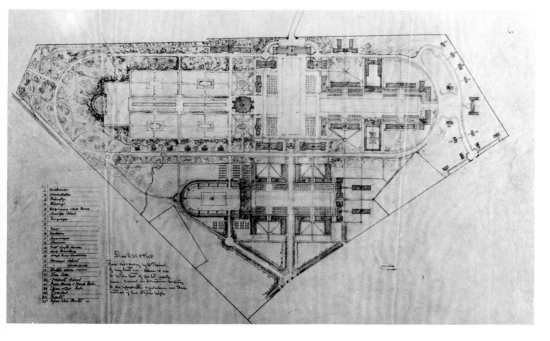

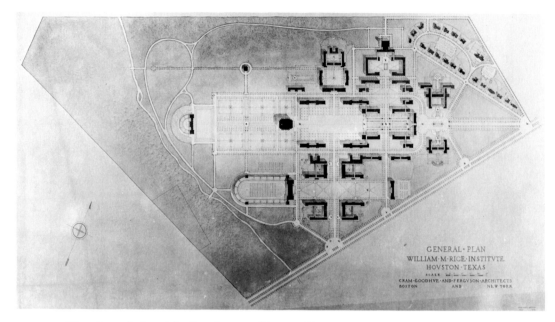

77. General plan of the Rice Institute, Houston, Texas, by Cram, Goodhue & Ferguson, 1909

entire house was one of refined simplicity and subdued color, devoid of any pretentious stylistic elements.[11]

In the period of 1903–1913, Goodhue participated in the design of two important groups of buildings: the Rice Institute in Houston, Texas, and the Panama-California Exposition in San Diego, California. Both display a sense of order different from the typical City Beautiful or Beaux Arts plan. In an article in *The Brickbuilder,* the architect and critic Alfred Morton Githens contrasted Goodhue's plans with more usual arrangements:

> . . . characteristic of the Paris ideal is a certain bigness and simplicity, evidenced in a desire to include all the buildings of a plan in one great composition rather than in a series of smaller arrangements of varied form, more or less closely knit together. A single great impression to the beholder of size and symmetry is preferred to this sustained interest in passing from group to group.[12]

In 1909, Cram, Goodhue & Ferguson was retained to design a new campus for the William M. Rice Institute in Houston. The Boston office sent three schematic site plans to the client, each characterized by complicated, irregular geometry. The New York office sent one. Its cross-axial arrangement, orthogonal geometry, and grandeur of scale formed the basis of the final plan. In it a major open space defined by buildings and massed trees was balanced by a series of secondary arrangements (Figs. 75–77).[13] The site plan is composed about a major east-west axis which is crossed by several secondary north-south axes. A series of large and small courts are positioned in relation to one or more of these axes and intimately connected one to another. Githens observed that in this composition "the several subsidiary courts can be finished one after another, so at no time may the group seem a great attempt impractical to carry out." The tree-lined walkways which formed the axes of the scheme were the fixed elements intended to provide continuity and a sense of completeness.[14] By contrast, a disadvantage of a City Beautiful plan, such as McKim, Mead & White's 1893 plan for the Morningside Heights campus of Columbia University in New York City, was that the grouping of buildings had to be carried out at once or the composition inevitably looked incomplete; then, once completed, such a composition was hard to enlarge.[15]

Goodhue's initial site plan for the Rice Institute was later revised by the Boston office, and after the firm dissolved, Cram & Ferguson retained the Rice Institute commission, designing several buildings for the campus in a fresh "Mediterranean Gothic" style.[16] However, Goodhue did design at least one building for the campus—the auditorium (Fig. 78).[17] The symmetrical building is placed at the end of an axis. At the center is a tall, arched portal flanked by massive pylons. Behind this sits an immense, cubelike volume which supports an octagonal lantern sur-

78. *Perspective of the auditorium for the Rice Institute, Houston, Texas, by Cram, Goodhue & Ferguson (New York), 1909*

mounted by a tiled dome. Arcades stretch across the facade to connect low side structures into a U-shaped group, raised above the landscape on a broad terrace. While the side buildings of concrete are austere, the central mass is encrusted with tiled ornament along the parapets and the dome forms a resplendent centerpiece. Although this design remained unbuilt, it is important nonetheless: Goodhue was beginning to shape the plan, massing, and ornament of a building to a tightly controlled order that possessed a sense of classical calm, even as he was exploring more romantic imagery that recalled his trip to Persia and his abiding fascination with Hispanic-Moorish architecture.[18] This design at once embodies Goodhue's recollections of Isfahan and presages the exotic classicism developed by Lutyens in Delhi.[19]

After the completion and publication of the chapel at West Point in 1910, Goodhue began to receive commissions in far-flung places that required him to be away from the office for long periods of time. From 1910 until his death in 1924 Goodhue crisscrossed America by train to tend to commissions. While hardly an unpleasant ordeal, train travel was, nevertheless, time-consuming and tiring, and it left him out of touch with his office. But in producing the working drawings for the buildings at West Point, Goodhue had organized an efficient, professional staff that did not require his presence on a day-to-day basis.

In April 1911, Goodhue received the commission to design a new hotel at Colón, in the Panama Canal Zone. This government job had resulted from the support of Frederick Law Olmsted, Jr., and the positive reception of the firm's work at West Point and Goodhue's Spanish Colonial designs in Cuba. In April, Goodhue sailed from New York for Panama, leaving the office to finish up the competition drawings for Northwestern University, in which he eventually placed second after Palmer & Hornbostel.[20]

After meeting with the clients, Goodhue sailed for New Orleans. On board, he prepared sketches and detailed notes for the hotel, both of which were forwarded to the office from port. The notes included fifty items relating to the design and construction of the hotel, and each was initialed to note whether the author was Goodhue or one of the clients. Most of Goodhue's suggestions reflected sound planning and construction, such as reinforced concrete construction throughout, cross-ventilation, impervious finishes on walls and floors, and the supply of chilled air to all public rooms. The hotel's plan was U-shaped around a court, with guest rooms clustered in pairs, each pair with a small private loggia. Despite this arrangement, and the use of the Spanish Colonial style, the completed hotel was a lackluster building, reflecting the fact that Goodhue's energies were directed toward other more important projects and that he did not get along well with the clients in Colón whom he appraised in a letter as "quite the vulgarest crowd you ever saw."[21] When his ideas were not received with enthusiasm, Goodhue could be abrupt and unwise in his dealings with the client, his manner working against his artistic intentions. His letter also revealed the stress of being away from the office and his family:

> To tell the truth, I'm distinctly homesick and hate the thought of starting west instead of east from New Orleans the moment I land. It's no fun being out of the scramble like this and no fun travelling with such a horrid crowd of my dear compatriots—the honeymooning Olmsteds are, of course, a constant delight—but I grow tired of being their "conductor."[22]

Sitting on the boat, Goodhue yearned to be back at his office. Instead, he was sailing toward New Orleans where he would board a train to Los Angeles and on to San Diego, where he was beginning work on the Panama-California Exposition.

In 1909, a group of citizens in San Diego decided to hold a fair in 1915 to celebrate the completion of the Panama Canal. This fair was intended to call attention to the city, which then had a population of only 35,000, and to its potential as the first western American harbor north of the canal.[23] The fair was to be located within the limits of the 1,400-acre Balboa Park in the center of the city, and to be called the Panama-California Exposition. Its purpose was to embody at the same time the romance of the past and the promise of the future. (After the San Diego fair had been announced, San Francisco decided to hold a fair of its own in the same year, consistent with the two cities' long history of civic competition. San Francisco's fair, called the Panama-Pacific Exposition, turned out to be far grander in scope.)[24]

San Diego had a talented local architect, Irving Gill, whose austere work had attracted the attention of some of the city's leading citizens. He had designed a house in 1904 for George Marston, a wealthy department store owner and an organizer of the fair. Gill also enjoyed the support of the Episcopal Bishop of Los Angeles, Joseph Johnson, an influential man in Southern California, as did Goodhue. At first, it was assumed that Gill would be the architect of the fair and that he would design a collection of simplified Mission-style buildings.[25]

In 1910, the San Diegans hired the Olmsted Brothers of Boston to lay out the site for the fair, and it was through his friendship with them that Goodhue heard of the post of consulting architect. At first, the Olmsteds' efforts on Goodhue's behalf were to no avail, and Goodhue replied regretfully to their letter, "I am sorry, too . . . because I consider myself quite a shark on the sort of stuff they ought to have and am pretty familiar with Californian conditions."[26] Accordingly, he tried another approach to obtain the commission. On December 28, 1910, he wrote to Elmer Grey, a prominent Los Angeles architect, about "a position I want very much . . . they have a perfectly lovely problem and one which Olmsted thought I was better fitted to deal with than any other architect, thanks to my studies of, and book on, Spanish Colonial architecture in Mexico."[27] Grey replied on January 4, 1911, that he had enlisted the help of his former partner, Myron Hunt, and noted that two men were being considered for the position: John Galen Howard of Berkeley, and Gill. Grey respected Howard's executive abilities but not his design capability; and he felt that Gill hadn't "a broad enough outlook."[28] Bishop Johnson, to whom Goodhue had written also, replied on January 2, 1911:

> I am devotedly attached to . . . Gill, who is by far the best architect . . . in San Diego. I have very frequently said to him that I thought he was a faddist . . . but should he be out of the way, I need hardly say that of all the men in the United States, you are the man to whom I would turn and for whom I would be pleased to use my influence.[29]

The San Diegans agreed to interview Goodhue, and in mid-January he traveled there by train, charmed the committee, and secured the commission. On January 28, 1911, *The San Diego Union* reported that Goodhue

> . . . had been engaged to give the general designs for the buildings; also the composite for the whole group. He will have the deciding voice in all questions of design and artistic effect. He also will give the complete plans and specifications for the most important buildings.[30]

The choice of Goodhue was fortuitous for the city. As Kevin Starr observed in *Americans and the California Dream*, "Goodhue was just at that stage where he could remarkably fulfill San Diego's needs: poised between past and present, glimpsing the modern but filled with nostalgia for an imagined past." By recalling a romantic Hispanic tradition, Goodhue created a new architecture intended to symbolize the city's future.[31]

Initially, the Olmsteds chose a site for the fair at the edge of Balboa Park, near the city center. This decision was consistent with their feelings about the role of an urban park: They preferred any buildings to occur at the edges, leaving the heart of the park as an unencumbered illusion of wilderness. The construction supervisor for the fair, Frank Allen, suggested an alternative site in the center of the park on a 400-acre mesa. Goodhue realized that the new site would allow a more dramatic grouping of buildings and concurred with Allen. Defeated on a matter of principle, the Olmsteds withdrew their services in September 1911.[32]

By the end of 1911, the general scheme of the fair had been worked out under Goodhue's direction, and it was different from the

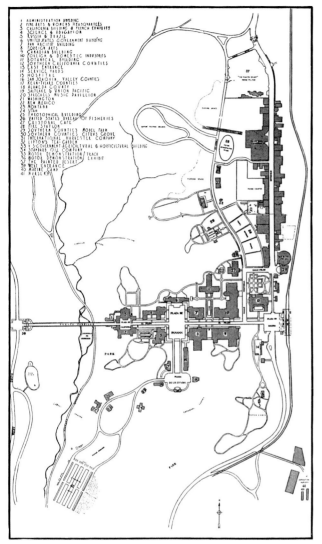

1 ADMINISTRATION BUILDING
2 FINE ARTS & WOMANS HEADQUARTERS
3 CALIFORNIA BUILDING & FRENCH EXHIBITS
4 SCIENCE & EDUCATION
5 RUSSIA & BRAZIL
6 UNITED STATES GOVERNMENT BUILDING
7 PAN PACIFIC BUILDING
8 FOREIGN ARTS
9 CANADIAN BUILDING
10 COLLEGE & DOMESTIC INDUSTRIES
11 BOTANICAL BUILDING
12 SOUTHERN CALIFORNIA COUNTIES
13 EAST ENTRANCE
14 SERVICE YARDS
15 HOSPITAL
16 SAN JOAQUIN VALLEY COUNTIES
17 KERN-TULARE COUNTIES
18 ALAMEDA COUNTY
19 SALT LAKE & UNION PACIFIC
20 SPRECKELS MUSIC PAVILLION
21 WASHINGTON
22 NEW MEXICO
23 MONTANA
24 UTAH
25 THEOLOGICAL BUILDING
26 UNITED STATES BUREAU OF FISHERIES
27 CRISTOBAL CAFE
28 FIRE STATION
29 SOUTHERN COUNTIES MODEL FARM
30 SOUTHERN COUNTIES CITRUS GROVE
31 INTERNATIONAL HARVESTER COMPANY
32 LIPTON'S TEA GARDEN
33 U S GOVERNMENT AGRICULTURAL & HORTICULTURAL BUILDING
34 STANDARD OIL COMPANY
35 MOTOR DEMONSTRATION TRACK
36 MOTOR DEMONSTRATION EXHIBIT
37 THE PAINTED DESERT
38 WEST ENTRANCE
39 MARINE CAMP
40
41 NURSERY

79.   General plan of the
Panama-California Exposition,
San Diego, California, by Cram,
Goodhue & Ferguson (New York),
1911–1915

usual fair plan. Alfred Morton Githens found "no French influence" in
Goodhue's "idealized Latin city." He compared Goodhue's scheme with
the experience of progression through sun, shade, and space in Rome,
where "out of the shadows of narrow streets and alleys between huge
palaces, one emerges on the Piazza Colonna, di Spagna or Barberini; a
vivid contrast is felt, the shadow intensifies the sunlight, and the sunlight
the shadow."[33] In this way, the San Diego fair stands in contrast to the
1893 Chicago fair where the paramount impression was the singular focus
of the Court of Honor.

Yet in another way, the San Diego fair possessed the same strong
sense of architectural unity that characterized previous exhibitions, as

Goodhue himself suggested:

> An artist, in creating a work of beauty, whatever it may be, chooses and eliminates his elements until he has formed a unified whole. Even in great old cities like Florence and Toledo there is manifest the result of just this same spirit, expressed in such cases however, not by a single artist but through centuries filled with artists working with the same ideal in mind against the same historic background.[34]

Goodhue eschewed what he regarded as the superimposed and singular unity of a City Beautiful plan in favor of a more variegated and natural order that appeared to grow up over time—a reflection of his belief that valid artistic ideas arise in a laissez-faire manner from the broad dimensions of history and culture.

The scheme was arranged around a major east-west axis called *El Prado* that linked the formal western approach from the city with a trolley station on the east (Fig. 79). Along this major axis were located two formal plazas and several secondary cross axes leading to more informal courts and patios. Every cross axis terminated in a building or a framed view of the landscape beyond. Unifying the various buildings and open spaces were a pair of long arcades lining the main axis. The arrangement

80. View of the entrance approach to the Panama-California Exposition, San Diego, California, by Cram, Goodhue & Ferguson (New York), 1911–1915

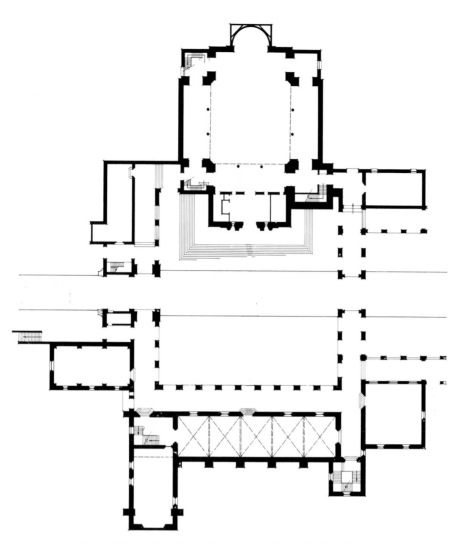

81. *Plan of the California Building at the Panama-California Exposition,*
San Diego, California, by Cram, Goodhue & Ferguson (New York), 1911–1915

of spaces and building groups adhered to an orthogonal geometry
throughout, but the peripheral groups of buildings were placed to conform
more or less with the shape of the flat mesa on which the fair was sited.
Goodhue's intention was to compose a rational plan fitted to the shape of
the site that would yield a "city-in-miniature wherein everything that met
the eye and ear of the visitor were meant to recall to mind the glamour
and mystery and poetry of the old Spanish days."[35]

Entrance to the exposition was from the west across a 1,000-foot-
long concrete bridge spanning Cabrillo Canyon, terminating at a picturesque pile of buildings that seemed to be based on Goodhue's drawings
of dream cities (Fig. 80). Through a monumental gateway, one entered
the *Plaza de California* around which the theme buildings were tightly

grouped. On the south side of the plaza was the low, massive, and rather chaste Fine Arts Building. On the north side was the California Building, composed of a striking combination of highly decorated tower, dome, and facade (Figs. 81–83). Its ecclesiastical format, a Greek-cross plan with shallow transepts, was modeled on the various Mexican churches Goodhue and Baxter had analyzed in 1899. The plain, 200-foot tower, placed in the angle formed by the south and east transepts, burst into flamboyant ornament at the top; an exuberantly Churrigueresque front facade displayed a profusion of carved figures depicting events in California history; and the dome was covered with blue, green, yellow, black, and white tiles and the inscription: "a land of wheat, and barley, and vines, and fig trees, and pomegranates; a land of oil olive [sic] and

82.   *Section of the California Building at the Panama-California Exposition, San Diego, California, by Cram, Goodhue & Ferguson (New York), 1911–1915*

83.　View of the California Building at the Panama-California Exposition,
San Diego, California, by Cram, Goodhue & Ferguson (New York) 1911–1915

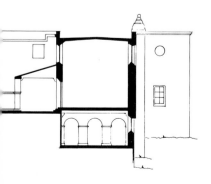

115

honey," an Old Testament description of the Holy Land and a prescription for Southern California. This grouping of permanent buildings was constructed of concrete, covered on the exterior with putty-colored stucco, and simply painted on the inside. The massing gave strength and dignity to the ensemble, while the concentrated ornament reinforced the plasticity and sculptural force of the major elements. [36]

Beyond the permanent entrance grouping, the exuberant and theatrical temporary buildings—designed by Carleton Winslow, Goodhue's site architect—were arranged along the acacia-lined pedestrian street, *El Prado*, and around the main *Plaza de Panamá*. Pearl-gray stucco was used throughout for the temporary buildings. This unity of color emphasized the effect of sunlight and shadow, provided a sense of overall harmony, and acted as a backdrop for the vivid colors of the tiled domes, the awnings, and the landscape (Figs. 84–86). Despite the festive effect of the temporary buildings, Goodhue felt they were fundamentally different from and inferior to the group of permanent buildings. He regarded the temporary buildings as

> . . . very close in certain directions to being actually stage scenery. The reveals of [their] windows and doors, when studied critically, are observed to be pitifully thin, while [their] various features and projections are, considered with reference to what is behind them, playful and meaningless rather than purposeful and logical expressions of their interior. [37]

Goodhue was particularly interested in the quality of light, especially full moonlight, as it fell on the fair buildings. He had described the effect he sought years earlier in "The Villa Fosca":

> In the hot glare of day, every imperfection, every sordid bit of plaster pretense . . . is pitilessly laid bare; but at night, in the tender light of the southern moon . . . all is changed. Then . . . the building gleams silvern and ghostly against the luminous purple of the starry sky, and something—the spirit of the dust-covered ages perhaps—seems to return. [38]

It was under such conditions that the romance of the fair buildings, resting "on the insubstantial shadow of the canyon," would be revealed. [39]

The fair opened on January 1, 1915, amidst blooming poinsettia plants and acacia trees, and it was a resounding critical and popular success despite its modest scope. George Edgell claimed in retrospect that "it made the most vivid impression upon the public mind of any exposition since the White City at Chicago." [40] The fair launched a revival of the Spanish Colonial style in California, eliciting Henry-Russell Hitchcock's subsequent observation that "the emulation [of the fair buildings] . . . turned most local architects away from innovation for almost twenty

84. *View along* El Prado *looking toward the California Building at the Panama-California Exposition, San Diego, California, by Cram, Goodhue & Ferguson (New York), 1911–1915*

85. *View of the Panama-California Exposition, San Diego, California, by Cram, Goodhue & Ferguson (New York), 1911–1915*

117

86.   *View of the Panama-California Exposition, San Diego, California,
by Cram, Goodhue & Ferguson (New York), 1911–1915*

years."[41] In contrast, Kevin Starr claimed that Goodhue's work in San
Diego actually confirmed and consolidated the architectural traditions of
the region, "moving California further along the path upon which it had
already set out through its revival of Mediterranean, toward simplicity of
line, drama of mass, and harmony with landscape."[42]

Had Goodhue's concept for the fair been fully realized, his work
might have been less influential. He had specified that all the temporary
buildings were to be razed after the exposition had closed and replaced
with gardens to complement the landscaping provided for the fair itself.
He had intended to transform the whole site into a 200-acre public garden
to rival those of Europe. Only the buildings at the entrance to the fair
were to remain—as a gatehouse—to mark the entrance to the vast

118

garden. The architect was disappointed when the San Diegans came to love the buildings so much that they refused to demolish them. [43] Ironically, this was fortuitous for his reputation and his influence upon California architecture. As the critic William Kent observed in 1920 in *Country Life*, Goodhue's influence could be attributed to two aspects of the exposition:

> . . . first of all, by the excellence of its grouping and design, and second, by the fact that many of the buildings at San Diego still endure, and several will continue to stand, as potent influences for delightful architecture. [44]

With the entire ensemble left in place, perhaps too much attention was focused on the florid ornamentation of the temporary buildings and too little on the superb massing and composition of the permanent group, its monumental dimensions, and its splendid siting. The excellence of Goodhue's fair buildings, finally, lies not so much in their scholarly regard for style as in their more fundamental architectonic qualities. [45] Nevertheless, Goodhue's designs prepared the way both for the more academic work of people like Myron Hunt and for the freer work of George Washington Smith and other domestic architects in subsequent years, and they provided all of California with the elements of an appealing and appropriate regional architecture. [46]

In the course of working on the fair, Goodhue came to admire the work of Irving Gill, and said so in a letter to Elmer Grey:

> . . . while I don't . . . coincide with all his views, and not at all with his theory that ornament is unnecessary, I do think that he has produced some of the most thoughtful work done in the California of today, and that for the average architect, his theories are far safer to follow than mine, or even perhaps yours. [47]

Grey disagreed, replying that he thought Gill's was "a dangerous kind of work," and resented "its evoking the admiration of such influential chaps as George Wharton James and Bertram Grosvenor Goodhue." All of Goodhue's subsequent work in California represented a move away from his own florid style and decisively in the direction pioneered by Gill. Indeed, by the opening of the San Diego fair in 1915, Goodhue had already begun to question the direction of his own work. It is ironic that Goodhue seemed to learn so much from Gill, while the latter's own views were met with silence in the wake of Goodhue's work at San Diego. [48]

As the 1903–1913 phase of Goodhue's career drew to a close, he was regarded by his peers and by conservative critics as a brilliant and unique talent working within the mainstream of American architecture. Of the many distinguished buildings he had designed to date, the West Point chapel and the San Diego fair had solidified his reputation, and had demonstrated anew that significant architecture could emerge from the wellspring of the traditional styles. They are highly personal accomplishments that demonstrate his ability to work in several styles, adapting the architectural heritage of Europe to American circumstances. Yet there are two negative aspects of Goodhue's success. First, he had avoided and even condemned the classical work of his peers, preferring to work within the boundaries of the freer styles. As a result, the range of commissions that he found congenial was limited. Second, as long as he continued to design within any of the established styles, he was avoiding that search for a greater freedom of expression which engaged the best of his peers. Lewis Mumford understood this completely when he observed retrospectively in 1925 that

> . . . had [Goodhue] died at that time [1913] he would have lingered feebly in our minds as a merely cultivated architect, distinguished by tact and delicacy and good taste, but after all in the same category as the X's and Y's.[49]

Goodhue might have agreed with Mumford. But as his steely independence of mind had caused him to resist an even stricter academic use of the traditional styles, so it caused him to resist the more radical direction of the modernists. He was still too confident about his ample talents, and therefore diffident about developing in a new direction.

Goodhue was about to experience a series of events that would cause him to reassess his talents, his commitment to his architectural goals, and the direction of his career. The first of these was his increasing dissatisfaction with his professional situation, which led to the dissolution of Cram, Goodhue & Ferguson and the establishment of his own office in 1914. As Goodhue turned forty, he naturally wanted to be recognized as an architect in his own right and to receive artistic credit for the work of the firm that he had accomplished alone. As Goodhue came to see that this goal was difficult to achieve within the framework of the firm as it had been established in 1898, he began to consider a revision in the terms of agreement binding the partners. The central issue was outlined by Goodhue in a letter to Cram and Ferguson in February 1910:

> . . . that while separate, the two offices were to be known each as that of CRAM, GOODHUE & FERGUSON; that while the working drawings, specifications and general directions were to emanate from the New York office in the case of West Point work and St. Thomas's Church, in which two cases all partners had an equal voice, all other things were to be solely in the hands of the representatives, or representative, of the firm dwelling near and controlling the direction of the office in which they were done, the profits, if any, however, being in all cases divided equally between all three members of the firm. . . . There is no real grievance against any

120

individual . . . I merely insist that the partnership shall be so constituted as to permit of my being given, and taking, the credit, or blame, for such work as I am directly responsible for.[50]

In January 1911, *The Architectural Record* devoted an entire issue to the work of Cram, Goodhue & Ferguson, and Montgomery Schuyler was meticulous in ascribing credit to the two offices.[51] Goodhue sent a copy of the magazine to Silas McBee, the editor of *The Churchman*, together with a letter:

My reason for sending you the "Architectural Record" was, of course, not merely that you might see that the firm of Cram, Goodhue & Ferguson is busy and has turned out a great deal of work, but that after this it will be impossible to credit it all to one hand and brain.[52]

Goodhue felt that this was the first occasion on which he had received adequate public recognition for his own efforts. Later that year, on July 3, 1911, the 1898 partnership agreement binding the three men was revised. The fourth article of the revised agreement clarified the responsibilities of the three partners:

The final decision in all matters of design in work carried on in the New York office shall rest in BERTRAM G. GOODHUE. The final decision in all matters of design in work carried on in the Boston office shall rest in RALPH A. CRAM. The final decision in all matters of engineering and construction in work carried on in both offices shall rest in FRANK W. FERGUSON.[53]

As in all contracts, this one also included a procedure by which any one of the partners could, through death, retirement, or withdrawal, terminate the partnership.

In the summer of 1911, Cram was appointed to be the consulting architect of the Cathedral of St. John the Divine, and this caused Goodhue some personal embarrassment. The death of Thomas Heins had left Grant LaFarge to carry on the cathedral commission they had won in competition in 1891. The cathedral trustees hastily and mysteriously dismissed LaFarge. After a perfunctory attempt at another competition, the trustees appointed Cram. LaFarge was well liked among architects in New York, and the decision was regarded as unpopular and unfair.[54]

That year, Goodhue had been proposed for membership in the Century Association, an important link with the New York establishment, and he was concerned that Cram's acceptance of the appointment might reflect badly and unjustly upon himself. Goodhue wrote to William Rutherford Mead, his proposer, who felt there was no problem, that Cram's actions were not related to or subject to Goodhue's control. On December 2, 1911, Goodhue was elected to the Century Association.[55]

121

Cram and Goodhue often worked independently as consulting architects—Goodhue for the Panama-California Exposition, and Cram for Princeton University—although all working drawings were completed in the firm's name, in one of the two offices. Goodhue perhaps felt threatened by Cram's possible motives in accepting the position at the cathedral. It may have occurred to him that by accepting a position in New York City, Cram was becoming too ambitious within the framework of the firm. Goodhue became distrustful and even paranoid about Cram's behavior. For example, when Cram was to deliver a lecture before the Royal Institute of British Architects in London in May 1912, Goodhue asked his friend Cecil Brewer to "make a point of hearing him talk and let me have a little report." He wanted to be assured that Cram claimed credit in the lecture only for the work he had done, "much of which is, of course, most excellent," and did not claim credit for that work coming out of the New York office. Goodhue's behavior was petulant and even childish, but there is no question that the issue of artistic credit was of great importance to him:

> I suppose I suffer somewhat (perhaps it is part of the damned neurasthenic fiddlesticks) from what Milton calls "the last infirmity of a noble mind," in other words, the desire for fame.[56]

The changes in the partnership agreement only postponed the inevitable, and on July 18, 1913, Goodhue notified Cram and Ferguson that he was withdrawing from the firm.[57] He presented his reasons in an interview in the August issue of *The Churchman:*

> The separation has occurred because I am convinced that the artistic individual mind works to best advantage when alone. With Mr. Cram I worked for ten years or more toward what appeared to be the same artistic ideal. But dating possibly from Mr. Cram's visit to England made at the instigation of *The Churchman* [in 1904] to write "The Ruined Abbeys of Great Britain," there came a divergence of ideas. Since the establishment of the office in New York . . . a difference in style has been more and more apparent in the firm's work. In any particular example, architects and most of the clergy have been able to recognize the dominant hand. While Mr. Cram and I recognize equally the practical requirements of the Church in our plans—and the name of these is legion, for they extend even into trifling details—yet in character, I may say in poetic character, the styles we employ are worlds apart.[58]

Goodhue was sure of his course, yet he also showed concern for his partners:

> I find myself happier than I have been for years. Just at present

R.A.C. probably feels a certain degree of bitterness and I know by experience he is a difficult person to convince of error, but I make no doubt that in the course of time he will be happier too, if indeed he is not so already. [59]

On December 31, 1913, at 5 P.M., Cram, Goodhue & Ferguson was dissolved. Cram and Ferguson remained together as a firm and subsequently designed a large body of distinguished work. [60] The firm later evolved to Hoyle, Doran & Berry, which remains in practice today in Boston. On January 1, 1914, Goodhue opened his own firm, retaining his office at 2 West 47th Street. He felt a mixture of emotions at dissolving his former partnership, which he related to Cecil Brewer:

> There is a certain solemnity about cutting off associations that have lasted so long. Cram and I for nearly a quarter of a century have worked together; we like the same things and the same people and if I could have possibly found a way of keeping on with him and at the same time preserving my self-respect, I would have done so. My case, however, was clearly strong and my own belief in the justice of my position and action has been reinforced time and time again since the event by letters and phrases of friends from architects and the like. [61]

One such letter was sent three years later by the Boston architect, Charles D. Maginnis, evaluating Goodhue's move:

> Now, more than ever it is interesting to watch what you are doing, as your identity is not so nebulous. You now stand quite clear and clean-cut in the artistic firmament, shining perhaps a little too brilliantly for all the rest of us. [62]

After a year on his own, Goodhue wrote to Cram in a reflective mood:

> Now that we are working separately, and by mutual confession both growing stouter in consequence, I am as ready to tell you as anyone (and I have told a number of people) that I often miss the stimulation of your companionship and controversion of my ideas, architectural and otherwise, that now pass as law. [63]

When Cram, Goodhue & Ferguson was dissolved, the assets in the form of commissions were valued and divided. Even as these matters go, it was a difficult, lengthy, and exasperating process for the three partners, and it was not completely settled for several years. [64] Nevertheless, Goodhue's attitude toward Cram continued to mellow over the years. In September 1921, Goodhue took the occasion of a visit to Boston to call on his former partner, and he wrote to his brother that he had had a pleasant time with Cram:

He seems busy and photographs and drawings he showed me represent very good work indeed. Most people suppose that I wish him ill but you know that this is anything but true.[65]

The dissolution of Cram, Goodhue & Ferguson was based in part upon the conflicts between the powerful and complex personalities of Cram and Goodhue. But it was also based upon each man's evolving attitude toward an essential architectural issue: the relationship between tradition and innovation. After 1913, Goodhue was professionally free to explore this critical issue on his own, and to produce work for which he alone would bear responsibility. His new independence did not result in an immediate change in his work, but it did mark the beginning of a period of restless search for a freer and less academic expression than he had used to date.

CHAPTER FIVE · THE IMPACT OF LIVERPOOL CATHEDRAL

I
N 1911, Goodhue was given the opportunity to design a major Episcopal cathedral in Baltimore: the Cathedral of the Incarnation.[1] The trustees had originally solicited sketches for a new building from Henry Vaughan. Vaughan's first drawings, approved on November 8, 1909, were for a synod hall—a component of a cathedral group—only the undercroft of which was completed by 1911. The trustees subsequently decided to seek a more imposing edifice than Vaughan had proposed, and turned to Goodhue, who developed a scheme in the fall of 1912.[2] The program called for a fully equipped seat for a bishop, and thus the programmatic elements ranged from a large nave and chancel down to small guest bedrooms in the staff quarters. Virtually every building type Goodhue had previously been asked to design was here assembled on one site: church, library, school, and houses. It was an opportunity to work at a grand scale (Fig. 87).[3]

The site had a gentle slope which fell away sharply to the southeast. The cathedral itself was placed on the highest spot, with the chantry, in line with the north choir aisle, thrusting out beyond the edge of the slope to create a picturesque effect. A spacious cloister garth was placed on the south side of the nave and, because of the slope, one level lower. This arrangement allowed the south porch to double as a pulpit for outdoor gatherings (Fig. 88). A diocesan library, the bishop's residence, and the choir school, including its dormitories, enclosed the cloister garth. To the east was a quadrangle of houses for three resident canons and to the south of the choir school was a synod hall. This complex facility was skillfully composed, each element—important or inconspicuous—finding its appropriate position.

The scheme for the cathedral itself was a blend of French and English characteristics. It had an English square termination and, in addition to the main transept, a secondary transept between the choir and sanctuary to introduce an extra burst of light, giving the interior the

125

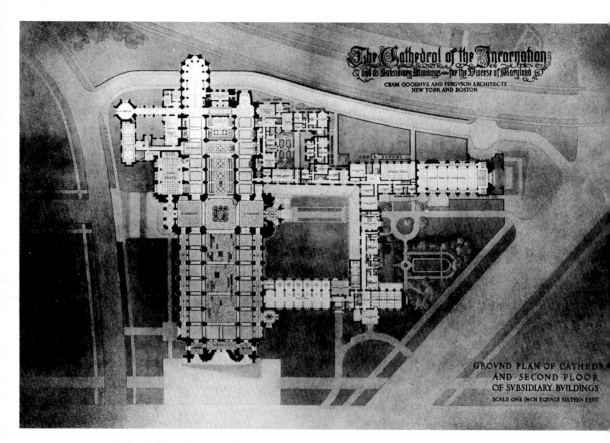

The Cathedral of the Incarnation
and its Subsidiary Buildings — for the Diocese of Maryland
CRAM GOODHVE AND FERGVSON ARCHITECTS
NEW YORK AND BOSTON

GROVND PLAN OF CATHEDRA
AND SECOND FLOOR
OF SVBSIDIARY BVILDINGS
SCALE ONE INCH EQVALS SIXTEEN FEET

87.   *Plan of the first scheme for the Cathedral of the Incarnation,*
Baltimore, Maryland, by Cram, Goodhue & Ferguson (New York), 1912

appearance of added length and complexity. The French wall system consisted of an arcade, triforium, and clerestory, with vertical proportions approaching those of Amiens, creating a majestic atmosphere. This was Goodhue's only design for which he used flying buttresses.

The rendering prepared the trustees for a medieval town, but while perfectly correct, the scheme seemed wrong, lacking the qualities Goodhue usually brought to bear in his work: freshness of spirit and expression. The cathedral design seemed dry and academic, and Goodhue knew it; he had deliberately produced a conservative and erudite scheme to clinch the commission. Once he had won the confidence of the conservative client, he would then propose a more original design for actual construction. It was a cunning tactic, and it worked. But, unfortunately, the initial project was widely published and it made its designer seem more academic and scholarly than he was. By early 1913, he was definitely assured of the commission, and immediately sailed for England to "have a look around at what the architects there are doing in the way of the most modern manifestations of the Gothic spirit."[4]

126

88. *Perspective of the south porch and outdoor pulpit of the Cathedral of the Incarnation, Baltimore, Maryland, by Cram, Goodhue & Ferguson (New York), 1912*

The most instructive and challenging example he saw was the new Anglican Cathedral under construction in Liverpool, designed by Giles Gilbert Scott, who was eleven years his junior. Goodhue came to regard this twentieth-century Gothic building as dauntingly original, and its design caused him to reevaluate his feelings about architectural form.[5]

In 1903, Scott, then twenty-two years old, had won the competition for the Liverpool Cathedral. At first the trustees were unwilling to allow Scott to carry out the work alone and required an association with George Frederick Bodley, the noted Gothicist, by then an aged and venerable architect, deeply admired and rigidly conservative. Bodley's influence surely would have dampened Scott's efforts at fresh architectural expression had the elder man not been distracted by equally large cathedral commissions in Washington, D.C., and San Francisco.[6]

The first stage of construction was the Lady Chapel, and upon its completion in 1910, the originality of Scott's design was apparent. After Bodley's death in 1907, Scott was able to develop an almost completely new overall scheme even less indebted to precedent than the competition-winning design (Fig. 89). When this was published, Goodhue thought it "to be a terrible mistake," and said so in a letter to Archdeacon Madden of Liverpool:

> . . . the first design was the wonder . . . of the architectural world and . . . the absence of certain features of Gothic so usual as to be almost regarded as clichés, such as for instance little crocketted pinnacles, formed the basis for one of my chief sources of satisfaction. On the new design, however, a number of these quite useless features are manifest and . . . the space, crossing, I suppose it would still be called, beneath the central tower will apparently be not lighted any too well, though in the original, quite the reverse was the case. No one, of course, can raise any objection to a central tower in place of the two transeptal ones in the original, but while the little account accompanying the reproductions states that this tower is enormously tall, it has no such effect in the picture.[7]

The Archdeacon passed the letter along to Scott, who replied that "I feel so confident of the advance made in the amended design as compared with the old scheme that even Mr. Goodhue's slashing attack leaves me unmoved."[8]

Goodhue traveled to England in January 1913, and had an opportunity to see the work completed at that time on the cathedral and to meet its architect. He changed his opinion of both:

> I . . . am quite mad over Scott's Liverpool Cathedral . . . [and] Scott himself . . . impresses me as one of the most quietly capable

128

89.   Perspective of the 1910 revised design for Liverpool Cathedral by Giles Gilbert Scott

young men I have ever seen. Certainly Liverpool is a perfect wonder. Baltimore will never be anything like so good. Of course, this is largely a matter of ignorant clients but the fact remains that Scott is a great deal better man than I am.[9]

Goodhue saw in the Liverpool design a big, boldly scaled modern building that was subsequently described in 1931 by the English classical architect Charles Herbert Reilly as

. . . so broad and monumental in its lines that, unlike the old Gothic cathedrals, it has much of the balanced beauty of a classical

129

building, while not abating a jot of the dynamic force of Gothic architecture in its most energetic form.[10]

Goodhue was stirred by this experience because the cathedral design represented what he himself wanted to accomplish in his own work, and he feared that "nothing I can do . . . will ever be able to rival Scott's work at Liverpool of which I am probably the most enthusiastic partisan in the world."[11]

Goodhue's reputation in England at that time was based primarily on his design for the chapel at West Point, which was admired for its massive forms, its bold silhouette, and its freshness of spirit. So it is ironic that Goodhue felt so challenged by Scott's design. Nonetheless, upon his return to America, spurred on by this new inspiration, Goodhue produced two remarkable designs, neither of which was to be built.

The first was a revision of the Cathedral of the Incarnation in Baltimore. Whereas the first scheme had been conservative, the second was bold, vigorous, and unconstrained. The primary structural system was simplified: the number of nave and chancel bays each was reduced from seven to four, and correspondingly increased in unit dimension, allowing large areas of glass; the flying buttresses were replaced with massive stepped and gabled piers; and the roof pitches were changed from steep to very shallow, thus drawing attention to the walls alone. The nave wall system included an aisle arcade with a small intermediate pier between each main pier, a triforium gallery, and a three-part clerestory above. The crossing was a very high space rising well into the tower and lighted by four large windows.

The exterior expression of the structure and space also was changed, especially in the crossing tower. The initial tower had risen as a continuous volume with strong vertical lines to a decorated top. The revised tower soared even higher, with an awesome, mountainlike quality, that dwarfed the body of the cathedral below. Everywhere in this second scheme, Goodhue's customary approach to form was pushed to a new level. The emphasis was on pure mass expressed by surfaces free of extraneous detail and enriched by sculpture at key places in the composition.[12]

The perspective drawings of the two designs reveal the significant change that took place in his work as a result of his trip to Liverpool (Figs. 90, 91). The initial sketch is drawn in a flat light with an emphasis on the detail and decoration, and from a vantage point which emphasizes the length of the cathedral and the intricacy of its parts: its flying buttresses, parapets, towers, and subsidiary buildings. The second perspective is drawn in a sharp, low light which emphasizes the modeling of the stepped and brooding masses, and from a vantage point which emphasizes the great height of the tower and the density of volumes boldly claiming the hilltop.[13]

130

90.   *Perspective of the first scheme for the Cathedral of the Incarnation, Baltimore, Maryland, by Cram, Goodhue & Ferguson (New York), 1912*

91.   *Perspective of the second scheme for the Cathedral of the Incarnation, Baltimore, Maryland, by Cram, Goodhue & Ferguson (New York), 1913*

Goodhue encountered resistance to the revised design.[14] Nevertheless, in November 1920 work began on Goodhue's design for the synod hall, to be built on Vaughan's undercroft, and almost immediately was halted because of severe foundation problems. With Goodhue's death in 1924, the commission was given to the firm of Frohman, Robb & Little, all of whom had worked for Cram & Ferguson and who had been given the commission of completing the Washington Cathedral after the death of Henry Vaughan in 1917. They revised the design of the synod hall in 1929, and it was completed in 1932. The Depression prevented any further construction, leaving the initial visions of the cathedral trustees unfulfilled.[15]

The second project was Goodhue's most romantic house: a medieval aerie for Frederick Peterson near Brewster, New York. The drawings of the house show a bold composition that takes command of a hilltop as though it were Mont St. Michel or a castle from *The Song of Roland*. They emphasize the tall, massive tower at the heart of the scheme, and show the gabled wings of the house and the stepped, terraced gardens reaching out across the craggy site (Figs. 92, 93).[16] Goodhue produced the drawings on "a sudden impulse brought about by the generally ideal character of the whole operation."[17] These designs for the Baltimore cathedral and for the Peterson House confirm that Goodhue's fertile imagination was governed by his fundamental sense of order and composition, his belief in the importance of structural expression and discipline,

92.   *Plan of the Frederick Peterson House, Westchester County, New York, 1915*

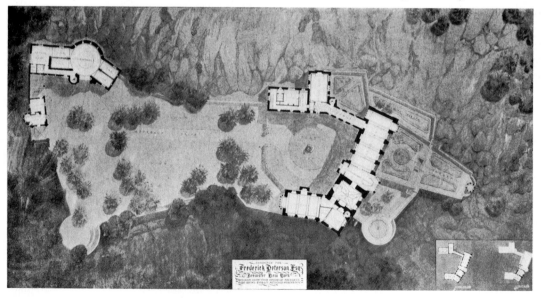

132

93.   Perspective of the Frederick Peterson House, Westchester County, New York, 1915

and a growing interest in surfaces and massing stripped of ornament and detail.

In 1914, Goodhue was asked to design the Church of Saint Vincent Ferrer for the Dominican Order of the Roman Catholic Church, on Lexington Avenue at 66th Street in New York City. This new building was to replace a church completed in 1869 by P. C. Keely, and to supersede plans by Allen & Collens and James W. O'Connor to remodel and enlarge the earlier church. Keely's design was a long, gabled volume with a north aisle and little triangular dormers, a modest, unarchaeological Victorian Gothic structure typical of the mid-nineteenth century. Allen & Collens and O'Connor proposed to add a new west front with two towers and to flank the nave with ambulatories and side chapels.[18] The demolition of the earlier church in 1914 confirmed the resolve of the Priory Council to create a new building instead, at once grander and more scholarly in conception. Because of his work at Saint Thomas's, Goodhue had the confidence of the clients and was given a free hand in his design, limited only by the complex liturgical requirements, the budget, and the difficult site. Goodhue found this commission to be a "sympathetic piece of work with lots of interesting little difficulties and quirks." He conveyed his enthusiasm for the project to his lawyer of many years, Henry Gennert, when he wrote that "as long as I give them their practical requirements for the money they can afford they are content to trust that

133

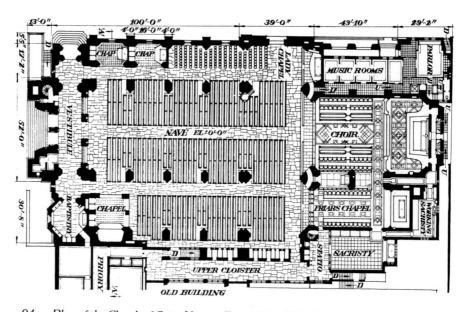

94.   *Plan of the Church of Saint Vincent Ferrer, New York City, 1914–1918*

I know more about architecture than they do." Goodhue had a large and distinguished body of church buildings to his credit by this time, and he was a natural choice for the commission. His professional capabilities secured the job, despite the obvious irony that Goodhue was, in his own words, "anti-religious and strongly anti-catholic."[19] The design was ready by 1915, and the completed building was dedicated on May 5, 1918.[20] Talbot Hamlin, the historian and critic, thought that in the result "there seems to be the perfect balance between freedom and academic style. Its proportions are so beautiful, the materials in its structure so well used and expressed, that the effect is profoundly satisfying."[21]

The church fills the site; almost every square foot of the property is used for interior space. The nave, composed of four bays and a crossing, seats 1,670; it is 130 feet long, 40 feet wide between piers, and rises to a height of 77 feet. The choir is 72 feet long and 37 feet wide. Two transepts increase the width of the church to 95 feet (Figs. 94, 95). The nave is placed slightly off center in plan, yielding a Lady Chapel and two side chapels in the north aisle and a side chapel and medieval-style friars' chapel in the south aisle. The confessionals are built into a cloister wall flanking the south aisle, minimizing their visual intrusion. An array of nostalgic paintings of religious subjects, seemingly created in different places at different times in the past, serve as the stations of the cross. They introduce variety and sentiment into the austere

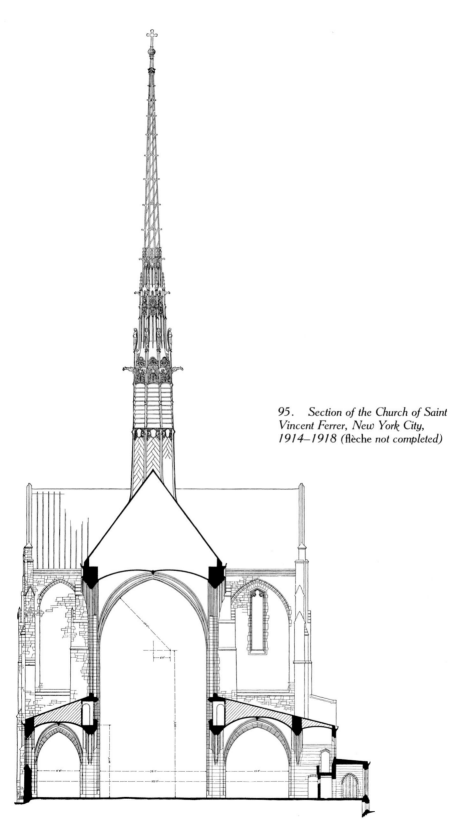

95. *Section of the Church of Saint Vincent Ferrer, New York City, 1914–1918* (flèche *not completed*)

135

interior of the building, which is built of warm-toned dressed sandstone with vaults of Guastavino tile and wall surfaces of a cocoa-colored porous tile called Akoustilith, another product of the association of Raphael Guastavino and the acoustician, Wallace Sabine.[22]

On the interior of Saint Vincent's, Goodhue experimented to see how far he could simplify the expression of structural forces without losing the atmosphere and spirit of Gothic space. In earlier churches like the West Point chapel, the elements of vault, rib, engaged shaft, and arcade molding had been expressed individually in an articulate composition. In subsequent designs, like the First Baptist Church, Goodhue had simplified the vertical elements into plain piers. In Saint Vincent's, the expression of the entire structure is simplified, even abstract. The Guastavino vaults are held by ribs which feather out into the massive piers, a system seen in earlier Goodhue churches. But integral to each rib and pier is a small, rounded, ornamental molding, which starts at the floor and soars up the piers, across the vaults on the ribs, and down the piers on the other side. This small ornament transforms the traditionally particulate elements of structure into a continuous fabric of incised lines and simplified moldings on the surfaces of the vaulting ribs and piers. Consequently, the surfaces have a stern simplicity bereft of applied ornament; the actual structure and the modeling of its masses create the primary impression. At the same time, the articulate structure traditionally regarded as the essence of Gothic architecture is abstracted to a cage of lines expressed as moldings.

The site for Saint Vincent's was afflicted with unusually bad soil conditions, with one of the many small streams that flow across Manhattan Island, and with vibration from the adjacent Lexington Avenue subway. These problems required expensive foundations and made towers on the west front impractical. Instead, Goodhue proposed a *flèche* over the crossing that would rise to a height of 265 feet. Framed in steel and sheathed in hand-hammered copper, the *flèche*, which remained unbuilt for financial reasons, would have been the highest in the world.[23]

The exterior of Saint Vincent's is sheathed in rough-textured, split-faced Plymouth granite, contributing to the brutal grandeur of this church (Fig. 96). Goodhue was probably attracted to its grim, unyielding appearance as a suitable material for the stern architectural expression he was developing. In contrast, the ornament and the carved figures atop the west turrets are rendered in smooth limestone. This use of different stone gives the exterior a welcome variety. The carved figures on the west turrets show Goodhue's and Lawrie's evolving ideas about the placement of such sculpture for ornamental effect (Fig. 97). The carved figures well up out of each turret as though they had grown out of the stone. The effect is not unlike the late statues by Michelangelo, where the figures appear to be struggling to be free of the stone. As on the interior, the

136

96.   *1930 exterior view from the northwest of the Church of
Saint Vincent Ferrer, New York City, 1914–1918*

ornament and sculpture are made to seem integral with the surfaces rather
than applied to them.

On July 5, 1918, while Saint Vincent's was under construction,
Goodhue was asked to design another large church, a chapel at the
University of Chicago. The 24-acre site of the university had been laid
out in 1891 by Henry Ives Cobb to embody the "ideal of a City of
Learning, one quadrangle opening into another, as though all the colleges
of Oxford were brought together into a continuous and unified whole."
The style of the early buildings was English Gothic, selected "to remove
the mind of the student from the busy mercantile conditions of Chicago
and surround him with a peculiar air of quiet dignity which is so notice-
able in old university buildings."[24]

137

Funds for the university chapel, or Rockefeller Chapel as it was named after the death of its benefactor, were secured as part of John D. Rockefeller's "Final Gift" of $10 million to the university in 1910.[25] As early as the summer of 1913, Goodhue had been in close pursuit of the commission, but the advent of World War I postponed any decision. Finally, in July 1918, Goodhue was hired, and by October he was prepared to begin work.[26]

A prominent site was chosen for the chapel: a full block on the southern edge of the campus facing onto the Midway, a spacious greensward that had been part of the grounds of the 1893 World's Columbian

97.   *1930 detail view of the sculpture on the west turrets of the Church of Saint Vincent Ferrer, New York City, 1914–1918*

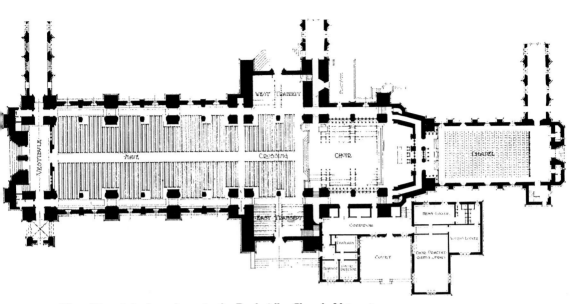

98.   *Plan of the first scheme for the Rockefeller Chapel, University
of Chicago, Chicago, Illinois, 1918*

Exposition. By the end of 1918, Goodhue had presented his first ideas
for the chapel in a series of sketches. The plan was composed of five
equal square bays, three for the nave and one each for the crossing and
chancel (Fig. 98). There were narrow aisles and two shallow transepts.
The dimensions of the bays were unusually large for a Gothic church,
permitting large clerestory windows to admit much light and creating a
serene, glassy hall.

The massing was characterized by the dramatic piling up of forms
typical of a Goodhue design (Fig. 99). Low, planar subsidiary buildings
flanked the periphery of the site. Rising behind was the immense five-bay
chapel with its turreted entrance facade. Looming up over the ensemble
was the crossing tower, startlingly tall and massive, even for the generous
chapel beneath it, housing one of the largest carillons in the world. The
imposing tower recalled that of Saint Kavin's Church and of the revised
Baltimore cathedral. The bold scale of the ensemble reflected the influence of Liverpool Cathedral.

There were problems with the first scheme. The chapel clients were
conservative and criticized Goodhue for not using the familiar forms of
French and English Gothic architecture. Goodhue defended his project
in a letter to an employee then serving in the war:

> . . . that you may know how safe and sound the scheme was I will
> tell you that the section and system was something like that of Albi

139

99. *Perspective of the first scheme for the Rockefeller Chapel,*
University of Chicago, Chicago, Illinois, 1918

or even Perpignan . . . [with] a very high and very narrow side
aisle with enormous windows and a little unarchitectural gallery of
inlaid wood and marble columns frankly inserted. I had intended
to cover the interior up to the spring of the vault with Akoustilith
. . . soft creamy white in tone . . . and then to blossom out in the
ceiling with dusky gold and color but all in tile: as you see, nothing
that need frighten anybody yet it seemed to shock the powers that
be.[27]

Goodhue was broadening his formal resources by introducing Romanesque and Byzantine elements. While not Gothic, these were still medieval, at least as defined by his mentor, William Lethaby, in *Mediaeval
Art.*

The clients also objected that the chapel's cubic volume was excessive, and that its seating capacity was insufficient. Accordingly, in January 1919, Goodhue submitted four alternative designs. In design A, the
seating was increased from 1,600 to the desired 2,000 and the aisle
space was reduced; in B, the overall width of the building was reduced
with a further reduction in the cubage; in C, the cubage was drastically
reduced by eliminating the central tower; and in D, the tower was
retained but placed over a transept. In the letter accompanying the four
alternatives, Goodhue noted "that everything in all the designs is most
tentative, not only from your point of view but from my own, for I
invariably study and re-study until the result I hope to achieve is attained." Nevertheless, he did not like to have his scheme challenged, and
concluded somewhat brusquely:

> I shall be glad to welcome any and all criticisms that may be made
> upon this design by you and the others of your Committee but I
> trust that such criticisms will be constructive rather than destructive
> with, in addition to the bald statement, the reasons given therefor.[28]

On August 26, 1919, Goodhue received permission to proceed
with working drawings, using design B, and these were complete by May
1920. The cost estimates were far larger than the available funds.[29]
Work on the chapel did not resume until late 1923, by which time the
crossing tower had been replaced by a transeptal tower, and the building
was completed in 1928 (Fig. 100).[30] Despite the restrained use of
marble and tile ornament, the brusque appeal of its plain, massive structural elements, and the serenity of its main space, the chapel remained an
unsatisfactory and transitional design.

In Saint Vincent's and the Rockefeller Chapel, the structural elements were composed with concern for overall effects of mass. At the
same time, the decorative aspects—the iconographic figure sculpture and
surface ornament—were reduced in quantity. The result in each case was

*100.   View of the completed Rockefeller Chapel, University of
Chicago, Chicago, Illinois, 1918–1928*

a stripped-down, austere, less scholarly version of his earlier ecclesiastical
designs that revealed the direction but not the resolution of Goodhue's
search for a new architectural expression. A church was no longer a
particularly challenging commission for Goodhue. Such a program had
certain inherent formal characteristics and a predictable sense of order in
plan and section, which he had long since mastered. The resolution of his
search lay along other lines—grappling with styles other than Gothic and
with building types other than churches.

In 1905, in an article written for *The Craftsman* long before this search was resolved, Goodhue had suggested the broad characteristics of a new architectural expression:

> It is possible that we shall never again have a distinctive style, but what I hope and believe we shall someday possess is something akin to a style—so flexible that it can be made to meet every practical and constructive need, so beautiful and complete as to harmonize the hitherto discordant notes of Art and Science, and to challenge comparison with the wonders of past ages, yet malleable enough to be moulded at the designer's will, as readily toward the calm perfection of the Parthenon as toward the majesty and restless mystery of Chartres.[31]

Ultimately Goodhue was able to bring forth a new architectural expression that embodied these two contradictory qualities of "calm perfection" and "restless mystery," but only after a period of haunting and often vexing search.

CHAPTER SIX · A SEARCH FOR NEW DIRECTIONS

IN 1914, Europe was plunged into a war that ruined the economies of most of the participating nations and called into question their political and philosophical structures. America entered the war late, was spared physical turmoil, and emerged confident in its traditional order. Within this context, architectural progress in Europe developed into a radical, revolutionary rejection of the past, while in America, progress was seen as an improved adaptation of forms which retained and reaffirmed a connection to the past.

In response to this, Goodhue pondered a number of architectural questions which proved increasingly troublesome to many other architects as well: the validity of historical forms in relationship to modern building programs, the relevance of new technology and constructive processes and materials, and the proper role of ornament. All of these issues seemed to him to suggest a new kind of architecture, but one that grew out of tradition. In an article written in 1916 for *The Craftsman,* he observed:

> I think you may expect me to say "Throw away traditions," but that I cannot do. I feel that we must hold tradition closely, it is our great background; as a matter of fact, good technique is born of tradition. We cannot start each generation at the beginning in our mastery of workmanship. The big universal progress in art moves on the wings of tradition. The nervousness about tradition in America springs from the fact that we have used it too much in place of imagination, in place of solid practical thought. Tradition has made us a little lazy about our own needs and our own inspirations. I feel that we should use tradition, and not be used by it. . . .[1]

Goodhue attempted to find a new architectural expression based upon imagery rather than technique. He had already routinely incorporated into his designs new building technology, but he felt that such elements in and of themselves did not constitute a basis for new expression. Instead, he continued to seek an architecture that combined appropriate craft and technique with an expression of time, place, and cultural purpose. This search for new form took two directions. In monumental work, Goodhue sought a way to adapt anew the architectural patrimony of England and the Mediterranean world to the scale of the twentieth century and to modern American circumstances, and in this he looked in part to the work of Edwin Lutyens and Giles Gilbert Scott. In work of more modest scope, Goodhue avoided the hegemony of the orthodox styles altogether and sought to adapt the primitive character he found in such vernacular forms as the Indian adobes of the American Southwest and the colonial stone buildings of the East, and in this he was inspired by the work of Irving Gill and Harrie T. Lindeberg.

In 1914, Goodhue's firm was busy with several projects, notably the buildings for the Panama-California Exposition in San Diego and those for the Virginia Military Institute in Lexington, Virginia,[2] when an even more important commission came to it: Saint Bartholomew's Church in New York City, which he anticipated could not be Gothic, "owing to the fact that the present triple doorway in the present church, a very beautiful affair in Southern French or possibly Italianate Romanesque, must be used and so sets the key for the new building."[3]

On March 30, 1914, the Vestry of Saint Bartholomew's Church met to consider the selection of an architect to design a new building on a site on Park Avenue then occupied by a brewery. Fourth Avenue had been renamed Park Avenue in 1875, but it did not fully come into its own as one of New York City's more prestigious streets until the submerged tracks of the New York Central Railroad were covered over in 1913.[4]

Although Goodhue was interviewed, he was fearful of losing the commission because of his reputation as a Gothicist. In a letter to Arthur C. Jackson, a member of the Vestry committee, he wrote:

> It occurs to me that certain of your committee may be prejudiced against me because of the undoubted fact that most of my churches have been in a sort of Gothic. By "a sort of" I mean a Gothic that disregards Mediaeval precedent when such conflicts with modern practical requirements and methods. I trust, however, that you will be able to convince them that I can work in the Romanesque of Italy and Southern France as freely and in no worse fashion than in Gothic.[5]

On June 4, 1914, he was appointed architect and embarked on a fresh stylistic challenge.[6]

The Romanesque-style triple portal, a gift from the Vanderbilt family, had been designed in 1909 by McKim, Mead & White and incorporated into the old church on Madison Avenue at 44th Street, designed by James Renwick in 1872. In reusing the portal, Goodhue did not wish to replicate its position in the old church, where the arches bore the mass of the facade above. Instead, he was inspired by the original example at Sainte Gilles where the portal stands as the front of the narthex, separate from the wall of the church proper. This strategy at the same time honored the triple portal and freed Goodhue to develop a harmonious but personal design.[7]

Once the style had been established, Goodhue turned his attention to the massing on the site.[8] He was interested in using as much of the site as possible to create a commanding group of church and auxiliary buildings, but the Vestry wished to reserve a portion of the site for income-producing development. While the block plans were studied, the broad architectural features of the church were resolved, inevitably suggesting comparisons with precedents. In a letter sent to the rector, Dr. Parks, on vacation in Europe, Goodhue suggested he see a number of churches in Italy which contained "wonderful bits of the style McKim, Mead & White had in mind when doing your triple portal," including "Saint Mark's, Venice, the church whose plan undoubtedly inspired that of Perigueux and, as undoubtedly, the one I am now working on for you."[9]

For inspiration in the design of Saint Bartholomew's, Goodhue also looked to England, this time to the example of the Byzantine-style Roman Catholic Westminster Cathedral (1895–1902) in London, by John Francis Bentley.[10] The decision that Westminster Cathedral be Byzantine was based on three points: the wish to avoid comparison with the Gothic Westminster Abbey; a need for a wide nave unimpeded by columns; and the intention to construct the entire structural fabric at once, leaving the ornament to be added over time as funds were available. Bentley was chosen to design the Byzantine cathedral despite his reputation as a Gothic architect, and when he toured Italy in 1895 to seek precedent for his project, he carried with him Lethaby's book on Sancta Sophia.[11] Bentley's design resulted in the largest Byzantine-style structure constructed since Sancta Sophia; it was described upon completion as "a work which must be for all time an architectural landmark emphasizing the passing of the nineteenth and the opening of the twentieth century."[12]

Emboldened by Westminster Cathedral and the Byzantine and Italian Romanesque examples it evoked, Goodhue began work on the design of Saint Bartholomew's in the last months of 1914. As presented to the Vestry on January 17, 1916, at Goodhue's office, it consisted of three elements: a description and drawings of three alternative site plans; samples of the stone and brick to be used; and, as the *pièce de résistance*, an unusually large model. The next day, *The New York Times* reported that the model showed an apartment house with 75 feet of frontage on Park Avenue, 32 feet back from the sidewalk, sharing the site with the church; that members of the Vanderbilt family were pleased with the incorporation of the triple portal; that the church would not cost the rumored $3 million; and that "it was denied also that any attempt had been made to rival Saint Thomas's either in cost or architecture."[13] Goodhue described the unveiling to the English architect Cecil Brewer:

> For the past two weeks my reception room, ordinarily a very attractive room, has been cluttered up by a model at twenty-fourth full size of the new Saint Bartholomew's, a strange aberration in Italian Romanesque of sorts . . . [and] it seems to be creating an enormous sensation. . . .[14]

Among the letters of congratulation came one from William Mitchell Kendall, principal design partner at McKim, Mead & White:

> I waited until I could see the model of Saint Bartholomew's at the League, which I did last week. It seems to me an extremely interesting design and you certainly have gone to the extreme of leaving the triple portal untouched.[15]

Three alternative site plans were studied. Scheme A, formally presented to the Vestry, used 125 feet of frontage along Park Avenue for the church, with the remainder to be used for other development. Scheme B made use of the entire site for the church only, with no income-producing tower. Scheme C proposed use of the full Park Avenue frontage but only 200 feet of depth, selling off lots on 50th and 51st streets. Goodhue preferred Scheme B because it allowed for a longer church and chapel with increased seating capacity and improved architectural proportions. Because of the site's adjacence to the underground railroad tracks leading into Grand Central Terminal, the question of vibration in the foundations was evaluated, and the location of the church at the corner of Park Avenue and 51st Street (as in Schemes B and C) was advocated. A cost estimate for each alternative was included; each was more than the parish anticipated spending. During the spring of 1916, the Vestry wavered between the affordable Scheme A and the more ample and splendid Scheme B, ultimately deciding in favor of the latter. Bids were received on September 7, 1916, and all were rejected as too high. Goodhue was requested to simplify the plans further, which he did within the month. After revised bids were accepted, construction began in early 1917 and was substantially complete by October 1918 (Fig. 101).[16]

The plan of Saint Bartholomew's is centered on a crossing space which is encompassed by four stone arches resting on large square reinforced concrete piers faced with stone and rising to a polychromed ceiling (Figs. 102, 103). Emanating from the crossing are a short three-bay nave, an apsidal choir, and two shallow transepts, all covered with barrel vaults of Rumford tile. Low aisles surmounted by galleries flank the nave.

147

101. *1926 view from the northwest of Saint Bartholomew's Church, New York City, 1914–1919*

102. *Plan of Saint Bartholomew's Church, New York City, 1914–1919 (cloister not completed)*

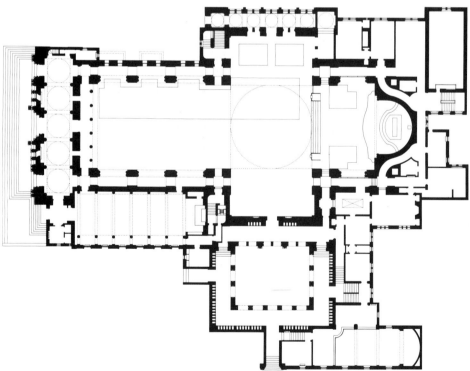

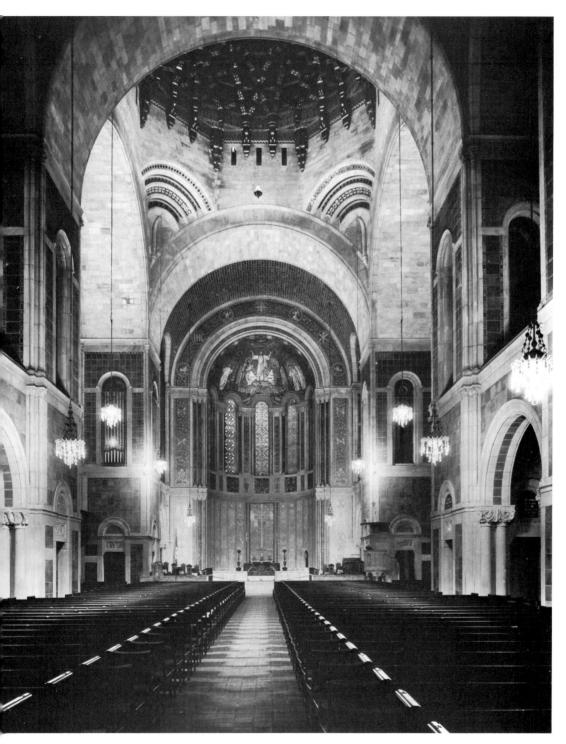

103. *Interior view of Saint Bartholomew's Church, New York City, 1914–1919*

104.   Interior view looking toward the altar of the side chapel of
Saint Bartholomew's Church, New York City, 1914–1919

The rhythm of the nave is accented by the transverse barrel vaults over
each of the nave windows and by the piers which support the ceiling
vault. These piers and the crossing piers have a tripartite vertical division:
the lower portions are plain; the middle portions have attenuated columns
at their corners; and the upper portions have decorated tile borders. The
wall surfaces of the church are faced with cocoa-colored Akoustilith tile
trimmed with stone. The decorative ornament follows Byzantine precedent: the surfaces around the altar are sheathed in sheets of marble; the
columns surrounding the altar are of various colors of marble; and each
of the capitals of the nave columns has a unique design. In the small

150

adjacent chapel, Goodhue developed a more decorative scheme. He incorporated the marble shafts of the columns of the old church, omitted their bases, and fitted them with new capitals of carved stone. He covered the chapel with a painted and gilded timber roof (Fig. 104).[17]

The scheme of this church is distinctly different from that of Saint Thomas's or the West Point chapel. In the earlier examples, the repetitive, modular structural bay is of prime importance in establishing the linearity of the space; at Saint Bartholomew's, the absence of a repetitive module, the cross-axial plan, and the great height of the crossing all help to establish the centrality of the space.

The exterior treatment of the masses and surfaces was fundamental to Goodhue's conception of the building. He observed that "we too often forget that New York is blessed with the brilliant skies of Italy," and used a mixture of stone and varied sized brick to achieve "a somewhat similar effect of richness to that which one finds in the Romanesque churches of Milan and Bologna," and, at the same time, "to keep the building in harmony . . . with the atmospheric effects of New York." The two exterior materials—warm gray Indiana limestone and light salmon-colored brick—were composed by Goodhue in such a way that the almost complete use of stone on the lower walls yielded to the nearly exclusive use of brick in the upper portions of the building. He felt that the church could not be built of stone alone, as "even so picturesquely varied a mass as is contemplated . . . needs the color and contrast of the various materials."[18]

The completion of Saint Bartholomew's in 1918 was not a particularly satisfying moment for Goodhue, in part because he had had several sharp clashes with the rector, in part because so many important finishing touches were not completed (the tiled dome and the community house were completed in 1930 by Goodhue's successor firm, Mayers, Murray & Phillip); and because by then he had become less traditional in his approach to architectural form.[19] Nevertheless, this church holds an important place in his career, because its design forced him to rethink the fabric of a church in a different architectural idiom. As he genially conceded, "Saint Bartholomew's is anything but Gothic, indeed when completed, if ever . . . it will look more like Arabian Nights or the last act of *Parsifal* than any Christian church."[20] For this building, Goodhue began to develop a bolder sense of scale in planning and massing, a wider palette of materials, and a greater feel for broad, plain surfaces.

In 1915, while Saint Bartholomew's was being designed, the Panama-California Exposition opened, and the buildings and grounds were well received by the press and the public. The fair generated several new commissions for building groups in the West: an opera house, agricultural college, and railway station in Riverside, California (1915), none of which was built;[21] a campus for the Throop College of Technology (after 1920 the California Institute of Technology) in Pasadena, California (1915–1939); a company town in Tyrone, New Mexico (1914–1918); a Marine Corps base and naval air station in San Diego (1918); and two colleges and a museum in Honolulu (1917–1927). For these projects, Goodhue began with the Spanish style of the San Diego fair and moved decisively toward greater simplicity.

The project in Tyrone was the first among these to proceed. Commissioned by the Phelps Dodge Corporation, the town had two components: the communal facilities, including a hotel, motion picture theater, bank, school, church, shops, and clubhouse; and the workers' housing.[22] This commission offered Goodhue the splendid opportunity to explore his ideas about urban form, albeit at a small scale, and at the same time to confront the problems of the modest individual dwelling unit—its fitness, functional layout, and simplicity of style—plus the arrangement of the various houses on the site.[23]

The town was sited in a narrow valley close to the Burro Mountain copper mines operated by the client. The strength of Goodhue's design was its arrangement into the image of an idealized Mexican town, with all the small-scale urbanity that image evokes. The communal facilities were housed in two-story buildings joined by a continuous arcade around the generous central plaza—140 by 250 feet—containing a fountain and bandstand (Figs. 105, 106). Goodhue located this plaza at the terminus of the railroad serving the valley, making the station an important element in the plan and rewarding the train passenger with a lush, green oasis for a destination. The plaza was approached axially from two directions by a wide, tree-lined street; two cross streets led out of the square to the housing areas. Perched on a hillock above was the church, modeled on the theme building at the San Diego fair. Around the plaza, the general store and the bank had ornamental elements in the same Spanish Baroque style used for the San Diego fair, and the administrative building had a heavy cornice and window moldings, but Goodhue designed the other buildings with "not an ounce of ornament anywhere, nothing but plaster walls with tile or flat parapeted roofs . . . not unlike the English cantonments I remember seeing at such places as Madras."[24] With little ornament and a bland surface texture, the buildings relied upon the composition of volumes and upon color for interest. Each was finished in a different pale tint: the store building was pearl white, the clubhouse a grayish neutral tone, the movie theater a bluish tint, the warehouse a yellowish buff, the bank and shop building were purplish, and the post office and railroad station were a pinkish buff. This subtle kaleidoscope of color was particularly suited to the soft nuances of western sunlight, which Goodhue found so different from the brilliant skies of the East.[25]

In contrast to the orthogonal geometry of the town center, the areas

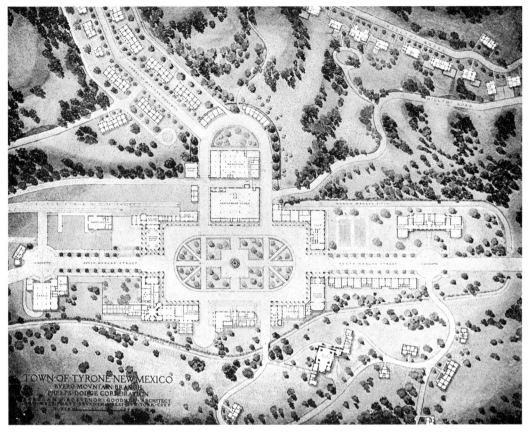

105. Plan of the town of Tyrone, New Mexico, 1914

106. Perspective of the town of Tyrone, New Mexico, 1914

153

of housing were fitted to the land in a more picturesque arrangement. Housing for the Mexican workers was built in an arroyo to the southwest and was composed of four types: a single-family house, a two-room duplex, a three-room duplex, and a twelve-room six-plex. Houses for the American workers varied in size from three to six rooms and were built on the crest of a nearby ridge, which allowed the two-family houses to be designed on two levels. The houses were extremely chaste and reflected at once the program and Goodhue's encounter with the work of Irving Gill in and around San Diego. Clarence Stein was the chief assistant on the Tyrone commission, and that experience together with his work on the San Diego fair undoubtedly contributed to his later work in town planning.[26]

Goodhue's use of a simplified style in Tyrone reflected his interest in the architecture of the Southwest, where he traveled to New Mexico to photograph the Indian adobes at Taos and elsewhere as research for his new commission. For the San Diego fair, Goodhue had rejected the California missions in favor of the earlier Mexican style; in Tyrone, he rejected the latter for the even earlier Indian adobe. Paradoxically, the austere simplicity of form and materials found in the adobe was exactly the quality sought by the most advanced architects like Irving Gill. A reuse of vernacular forms seemed a way to revitalize at least the design of modest buildings, but it would be premature to assume that Goodhue had by then evolved a new attitude about architectural form in general.

Two fairly large commissions in San Diego were awarded to Goodhue by the Bureau of Yards and Docks: a Marine Corps base and a naval air station. In the Marine base, Goodhue used plain stucco arcades to link the more embellished major buildings placed around a vast parade ground. He regarded both commissions as

> . . . strictly workaday propositions but not unamusing in spite of it . . . especially the Aviation Buildings where we have to have doors over 100 feet wide, a stable to keep a balloon in and various problems that did not trouble the architects of old.[27]

While working on these commissions, Goodhue had an opportunity to fly in an airplane for the first time, and it proved a momentous experience:

> Flying, by the way, has my whole heart. I went up . . . in San Diego last summer to view the site . . . for the Aviation Group. We sailed over [the] San Diego Fair and for a long time afterward this killed all taste for architecture in me. The tower, which you will remember was quite "some tower" looked like the end of a pencil, rather a small pencil at that, while the other buildings looked like rabbits' hutches or dog houses.[28]

From this new vantage point, Goodhue was impressed with the potential

154

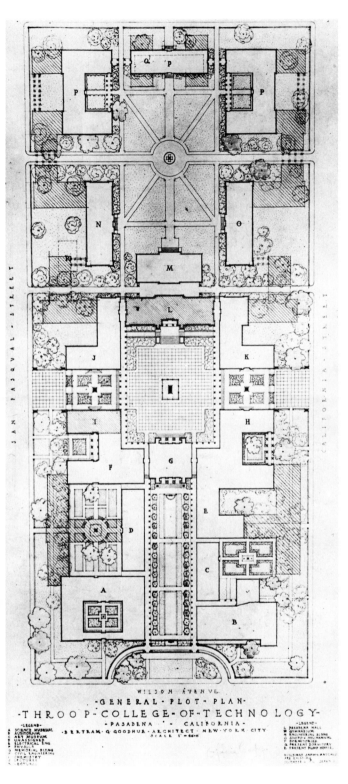

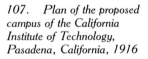

*107.   Plan of the proposed
campus of the California
Institute of Technology,
Pasadena, California, 1916*

impact of bold simplified forms of ample dimension, and the insignificance of the intricate, picturesque effects which had often characterized his work. One immediate result of his flight was that the two military groups were drawn from the vantage point of an airplane passenger and the renderings tended to accentuate the regularized, geometric composition of the ensemble of buildings in each scheme. In a more general way, his emerging interest in an architecture stripped of extraneous detail was undoubtedly reinforced by what he saw from his aerial vantage point, even though buildings are not usually seen from the air.

In 1915, Goodhue was asked by George Ellery Hale to become the consulting architect for the campus of the California Institute of Technology in Pasadena. Hale, a trustee and a gifted astronomer, was responsible for the creation of the Mount Wilson Observatory, built high in the mountains above Los Angeles in 1902. But perhaps his greatest talent was his ability to influence the creation and direction of whole institutions. He left his mark on the California Institute of Technology, on the Huntington Library and Art Gallery in San Marino, California, and on the National Academy of Sciences at Washington, D.C. Hale and Goodhue had met as a result of the latter's work at the Panama-California Exposition. An initial meeting led to commissions for Goodhue and eventually to a close friendship between the two men. [29]

Goodhue's first project on the campus was to establish a location for and to redesign the exterior of the proposed Gates Chemistry Building, which had already been designed by Elmer Grey of Los Angeles. Grey's scheme was a two-story Spanish Renaissance block surmounted by a continuous entablature. A central door with decorative surround was flanked on each side by four windows on each floor and small windows at the corners. Goodhue respected Grey's planning and the strict geometrical symmetry and classical calm of the facade, but he increased the depth of the ornamental relief, resulting in a greater sense of plasticity. [30]

The Gates Chemistry Building (1917) was part of the plan for the entire campus. When the Institute was established in 1908, Myron Hunt and Elmer Grey, then partners, were retained to plan the campus. Their initial ideas were embodied in a perspective that showed a domed, Mission-style central building—Throop Hall—facing a long, rectangular greensward flanked by arcades and academic buildings. These ideas were further developed by Hunt in a plan of 1912. [31]

Goodhue's scheme for the campus was presented in a site plan in December 1916, followed by a report, various sketches of individual buildings, and one of the dazzling perspective drawings produced in his office (Figs. 107, 108). Taking inspiration from universities in Spain and Latin America, the heart of the plan was a paved quadrangle, 180 feet square, surrounded by arcades, or *portales*. On its eastern side was the

108.   *Perspective of the proposed campus of the California Institute of Technology, Pasadena, California, 1917*

existing administration building, Throop Hall, while on the west was the proposed Memorial Building and library with its elaborate colored-tile dome and Churrigueresque ornament. In contrast to the rich sculptural effect of this domed centerpiece, the academic buildings were treated as unornamented concrete volumes. Connecting the Memorial Building with the western entrance to the campus was a second major court, off which intimate patios and gardens were placed. Along its major axis were three pools of water, which for Goodhue recalled Moghul gardens and best exemplified the approach to the Taj Mahal (a motif that was to be fully realized in the National Academy of Sciences and the Los Angeles Public Library). The long, narrow, western court was flanked by arcades which were terminated at one end by tile-domed aedicular porches. At the other end, the arcades penetrated the Memorial Building to join with those encompassing the main quadrangle. The arcades were the unifying elements of the plan, providing for sheltered movement while gathering the asymmetrical disposition of academic buildings into a formal, east-west spine. The boundary of the campus was marked by a combination of walls and fencing that established a strict division between town and

157

gown. In the varied spaces between the buildings and the bounding walls
Goodhue envisioned gardens and dense landscaping that in some cases
would obscure the architecture. In planning and design, Goodhue's proposal for the California Institute of Technology was an extension of his
work at the San Diego fair. The strong feature of the scheme was its
fusion of a regional and climatic architectural expression with sound
planning for a dense urban campus that was required to grow slowly over
time.[32]

While the Gates Chemistry Building was under construction,
Goodhue developed plans for a spacious auditorium building at the western edge of the campus which eventually was realized (1922) as the more
modest Culbertson Hall. Subsequently, he designed the Bridge Physics
Laboratory (1922) and its additions (1924, 1925) and the High Potential Research Laboratory (1923). The last building, especially, is notable for its severe composition and its flattened, abstracted ornament,
anticipating Goodhue's more advanced ideas of the 1920s. After his
death in 1924, several other buildings were completed in the 1920s and
1930s by his successor firm, Mayers, Murray & Phillip, using the stripped-
down forms Goodhue ultimately came to favor, despite the insistence of
the trustees that the style of the proposed Memorial Building as shown in
the 1917 perspective should set the direction for the remaining structures.
The buildings completed by Goodhue and by Mayers, Murray & Phillip
were essentially the background elements of the campus. Built in antici-
pation of the dominant central structure, they are plain, understated, and
somewhat dry. Ironically, the Memorial Building was never completed in
the form Goodhue envisioned. Instead of a splendid domed and tiled
mass, it was constructed in 1967 as a tall, slim tower, unconnected in
form or material with the surrounding buildings.[33]

Just after he started work in Pasadena, Goodhue was invited by
members of the Bishop and Dillingham families to come to Honolulu to
discuss a number of projects, and he traveled there in the summer of
1917. That fall, work began on the first two commissions, block plans
for two colleges: the Kamehameha Institute, a school which included the
famed Bishop Museum, founded by the Bishop family and located upon
a site of 860 acres within the city; and Oahu College, a school founded
by Connecticut missionaries early in the nineteenth century.[34]

While in Honolulu, Goodhue gave a speech on his ideas for a new
Hawaiian architecture, and after he returned to New York, he prepared
some drawings of Honolulu as he thought it ought to be, based on picture
postcards of Honolulu as he had experienced it (Fig. 109). These drawings were ill-received by the Hawaiians, as Goodhue recalled in a letter
to Cecil Brewer:

It seems that while the talk I inflicted upon them at the Club there last summer was well-received and accepted as Gospel, when it came to approving the drawings I sent out, they could not stand the simplicity I had advocated verbally. I am sorry because I am sure I am right and that simple white-walled buildings with tile roofs and no, or practically no, ornamental features whatsoever would be the rightest thing for them. [Louis Christian] Mullgardt of San Francisco . . . had made . . . some designs for four commercial buildings . . . that clearly pleased the populace much bet-

109.   Perspective of proposed commercial development for
Honolulu, Hawaii, 1917

ter. Mullgardt is a fine fellow and a good architect and if he is right no doubt I'm hopelessly wrong; anyhow his buildings, one of which is going to be built, are loaded with *soi-disant* "spinach."[35]

Goodhue's clients in Honolulu proved to be far more conservative than he, preferring the richly ornamented surfaces of the San Diego fair, which, ironically, he had done so much to popularize. It also possibly seemed startling to his would-be clients that a high-style architect, whose work was associated with the suave deployment of ornament, would now advocate the use of so little. His ideas were premature for the Hawaiians; but six years later, Goodhue was called again to Honolulu to design a museum, which benefited from the rapid evolution of his thinking in the intervening years.

In 1923, Goodhue began work on a building for the newly established Honolulu Academy of Arts, founded by Anna Rice Cooke, a native Hawaiian and the daughter of New England missionaries. Early in 1920, Mrs. Cooke began to envision a museum, using her collection of Oriental and Occidental art as the basis of an institution to embody the cosmopolitan heritage of the Hawaiian Islands, one that would be inviting and free of the stiffness and formality of a traditional museum. On March 16, 1922, the Territory of Hawaii issued a charter of incorporation to the new institution. The site for the new Academy building was that of Mrs. Cooke's family home, in which her collection had been informally displayed for years. The Academy was completed to Goodhue's design in 1926 and opened to the public on April 8, 1927.[36]

The museum has a spacious plan with galleries and subsidiary spaces grouped around a series of open courts (Fig. 110). Entrance to the building is through a south-facing loggia beneath an immense tiled roof into a central courtyard—60 feet square—that forms the heart of the building (Fig. 111). Two courts are placed on an east-west axis, and the thematic imagery of each serves to organize the display of art. To the east is the Spanish Court, encompassed by the galleries of American and European art (Fig. 112). To the west is the Chinese Court, the focus of the galleries of Oriental and Pacific art (Fig. 113). The axial composition of the courts and the serial arrangement of the galleries around them provide for a clear sense of circulation, accented by the progression of sunlight and shade.

The thick, massive, highly textured walls of the Academy are made of handlaid local lava rock covered with a thin coat of stucco. The columns at the entrance and around the central court are sculpted piers of rock with carved capitals—at once archaic and modernistic in character. Flashes of brilliant color in the cream-colored building are provided by tilework and by the floral landscape. The large, simple roofs are modified in section to include a set of clerestories which suffuse the galleries with indirect natural light.

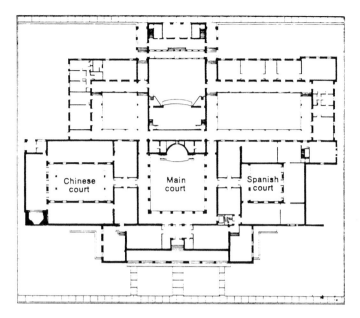

110.   Plan of the Honolulu Academy of Arts, Hawaii, 1922–1927

*111.   View of the south facade of the Honolulu Academy of Arts,
Hawaii, 1922–1927*

112. View of the Spanish Court, Honolulu Academy of Arts, Hawaii, 1922–1927

In the Academy of Arts, Goodhue was able to realize his ideas for a specifically Hawaiian architecture that he had discussed in Honolulu in 1917: a building that was regional in its use of materials and response to climate; freely classic in its plan, its details, and the composition of its masses; and romantic in its use of stripped-down, primitivistic forms.

Goodhue's evolution toward a simpler, freer mode of expression was reflected in an article he wrote for *The Craftsman* in February 1916 on the future of American domestic architecture. He observed that "all art is to be a varied expression of the one great impulse toward beauty," and that "today what we lack in America is poetry in our architecture, in our painting, in our homemaking." He thought that poetic impulse could not be reclaimed in houses that were "too extravagant, too osten-

162

113. View of the Chinese Court, Honolulu Academy of Arts, Hawaii, 1922–1927

tatious." He wanted to address "the problem of building a good, moderately priced house for a man of moderate means." The crux of the problem lay in the plan and the appearance of the house:

> In building the simple house, the plan is the beginning of wisdom. The person building should study every detail of the plan. He should know just what is absolutely essential for him and his home and what he is willing to give up. He must consider the best way to use every foot of space. . . . The moderate house is successful in its appearance just so far as the outside of it fails to suggest a lack of space within.[37]

These thoughts were reinforced by simple vernacular buildings he saw in

163

magazines. For example, he saw in the *American Institute of Architects'*
Journal "several designs . . . for houses in France that were . . . excellent; quite small, white-washed stone or brick with slate or tile roofs, all
absolutely without frills or any sense of style. . . ."[38]

In a series of large house commissions, Goodhue began to apply
the simpler mode of expression he had used for the modest buildings in
Tyrone. The first was a house for Henry Dater in Montecito, California,
North African in character rather than the Spanish Colonial style so
favored in Southern California (Figs. 114, 115). The simple blocklike

114.   Plan of the Henry Dater House, Montecito, California, 1915–1918

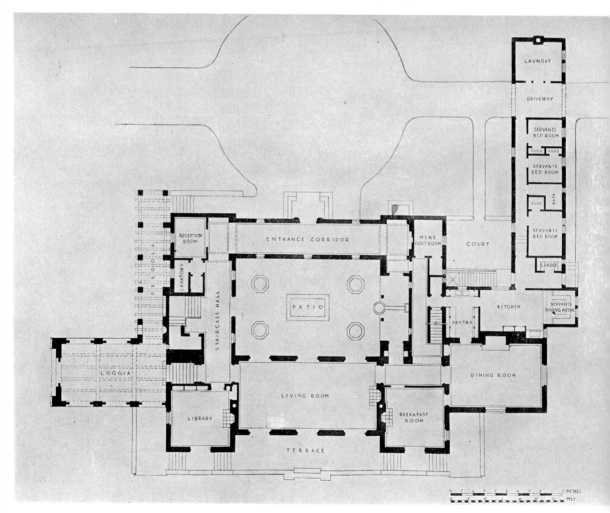

forms of the house are covered with tan stucco and encompass a central patio resplendent with Moroccan tiles. Generous gardens are terraced down an east-facing slope to a large reflecting pool. The exterior has no ornament at all, and the interiors are spacious and spare. William Kent claimed in 1920 in an article, "The Modern Country House in California," that the Dater House embodied

> . . . the main characteristics of the country house of the future
> . . . [and] chief among them is the simplicity, quite unforced, of

115. View of the Henry Dater House and its gardens, Montecito, California, 1915–1918

116. View of the Philip Henry House, Scarborough, New York, 1918

the entire design, due to the effect of plain wall surfaces, pierced by only as many and as large openings as are necessary for entrance and for proper lighting respectively.[39]

The second such house was for Mrs. Philip Henry in Scarborough-on-Hudson, New York, "a sort of Eastern and Anglicized version" of the Dater House. Perhaps Goodhue's finest house, it was favored by him for its spare, laconic forms and its simple walls constructed of rough, random local stone (Fig. 116).[40] A third house and garden with terraces, also in Scarborough, for Walter Douglas, was described by Goodhue as

> . . . somewhat Lindebergish . . . even more in the 1900–1905 manner of . . . Lutyens, though by no means so splendid as his clients usually demand, being built of almost anything handy, split stone from pasture walls, second-hand brick with a little terra cotta and the like, all whitewashed with a wobbly and irregular slate roof.[41]

Goodhue was striving for those qualities found in the domestic architec-

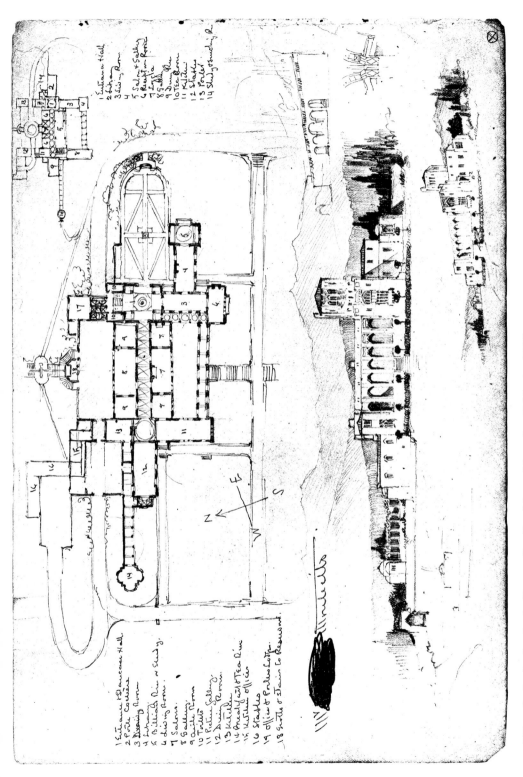

117. *Study sketches for the Bertram Goodhue House, Montecito, California, 1918*

ture of Harrie T. Lindeberg, which the critic Royal Cortissoz described in the introduction to a book on Lindeberg's work:

> To gain the effect of simple unity for which he is always striving he looks to the proportions of his walls, with their doors and fenestrations, to the crowning grace of his roofs and to the fullness with which these things speak for themselves . . . a house of his leaves an impression of romanticism . . . counterbalanced by the classical tincture . . . and by the deeply practical strain running through his practice. [42]

Of all the houses Goodhue designed at this time, he seemed most intrigued with his own in Montecito (Fig. 117). As he observed in 1918 in a letter to an employee serving in the war:

> Of late I have been sitting up way into the night, after my fashion of ten years ago, over the design for this house. It's about 170 feet long by about 40 feet deep, all of whitewashed stone (possibly inside as well as out) and without one particle of ornament beyond a little semi-Spanish wrought-iron work. It probably never will be built, but at least it's fun to do and certainly good practice to see how good a design can be made without recourse to ornament to pull things together with. [43]

Goodhue's own large house was never built, although in 1920, he did enlarge a small house in Montecito—*La Cabaña*—in the same plain style which relied upon the vigorous texture of the wall surfaces to act as a surrogate for conventional applied ornament. [44]

In contrast to the series of projects just described, at least four of Goodhue's designs in the period of 1913–1919 represented little or no attempt to break free of tradition, and these reflect the architect's natural hesitancy as well as the commissions themselves. The Congregational Church in Montclair, New Jersey, was an orthodox design, of interest mainly for the use of Akoustilith tile on practically every interior surface, resulting in excellent acoustics (Fig. 118). [45] The parish house for Saint Peter's Church in Morristown, New Jersey, was a simple, Tudor design enlivened by integral figurative sculpture in the assembly hall. [46] The new building for the Grolier Club in New York City was little more than a polite brick townhouse with Georgian ornament and detail. The budget was modest and Goodhue was only allowed to oversee the design of one major space—the main reading room, "Wrenaissance" in style. [47] The competition entry for the Waterbury City Hall was also a polite, formal brick building with a large, gambrel-roofed central volume surmounted by a Colonial cupola and flanked by symmetrical wings. [48]

A part of Goodhue's timidity about a new approach to architectural form was due to a psychological restlessness. It is common for men

118.   Interior view of the Congregational Church, Montclair, New Jersey, 1916

in midcareer to experience a kind of identity crisis, a sharp awareness of the limitations of life and work. Goodhue was no exception; his personal crisis was symbolized by the publication in 1914 of *A Book of Architectural and Decorative Drawings by Bertram Grosvenor Goodhue*, a volume he referred to as the "ME Book." This volume contained the drawings of imaginary places, sketches of buildings and gardens, and a section de-

169

voted to his designs in typeface, decorative initials, page borders, and bookplates. Many of the drawings in the book had been completed in the 1890s when his professional practice was just beginning. It had been assembled by several assistants, and Goodhue had looked askance at the undertaking:

> . . . you can't imagine what a curious feeling the getting out of this book gives me of extreme old age, and at the same time, the impression of being a disembodied spirit looking on at the antics of posterity. [49]

To a fellow architect to whom he gave the book, he complained:

> I, alas, have grown too old, but it *was* fun to dream out imaginary places—and this, I guess, is one of the peculiar prerogatives of youth. [50]

Goodhue was friendly with Ruth Baldwin, a poet and free spirit whom he had met in Boston in the 1890s, and his feelings about aging surfaced in a letter accompanying the "ME Book":

> You will notice too perhaps that the date of everything is a way back twenty years or so, that is to the days when pep and zip, etc. still existed for me, when ideals were comely vessels and not such shards as they are now—all of which is very mournful, but I am afraid quite true. [51]

In a second letter to Baldwin, Goodhue continued in his gloomy tone:

> . . . the sad fact remains that the "White Moments" are gone irrevocably and all I can do now is to try to refine and perfect what I once did spontaneously and to settle into a middle, and then old, age full of wise saws and modern instances and keep the lean and slippered horror as far in the future as I can. [52]

He sensed that the relentless demands of his life as a successful New York architect seemed antithetical to his artistic nature. Still, as he confided to his brother, Edward, "I am not a very cheerfully inclined person, and Lydia says that my mind dwells altogether too much on old age and death."[53] In some of his correspondence, and indeed on his personal bookplate, there is the suggestion of a competition with death, a heightened sense of individual initiative against tough odds, a sense of a race against time and against the fading of talent.

Some of these feelings may be attributed to his very success. By 1914, he was the head of a moderately large office of twenty to thirty employees, with commissions all across the United States. He had organized a thoroughly professional staff capable of handling large commissions, and he had an efficient office manager, Francis S. L. Mayers, who took care of the day-to-day operation of the office. This freed Goodhue to meet with clients and contractors, oversee the work as it progressed through the office, and engage in extracurricular professional activities.[54] Mornings were reserved for reading his mail, after which he would move through the drafting room, criticizing and revising the work of his staff, encouraging them as he went. Depending upon Goodhue's somewhat unpredictable moods and the state of the project, these sessions could be instructive and illuminating or a flurry of tense activity. Following lunch, frequently at the Century, afternoons were usually reserved for dictating letters and meeting with various people. There was almost no time during the day when Goodhue actually could work at a drafting board by himself, and he contented himself with sketching in notebooks and working up initial drawings in his studio at home in the evenings.[55]

Given his schedule, he rarely had the opportunity to produce the brilliant perspectives which had been the original source of his reputation as a young man. Like many other firms, Goodhue's began to rely upon architectural renderers, such as E. Donald Robb, Birch Burdette Long, and Hugh Ferriss, to produce formal presentation drawings.[56]

Goodhue's office had a spirited atmosphere. A number of employees were English, although Goodhue seemed to prefer Scottish draftsmen who had trained as apprentices like himself. He had a personal fetish against hiring graduates of the Ecole des Beaux Arts.[57] Although professional in the quality of its production, the office had the atmosphere of an *atelier*, and the staff seems to have been infused with an earnest enthusiasm for the work and a deep devotion to their employer. Thus, the structure of the office was similar to others in the early twentieth century: a strong, singular, creative leader, supported by a core of little-known, technically competent staff, and enriched by bright, energetic young people like Clarence Stein, Raymond Hood, and Wallace Harrison who came for a while and moved on to distinguished careers of their own. The *atelier*-like quality of the office was epitomized by the Twelfth Night Revels, held each January 5th. A combination of office party and farcical masque (usually with Goodhue portrayed as the hero and some feckless clergyman as the villain), the event brought the staff, the Goodhue family, and favored friends and clients together in a special spirit of camaraderie.[58]

The office itself, a reflection of "that absence of commercialism which the firm expresses in all its work," occupied the entire top floor of the Jackson Building at 2 West 47th Street, on what was then the northern edge of the midtown business district, and had been designed by Goodhue (Figs. 119, 120). The work spaces for the staff were spacious but utilitarian in nature, efficiently arranged and flooded with light. The rooms for receiving clients were more imposing. A cool green entrance foyer led to a reception room that resembled the hall of an English manor house, with a panelized ceiling of ornamental plasterwork.

171

The room's focus was a large fireplace surrounded by a painted and gilded mantel bearing the family arms of Cram, of Goodhue, and of Ferguson. Goodhue's private office was paneled and furnished with a desk and Windsor chairs, yet one element revealed his wit: each of the four fire sprinklers in the room was supported by a sculpted figure, personifying one of the four rivers that flow from Paradise. Both the reception room and the private office looked out onto a south-facing loggia and roof garden planted with "cedar and box and old-fashioned flowers."[59]

Goodhue enjoyed being in his office, but he was frequently away—occasionally for long periods of time. To make matters worse, his staff would inform him upon return—only half in jest—that the office seemed to run more smoothly in his absence. Away from the office, Goodhue faced the inevitable long train trips: four days across the continent to New Mexico and California, less to Chicago, Duluth, and Boston. A certain amount of paperwork, sketching, and reading was accomplished on these trips, and his effervescent and gregarious sociability in the dining and

119. *Plan of the New York office of Cram, Goodhue & Ferguson, 1913*

120.   *View of the reception room in the New York office of Cram,*
Goodhue & Ferguson, during the Twelfth Night Revels, 1913
(Goodhue is fourth from the right)

lounge cars eased somewhat the sense of long separation from his office
and family.[60] Still, he may often have thought to himself, perhaps on the
long run across the Great Plains to California, that he had taken on too
much, that he had too many irons in the fire, that he was diffusing his
energies instead of focusing them, that a true sense of artistic accomplish-
ment was being submerged in day-to-day events.

    To ease the stress of his professional life and to try and compensate
for his long absences from New York, Goodhue threw himself into his
family life. He had been raised with a strong devotion to familial connections and this sustained him in later years. He was a proud, affectionate,
and doting father to his daughter, Frances, and his son, Hugh.[61] He and
Lydia were an attractive couple and they moved gracefully through the

complicated social world of New York City, establishing a wide acquaint-anceship in the process. He was fond of good food and drink and took great pleasure in sharing his table with a host of friends.[62]

During the years 1914–1919, his search for a new architectural expression took two principal directions. In his monumental churches, he experimented with a stripped-down version of traditional styles and with ways of integrating purposeful ornament more fully into the fabric of the building. In his domestic work and in several western projects, he looked to a simple, regional vernacular for inspiration. Inherent in both approaches was a continuing concern with artistic expression, thoughtful planning, and sound construction, but the two directions remained distinct from each other. An impending confrontation with the classical language of architecture would serve as a catalyst to transform his career, to integrate these two currents, and to alter the shape and the meaning of his architecture.

CHAPTER SEVEN · CONFRONTATION WITH CLASSICISM

AS the second decade of the century drew to a close, two projects presented themselves to Goodhue which offered a profound challenge to his customary attitudes: a new building for the National Academy of Sciences in Washington, D.C., and a competition for the new Nebraska State Capitol in Lincoln. Both required a classical scheme: the first called for a background building that would be compatible with the Lincoln Memorial; the second was a monumental building of a type that usually resembled the domed Capitol in Washington, D.C.[1] Of the two, the Academy commission was the more troubling and cathartic experience, strongly altering Goodhue's views about architecture in general and about his own work. In designing the Academy building in a classical style contrary to the professed beliefs of a lifetime, the architect discovered to his own amazement that he was pleased with the outcome. Consequently, he relaxed his prejudices, releasing his mind to consider far broader architectural possibilities.

The National Academy of Sciences was established by Act of Congress in 1863. Without a building of its own for its first sixty years of existence, its offices were in quarters furnished by the Smithsonian Institution. The new role of science in World War I led President Woodrow Wilson to request the Academy to establish a subsidiary organization for the solution of war problems, which became known as the National Research Council. When the Council was perpetuated at the close of the war in 1918, the need for a new building to house both the Academy and the Council became apparent.[2]

The man most responsible for the growth and development of the Academy and for the efforts to secure a new building was George Ellery Hale, for whom Goodhue had worked on the California Institute of Technology. When it seemed possible that a new Academy building could be built, Hale, then chairman of the Academy's building committee, approached Goodhue to suggest a site and to prepare some preliminary sketch designs. Goodhue outlined the progress of the project in a comprehensive set of notes, dated April 7, 1920:

> Three or four years ago, Dr. Hale asked me to have sketch designs prepared for a building for the Academy of Sciences to be built in Washington. The site was indeterminate, and I was asked to look over the field of such and report. The summit of the hill on Sixteenth Street, about a mile from the White House, appealed to me most strongly, since it was almost ideal for a building of the irregular character in which I believe . . . irregular in this case means, of course, that the plan can be made as practical and convenient as may be, without regard for symmetry. [3]

Goodhue prepared a set of sketches for a building on this site which unfortunately have disappeared, but however appealing the sketches may have been, the site was not purchased—in part because a new building for an important national organization would be located more appropriately in the heart of the Federal sector of the city. Subsequently, Goodhue looked at a site on the Mall and found it "thoroughly unsatisfactory."[4]

After these two initial efforts at site selection, the project lay dormant for over a year while the Academy sought funds for the new building. With money for construction and endowment secured from the Carnegie Corporation in 1919, Hale and his committee selected a site without the advice of Goodhue:

> After considerable lapse of time, I was informed that a site had been definitely chosen . . . without distinction in itself beyond the fact that it lies within a thousand feet or so of the Lincoln Memorial. Contrasting it with the Sixteenth Street hill, I felt distinctly discouraged, for I recognized that any building here must needs be much duller and more formalistic in its character. Explaining this to Dr. Hale, he was good enough to express the belief that the added difficulty would only spur me and my young men on to greater and more successful efforts. [5]

The choice of the site was brilliant for the Academy and its future and fortuitous for Goodhue, although he did not think so at the time. The choice insured that the Academy would share symbolically and physically in the imperial composition of the city of Washington. It also forced Goodhue to confront the robust classicism in which the high ideals of the McMillan Plan of 1901–1902 were coming to fruition.

Senator James McMillan of Michigan lent his name to and fathered the 1901–1902 Senate Parks Commission Plan for Washington, D.C., which had been prepared by Daniel Burnham, Charles Follen McKim, and Augustus Saint-Gaudens. To ensure that the proposals of the McMillan Plan for the city were carried out, Congress created the

Commission of Fine Arts in 1910.[6]

One of the key elements in the new development of the Mall was the creation of a memorial to Abraham Lincoln at the far western end, where the Mall terminates at the Potomac River. The Lincoln Memorial (1912–1917), designed by Henry Bacon, joined the Washington Monument, the White House, and the Capitol as a key monument in the geometrical composition of the city. True to the ideals of the American Renaissance and the aims of the McMillan Plan, the Lincoln Memorial was never regarded by the Commission of Fine Arts as an isolated monumental building unrelated to its setting. The creation of the monumental form required, as a matter of course, the creation of its setting.[7] As the Ninth Report of the Commission noted:

> The completion of the Lincoln Memorial calls for the continuation along B Street of semi-public buildings architecturally in harmony with the Memorial, which shall serve as a frame for that structure. One such building has been provided in the headquarters of the National Academy of Sciences. . . .[8]

Goodhue faced a difficult challenge. On the one hand, the Academy building was to be the first background building for the Lincoln Memorial and thus a precedent for future buildings along B Street, now Constitution Avenue. This, of course, appealed to Goodhue. He would be free to "work with the idea of producing a modern and scientific building, built with modern and scientific materials, by modern and scientific methods for a modern and scientific set of clients."[9] On the other hand, the Academy building would have to be designed in some sort of classical style, and Goodhue feared he would have to subvert his personal vision to the more orthodox views of the Fine Arts Commission, which would have to approve his design.[10] To a certain extent he was right, given his initial ideas for the building as expressed in a letter to John D. Moore, a former employee:

> I have visualized a sort of loosely-knit and picturesquely-grouped classical affair with big courtyards and of very simple material. For myself I'd rather use rough stone, white-washed, than anything else but suppose this is too much to expect Washington to stomach.[11]

For the first time Goodhue was proposing to combine elements of vernacular architecture with an institutional program in a monumental setting. In the summer and autumn of 1919 he proceeded with another design, the broad outlines of which were well established by November of that year. The budget was not lavish, and in fact required a scheme that could be built in stages.[12]

Goodhue's plan for the building took the form of a hollow rectangle tied across the middle by a square containing a domed rotunda and seven small exhibition rooms. Two cross-axial loggias created four courtyards. With the limited budget in mind, Goodhue suggested that

> . . . the rear and therefore simpler portion of the building should be built first. It occurred to me . . . that it would be desirable to make the first construction include one of the four arches of the central feature with its abutting pylons leaving the other two pylons and three arches to be built later on; and to build a temporary vestibule of inexpensive materials across the lower portion of the great recessed arch, thus nothing of the first construction but the temporary vestibule would have to be demolished when the building would be finally completed.[13]

It is easy to imagine why Goodhue liked this proposal: a portion of the building could be constructed at once for the money available, while the design of the classical facade facing the Lincoln Memorial would be postponed. Although the building committee members were pleased with the general plan, they preferred that the front half of the edifice be built first, that white granite be used, and that a row of Corinthian columns be included in the composition of the facade. This last suggestion caused Goodhue to offer his resignation:

> My attitude toward the Classic style—that is, the usual formal Classic—is very definite and very well known. The row of Corinthian columns was the last straw, and I quite frankly stated my belief in my inability to build the sort of building evidently regarded as appropriate by the Academy of Sciences. However, I was prevailed upon to continue the work, the arguments used being somewhat as follows: that there was a strong desire on the part of somebody that "Goodhue come into the District of Columbia"; that the sort of Classic I could approve and would produce would be an interesting variant of, though by no means out of harmony with, the prevailing style of Washingtonian architecture. Greatly to my surprise, Dr. Hale supported this point of view. Rather downheartedly, it must be confessed, I then attempted something that would be a not unsatisfactory compromise between my own tastes and those of Washington, and began again.[14]

Goodhue had, of course, designed classical buildings earlier—the Deborah Cook Sayles Library and the Gillespie House—but his sulky attitude in this case stemmed from what he viewed as the attempts of the client to encroach upon his artistic prerogatives. In this regard, Goodhue had the support of the Commission of Fine Arts, who felt that he "should be permitted to design the building rather than have the building designed for him by the [client] Committee."[15] A second set of elevations was prepared along the lines of the original plan. The symmetrical front

178

*121.   1920 elevation of the proposed National Academy of Sciences Building,
Washington, D.C., 1919–1924*

facade stretched for 260 feet along Constitution Avenue. It had a central
door with ornamental surround flanked by three two-story windows on
each side and one on the slightly projecting pavilion at each end. The
third floor was expressed as an attic above a continuous entablature, with
pairs of windows repeating the rhythm of the main windows and a trio of
windows marking the central door. The principle ornament of this scheme
was a series of low-relief figure panels in bronze, modeled by Lawrie,
depicting a procession of the great founders of science and set between
the lintels of the main story windows and sills of the windows above,
which allowed the two floors of the building to appear as a single *piano
nobile*. There were no Corinthian columns. Goodhue was cautiously pleased
with the second proposal (Fig. 121):

> I believed the building would prove not unworthy of the site as-
> signed it since, as I viewed the problem, it would never be impor-
> tant enough to make any claims for itself but only as a central
> pavilion of a small but heavily planted park. Also I believed it to
> be decently proportioned and to have a certain interest, due mainly
> to its sculpture.[16]

Using the low budget to disguise his sense of horror at adding to
the monumental classicism of Washington, D.C., Goodhue proposed to
construct the building in plain concrete rather than in stone, and he
painted a beguiling picture of what it would be like:

> . . . the thing to do is to build the building as simply as possible
> and to rely on what the landscape architects call "planting it out"
> . . . and, after all, I don't know but that a simple building with

179

beautiful gardens and shaded walks in which the assembled scientists may pace, isn't perhaps more appropriate than a more pretentious building ever could be.[17]

In reply, James Angell, Chairman of the National Research Council and a member of the building committee, reaffirmed his desire for a simple, less costly building, but weighed the use of bare concrete against the proposed building's symbolic character and its proximity to the Lincoln Memorial. In the end, a warm-toned white Dover marble was used, laid in irregular courses to avoid the dull, chilly blue-white marble surfaces frequently used in Washington. The copper roof and the bas-relief bronze panels added a strong note of color.[18]

On March 26, 1920, Dr. Angell and Goodhue presented the proposed building to the Fine Arts Commission in a series of dry, lifeless, academic drawings. Although both men assumed the meeting would be a mere formality, the scheme was not approved and "after extended discussion the Commission took the plans under advisement." The criticism of Goodhue's design originated with the architects on the Commission, William M. Kendall and Charles A. Platt. They were able to persuade Charles Moore, the chairman, to adopt their view, bringing work on the building to a complete halt pending a revision of the design.[19]

Following the Commission meeting, Platt and Kendall met informally with Goodhue over lunch at the Century Club in New York to present their reservation with the design, which was essentially a demand that the facade be more "classic." Goodhue interpreted this, incorrectly as it turned out, to mean the application of the orders, and became more recalcitrant than ever, demanding to have a list of required changes placed in a letter. He felt beleaguered by his clients and by the Commission of Fine Arts, and put the project aside as the deadline for the Nebraska competition approached.[20]

A letter from Charles Moore was sent to Goodhue in late June 1920. In it, Moore reiterated the Commission's confidence in the architect's abilities, its respect for his freedom as an artist, and its reluctance to dictate a specific design to him. Moore identified the problem as follows:

> When your plans were submitted the Commission felt that you yourself had not taken the matter in the spirit we had reason to expect; that you were not working in the spirit of the city; and that you were hampered by the fact that you were not in thorough sympathy with the larger conception of the group as distinguished from the single building. They felt that you had not come up to your own high standard of excellence in the design submitted.[21]

Moore reminded Goodhue of the latter's own remarks about Florence and Toledo manifesting the work of artists across time working toward a common ideal, and concluded:

> All [the Commission asks] of you is the same spirit of subordination to the Washington ideal that you yourself recognize to be the right and even necessary attitude of an artist working for enduring success of the unified project. [22]

Goodhue remained obstinate. In December 1920, Moore wrote to Charles Walcott, Secretary of the Smithsonian Institution, to explain that

> . . . what the Commission of Fine Arts desires is a building with as much charm as the Pan American building and the Freer Gallery possess. Mr. Goodhue is capable of accomplishing this result if he will put himself in the attitude to do it. He has not put himself in that attitude and his sketches give no promise that he will handle the design in the spirit in which the designs of the two buildings named were handled. [23]

On May 12, 1921, Goodhue resubmitted the design, essentially unchanged but now rendered in two perspectives. One showed the overall building set amidst its dense landscaping as seen from the Lincoln Memorial (Fig. 122), the other showed a close-up view of the main approach flanked by tall cedars. The first set of drawings had presented

122.   1921 perspective of the proposed National Academy of Sciences Building, Washington, D.C., 1919–1924

123. *1925 exterior view of the National Academy of Sciences Building, Washington, D.C., 1919–1924*

the design as a lifeless, Beaux Arts composition, whereas the second set stressed the design's unpretentious, well-proportioned, almost entirely astylar mass, unified by its broad terrace and its entablature. The second set of drawings made evident Goodhue's dual concern with architectural clarity and with pictorial effect, and suggests that he had at last come to terms with the scheme. This time, the Commission approved the design, finding it "satisfactory, and in keeping with the Lincoln Memorial."[24]

In the end, the Commission had not wanted an Academy building of Roman scale; such belonged properly only to the Lincoln Memorial. As a result, Goodhue came to see that classicism need not lead to a dry and academic scheme but could be susceptible to a wide range of personal, individualistic, and original designs.

Before construction began in the spring of 1922, Goodhue revised the design further, improving it considerably. In the completed building, the corner pavilions have smaller, individual windows in place of the double-height windows elsewhere on the facade; the windows in the attic have their own rhythm related to but no longer repeating that of the major windows below; and the ornament around the central door is simpler and more severe (Figs. 123, 124). The plan underwent some minor modification in the arrangement of public rooms along the front facade (Fig. 125). Yet the finished building is less than completely satisfying. In particular, the overall massing is bland and the thin classical detail lacks conviction. The Academy is charming in its use of materials and in much

182

124.   Detail view of the main door to the National Academy of Sciences
Building, Washington, D.C., 1919–1924

125.   Plan of the National Academy of Sciences Building,
Washington, D.C., 1919–1924

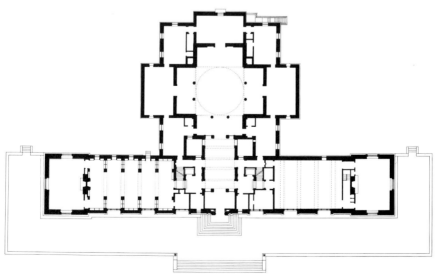

of its ornament, elegant in many of its proportions, but dry as an overall composition. It reflects the artistic struggle of its designer rather than the moment of his denouement.

For the interior, Hale had asked Goodhue to provide abundant, warm, rich colors in contrast to the cool, monochromatic exterior. As a result, Goodhue proposed a great deal of tiled and painted decoration which was subsequently designed by Hildreth Meiere, and which provided visual stimulation while preserving the spare, planar feeling of the rooms (Fig. 126).[25] Further, all the proposed ornament, inside and out, played a role in a program of symbolism which exalted the history, lore, and contemporary role of science. The preparation of an extensive program of secular iconography for this building was in itself an important development in Goodhue's work, because it paved the way for similar programs of art and symbolism which enliven his last and most accomplished buildings.

The design of the Academy took place in the months just preceding and in the early stages of the competition for the new Nebraska State Capitol. The Washington project forced Goodhue to attempt to personalize a style he had heretofore regarded as merely academic. While it is often suggested that Goodhue designed the Capitol tabula rasa, without the influence of previous efforts, it is clear that such was not the case. The Capitol was a breakthrough in Goodhue's career as an architect, correctly praised for its freely interpreted classical style and for its lively composition of stepped masses.[26] But the freedom embodied in its design was hard won on the shores of the Potomac: to a very great extent, the Capitol is the child of the National Academy of Sciences building.

In 1919, the Nebraska State Legislature realized that the existing Capitol building, designed by B. H. Wilcox of Chicago in 1879, was falling into disrepair and needed to be replaced. On February 20, 1919, a Capitol Commission was created consisting of the Governor, the Secretary of the Department of Irrigation, Highways and Drainage, and three citizens, empowered "to proceed with the preparation of working plans and specifications for the erection and completion, at the existing site, of a suitable building for a State Capitol."[27]

An architect was to be selected by competition and an architectural adviser was sought. Thomas R. Kimball, of Omaha, Nebraska, and then president of the American Institute of Architects, was appointed on June 24, 1919. Kimball developed a two-stage competition. The first stage began on September 30, 1919, and was open to all architects practicing in Nebraska. Eight entries were received and in the judgment held on December 2, 1919, three were premiated. The second stage consisted of these three local architects plus seven invited competitors chosen from elsewhere in the country. The seven nationally known architects were chosen from a list of thirty-two names prepared by Kim-

126. *Perspective of the rotunda of the National Academy of Sciences Building, Washington, D.C., 1919–1924*

ball.[28] The final stage of the competition included the following ten archi-tects: Bliss & Faville, San Francisco; Ellery Davis, Lincoln; Bertram Goodhue, New York City; John Latenser & Sons, Omaha; H. Van Buren Magonigle, New York City; John McDonald & Alan McDonald, Omaha; McKim, Mead & White, New York City; John Russell Pope, New York City; Tracy & Swartwout, New York City; and Paul Cret and Zantzinger, Borie & Medary, Philadelphia.[29]

On January 10, 1920, the Capitol Commission and eight of the ten competitors met in Lincoln (Goodhue and Pope were unable to attend) when the competition program was distributed. The aim of the competition itself was described in a statement by Kimball:

> . . . its solution is to be the test whereby the vision, skill, experience, and wisdom of the competitors are to be evaluated and compared, in order that the architect best qualified to guide the Capitol Commission to a worthy conclusion of its great undertaking may thereby be justly determined. [30]

Put more succinctly, the Commission sought the man rather than the scheme. In the event, the Commission achieved both at once. The program requested the competitors to provide "for real collaboration of Architect, Sculptor, Painter, and Landscapist," and urged each competitor to associate with any or all of the above in the actual competition. In essence, the Capitol Commission was seeking not only an architect, but a compatible artistic team under the "guidance and control of the Architect" to create the new Capitol building. [31]

For Goodhue the noteworthy feature of the program was that

> as to plan, scope, style, type, or material, the Capitol Commission will offer no suggestion. Even in the matter of tradition, it is clearly the desire of the Commission that each competitor shall feel free to express what is in his heart, unmindful of what has been inherited in this regard, willing even that the legacies of the Masters should guide and restrain rather than fetter. [32]

The competition offered an opportunity of unparalleled freedom, and it came at a moment when Goodhue was prepared to take full advantage.

The jury was composed of three architects, "one chosen by the Capitol Commission, and one by the competitors, and the third by the two thus chosen." The Commission chose Waddy B. Wood of Washington, D.C.; the competitors chose James Gamble Rogers of New York; and the two jurors chose Willis Polk of San Francisco. [33]

The entries were due in Lincoln by June 15, 1920. On June 23, the jury began three days of study of the ten sets of drawings, reporting to the Commission on June 26, 1920. The jury noted that while the winning architect

> . . .sacrificed nothing in area and nothing in utility and nothing in beauty, he has been able to produce a building that is less than 75% of the size of the average building in this competition. He has produced for this land a building as free from binding traditions as it is from prejudice, an edifice that expresses his capability of designing any type of a monument that may later develop as suitable. [34]

186

In their report, the three men noted the difficulty of the judgment process, but later, Waddy Wood gave a different interpretation:

> When we came into the room where the designs were displayed, we all ran over to the design with a tower. It took all of us, right off the bat! But Mr. Rogers, always careful and cautious, said, "Well, we have got to look at them all, haven't we?" So we looked at each one for awhile, but always came back to that tower. It was the easiest judgment of my experience.[35]

The competition rules allowed each competitor to accompany his drawings with approximately five hundred words of descriptive text. Goodhue's text was reprinted in the *American Institute of Architects' Journal* along with the illustrations of his winning design:

> The site is a square in the heart of the city of Lincoln, the point of intersection of two great avenues, while the surrounding country is generally level. Therefore, from the very beginning, the authors of the design herewith submitted have felt impelled to produce something quite unlike the usual—and, to them, rather trite—thing of the sort, with its veneered order and invariable Roman dome.
>
> As their studies have progressed, this impression has but deepened, finally taking form in a vast, though rather low structure, from the midst of which rises a great central tower. . . . Though everywhere monumental, no element of the practical or convenient has been sacrificed to this end. Even the tower is no mere useless ornament, for its shaft contains the glass-floored, many-storied Library book-stack.
>
> It has seemed to the authors that the traditions of ancient Greece and Rome and of Eighteenth Century France are in no wise applicable in designing a building destined to be the seat of Government of a great western commonwealth: So, while the architectural style employed may, roughly, be called "Classic," it makes no pretense of belonging to any period of the past. Its authors have striven to present . . . a State Capitol of the Here and Now, and naught else.
>
> Throughout the building's interior arrangement, the authors have striven to achieve the greatest degree of directness, compactness and economy consistent with convenience and dignity.
>
> This design is essentially that of a finished entity, as such scarcely susceptible of extension in the form of wings certain to encroach seriously upon the pleasant tree-shaded space, which the authors regard as quite vitally part-and-parcel of the whole. If in coming years, additions prove desirable, these should take form as quite separate, though harmonious, structures, set about the square

127. *Elevation of Goodhue's competitive design for the*
Nebraska State Capitol, Lincoln, 1920

and lining the main avenue of approach.[36]

   The drawings showed a tall marker on the plains of Nebraska: a
horizontal building 400 feet square, stepping up to and dominated by a
tower 79 feet square and 400 feet tall. The horizontal base had hard,
crisp shapes and flat, broad surfaces, giving it stability as à foil for the
soaring lines of the tower, which terminated in a resplendent tiled dome
and Lawrie's statue of "The Sower." The sculptural solidity of the whole
was enhanced by the battered walls of the corner pavilions and tower as
they rose in a stepped, pyramidal silhouette. Apt vernacular ornament,
like the buffalo sculptures that flanked the steps cascading from the main
door, enriched the quixotic gesture of the tower (Fig. 127).

188

The Capitol became widely perceived as a free and original work. By a supreme irony, Goodhue realized his deepest, most romantic architectural dreams in a design that was governed by the austere discipline of the classical tradition: in the abstract geometrical composition of the whole, in the hierarchical and ceremonial arrangement of parts, in the shading of architectonic expression, and in the remorseless elimination of the merely picturesque and sentimental. Although the design seemed a radical departure from a typical capitol building, in fact the tower allowed for two central ceremonial spaces instead of the usual one: the domed rotunda in its base and the Memorial Hall, dedicated to the war dead from Nebraska, beneath the dome at its summit. The tower did not imply a rejection of classical precedent; on the contrary, it was the central element of a scheme that integrated the traditions of classicism with Goodhue's romanticism. Nevertheless, the Capitol design was essentially astylar, and it proved that monumentality could be achieved without resort to an academic or archaeological system of expression.

The cross-axial plan was a more advanced development of the National Academy of Sciences building (Fig. 128). Four arms radiated from a domed rotunda at the center of the building in the base of the tower: one for the Great Hall leading to the main door; two for the

128. *Plan of the completed Nebraska State Capitol, Lincoln, 1920–1932*

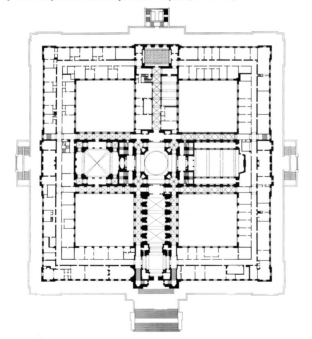

legislative chambers; and a fourth which led to the Supreme Court. These cross axes extended out from the Capitol to form the entry approaches and linked the building to the city's square grid of streets, itself a miniature of the national grid that divides much of Nebraska into square plots of land. From every direction as one approached the Capitol, the symmetry of the composition and the centrality of the tower were apparent. The Supreme Court chamber, special lounges for the legislators, and the main entry foyer were located in engaged pavilions at the cardinal points of the plan, where the Greek cross intersected the square. The encompassing square contained the state offices and created four large exterior courts.

The competition drawings heralded a resolution of Goodhue's search for a new architectural expression, one that implied a new sensibility. The Capitol design was "traditional" in its reflection of the timeless qualities that classicism embodies, yet it was undeniably fresh in its departure from the classical repertory. Although Goodhue's work seemed characterized by an unconstrained freedom, from this point on, it could be seen more correctly as a rigorous and complex synthesis of the classical, the romantic, and the vernacular that resulted in a fresh traditionalism.

Of the other Capitol schemes, those by John Russell Pope and Ellery Davis were the most interesting.[37] Pope's second-place scheme was serene and academic, composed to accentuate the noble porch and lofty dome (Fig. 129). Davis's scheme incorporated, like Goodhue's, a tower as its major feature (Fig. 130). Davis's tower was an actual office tower, like a small skyscraper with large public spaces in an enlarged base, at once more functional and less poetic than Goodhue's. Goodhue's tower was to hold the library stacks, true, but its real impact was as a symbol.

During the summer of 1920, the Capitol began to attract the attention of the press. On July 16, 1920, an article in *The New York Times* entitled "Architectural Derring-Do" commented that

> . . . in spite of Mr. Bertram Goodhue's devotion to the Gothic tradition, in accord with which he has done excellent work, the spirit of an architectural *vers librist* is said to have been manifested in his designs for the new Nebraska State Capitol.[38]

The same article included conflicting comments from Nebraska newspapers. The Omaha *World-Herald* thought the Capitol contained "something of Egypt and something of Spain [yet] Egypt and Spain have nothing like it." The Kearney *Hub* was unimpressed and thought the proposed building looked like "a powerhouse with an overgrown smokestack . . . severely plain . . . somewhat squatty."[39]

Eleven days later, another article in *The New York Times* noted that "Bertram G. Goodhue, architect of the Gothic and the Hispanic, has of late ceased to be content to copy tradition—even the best tradition," that nowhere "does the stern mood of this building yield to the blandishments of the gracious," and that its beauty "lies in the final rightness of good proportions and in consistency." The base with windows facing into courtyards was defended on the grounds that a window-filled facade would have looked too weak to carry the tower, and similarly, a colonnade casting "delicate shadows" on the facade would have weakened the composition. The "crude vigor" of the stepped masses of the Capitol was seen as a recollection of the chapel at West Point. The

129. Elevation of John Russell Pope's competitive design for the Nebraska State Capitol, Lincoln, 1920

130. Elevation of Ellery Davis's competitive design for the Nebraska State Capitol, Lincoln, 1920

style of the new building remained enigmatic for the critic, for whom the design evoked Egyptian and Romanesque forms as well as "the ruins of Roman construction in Northern Africa." The article concluded that

> . . . what the architect has done is to select a mood and use form to create the mood. . . . The mood which Goodhue seems to be developing in this structure, as in his other recent work, is of a stern—almost of a brutal—nature.[40]

Regardless of the confusion as to what style, if any, the new design embodied, there was nearly universal agreement that it represented an act of daring. The feeling was that

> Goodhue, who wrought so beautifully in several traditional styles, has now thrown them all to the winds in order to create a new style—or, as he more modestly says, in order to give untrammeled expression to an individual mood.[41]

A year later, C. Matlack Price wrote a considerably less sanguine review of the Capitol design. He thought the building "seems in some subtle, yet insistent, way to contradict itself. Is it a tall, vertical building or a low horizontal building with a tower? Somehow it seems to be neither," which dismayed Price. He concluded that "probably two fundamentally different types of buildings cannot consistently be combined in one design." But this fundamental contradiction was part of the challenging spirit of the Capitol, perhaps its most remembered feature. Price was even less pleased about its so-called new style. While he praised the lack of historical stylistic precedent, he thought "this avoidance has not been carried to the radical extreme," resulting in a "sort of 'middle grayness,' a position of something like architectural neutrality."[42] For Price and for other critics, the Capitol design remained an enigma, precisely because it combined the two contradictory qualities that Charles Herbert Reilly had ascribed to Scott's Liverpool Cathedral, "the balanced beauty of a classical building" and "the dynamic force of Gothic architecture."[43]

On June 26, 1920, the Goodhue office received the news from Lincoln ecstatically. Goodhue, informed of his selection while in Montreal, enroute to California, wrote confidently to his brother Edward: "I was called up in my [hotel] room from New York to hear the entire office giving three cheers over our having won the Nebraska Capitol commission. Let me tell you that this means 6% commission on $10,000,000, add this amount to Yale to the Academy of Sciences and our other work and we have close to $30,000,000."[44] The ever competitive Goodhue realized the full implications of his success in Nebraska: he had achieved a major artistic victory that refocused the direction of his career, and he had secured once again the fortunes of his office. Most important of all, he looked forward to an architecture free of specific stylistic references, one that relied upon an expression of pure mass and volume for its principal effects. In full control of his aesthetic sensibilities, Goodhue seemed ready to sail confidently into his maturity, the triumph at Lincoln preparing the way for buildings in a style uniquely his own.

Goodhue's search for a new architectural expression was hardly unique among the best architects of his generation, and indeed, the resolution of his own search came later than for many of his colleagues. Despite the reservations of such critics as Fiske Kimball, this is not to suggest that Goodhue was following the lead of others, or that his resolution was identical to any of theirs. As has been pointed out by Hitchcock, the generation of architects born around 1870 was characterized by an intense individuality.

Perhaps the experience that Goodhue and his peers share is that each, in an attempt to move beyond both a picturesque romanticism and an archaeological traditionalism, had to confront the problem of classicism. Each emerged from this confrontation with a belief, not so much in the "rules" of classicism per se as in the resources of classicism as an architectural language which could discipline a composition while permitting fresh formal expression. Very often, this led to an emphasis on the expression of pure mass and to ornamentation of an exotic or stylized character.[45]

During the first decade of this century, both Lutyens and Wright moved decisively away from picturesque, asymmetrical designs to more axially controlled classical compositions. Lutyens had used classical elements in his early, picturesquely composed houses, but after the turn of the century, classicism became quintessential to his work. Wright, in some of the suburban houses he designed between 1902 and 1910, and more particularly in his public buildings of the century's first two decades, went even further in achieving an intrinsic classic quality while eschewing the use of classical forms.[46]

Auguste Perret and Irving Gill, other contemporaries of Goodhue's, arrived at fundamentally a classical method of composition, in part through a rigorous exploration of the possibilities of ferro-concrete construction. Perret's Garage Ponthieu (1905) and his later Church of Notre Dame at Le Raincy (1923) were built of concrete with a simplified, slightly abstracted classical format. Gill's two great works, the Dodge House (1914–1916) in Los Angeles and the Scripps House (1915–1916) in La Jolla, both made of concrete, were composed of crisp, cubistic, completely astylar forms which were as fresh in their way as any of Loos's work in Vienna, with plans that were disciplined but informal.[47]

Over and over again, among Goodhue's contemporaries, one sees evidence of the search for a fresh traditionalism in a manner similar to his own, that is, through a simpler and bolder composition of mass, a reduction but not an elimination of ornament, and an increased formality in planning. This search characterizes Eliel Saarinen's move from the romantic, picturesque manner of his house and studio at Hvittrask (1902), to his proposed Finnish Parliament House (1908), which had stripped masses, composed quite formally, piling up to a tower crowned by stepped setbacks, and his Helsinki Railroad Station (1906–1914), both of which were quite premonitory of Goodhue's Capitol. [48]

Although the Capitol design bore similarities to the work just mentioned, it had distinctive aspects as well, many of which grew from Goodhue's efforts to express the building's role as war memorial, public monument, and regional symbol. As such it could not be as freely experimental as a house; it could not totally ignore time-honored precedents, nor could it be stripped of all iconographic ornament.

Viewed in this way, the Capitol can be compared to Lutyens's immense Viceroy's House (1914–1930) in New Delhi. Despite the obvious differences between the ancient traditions of Moghul architecture and the newer ones of Nebraska, in each building there is a fusion of a classical discipline with a sensitivity to local conditions. Each is a pure mass enlivened by familiar forms recast in a fresh manner. The introduction of Indian themes in the Viceroy's House, for instance, is paralleled by the use of Nebraskan themes in the Capitol. In achieving this fusion of the classical and the vernacular, each avoids the sentimental picturesqueness of too strong an emphasis on local traditions, as well as the dryness and abstraction of too close an adherence to a canonical or archaeological view of classicism. In doing so, each confirms the value and vitality of the classical tradition in contemporary monumental architecture. [49]

After the initial excitement over the Capitol design had subsided, the design underwent four important changes. First, the entire building was rotated 90 degrees at the request of the client so that the entrance faced north toward the campus of the University of Nebraska, instead of west as Goodhue had proposed. [50] It is not known why he faced the building west. He may have viewed it as a secular cathedral and used a traditional liturgical orientation, or he may have intended the building to embody the American sense of westward movement. Facing west, the ecclesiastical format and liturgical orientation of the Capitol would have been apparent, with the west front giving onto the nave that led to the rotunda or crossing in the base of the great tower; the legislative chambers occupying the transepts; the Supreme Court in the position of the sanctuary; and the offices of the bureaucracy gathered about and supporting the main body of the building (Fig. 131). In any case, with the new orientation the Supreme Court chamber faced south, the legislative chambers faced east and west, and the quality of light in the rotunda and Great Hall was substantially diminished by harsh glare.

131. 1934 view from the northwest of the Nebraska State Capitol,
Lincoln, 1920–1932

In the second change, the dimensions of the square plan were increased by 40 feet on each side, with the result that the horizontal base assumed slightly too much prominence; when seen from certain angles, the tower now seems somewhat detached from the broad base. In the third change, the main entrance was redesigned. Goodhue had received considerable negative comment on the flat, half-hearted classical front shown in the drawings, and it was changed to a high, deep, arched recess flanked by massive piers, a more accurate and dramatic expression of the domed vestibule within.

A fourth change was in the termination of the tower. The original design showed the dome flanked by four cupolas, and the final design employs octagonal turrets. There were two intermediate stages. In one, Goodhue proposed to use four buffaloes, and when the Commission thought they looked unsteady on the corners of the tower, he changed them to winged buffaloes. The Commission was not pleased with this change, and the final design was chosen. The winged buffalo was also

195

proposed as an alternative to the piers flanking the entrance stairs (Figs. 132, 133). In the end, this motif was not used anywhere, and Goodhue regretted "the loss of the poetic quality the winged buffaloes would have given."[51] However original a winged buffalo might have seemed, Goodhue knew familiar precedents for such a motif: in ecclesiastical iconography, the four Evangelists were often depicted respectively by a winged man, a winged lion, a winged ox, and an eagle, to symbolize the spread of the gospel. Goodhue was merely attempting to combine a vernacular creature with an ancient format as a fresh, imaginative symbol for Nebraska.

The Capitol was designed to be built in five stages: the north entrance, Great Hall, and the northern half of the low office wing; the Supreme Court chamber and the southern half of the office wing; the Senate Chamber and tower base; the tower shaft; and finally, the Legislative Chamber on the western side. This staging allowed the office accommodation to be built around the old Capitol while it remained standing. The state offices were able to move into the new quarters before the demolition of the old building, saving the state $750,000 in rentals for temporary space.[52]

The first stage of construction began in November 1922, and by February 1923 it and its architect were the subject of state investigations. Among the ten charges leveled against Goodhue, one dealt with what was perceived to be wide variations in the stone. Goodhue had selected three grades of stone—all of which met the loading tests—because each grade contained a different amount of shell material and tiny spots of color. He wanted even the monochromatic surfaces of the building to have a degree of subtle variation. The lack of consistency in the stone gave George Johnson, a member of the Commission and acting State Engineer, the opportunity to raise questions.[53] Goodhue described his view of the investigations in a letter to an English friend in 1923:

> George Johnson was anxious to act as general contractor for the building, in other words to have the various figures from the various subcontractors assembled by himself and the building built under his direction: to this end we wrote . . . twenty-seven different specifications one covering each trade; but, having heard in the interim that Mr. Johnson's record was not good and that although no investigation had been able to actually pin anything on him, he was known as a grafter, and powerfully strong in local politics; as soon as the opportunity arrived therefore, I opposed the work being done in this way . . . and the commission voted to award the work to a general contractor. [Ever since] he has been "after me" with undying hatred.[54]

On February 23, 1923, Johnson charged Goodhue with dishonesty, gross negligence, and gross incompetence. In an unusual meeting on

132. *View of the study model for the north portal of the Nebraska State Capitol, Lincoln, 1921*

133. *View of the buffalo sculpture flanking the north steps of the Nebraska State Capitol, Lincoln, 1920–1932*

134.   *1947 view of the north facade of the Nebraska State Capitol,
Lincoln, 1920–1932*

March 23, open to the press, the Commission supported Goodhue against
Johnson's claims. Subsequently, a legislative investigating committee was
appointed to review the charges. This committee found nothing wrong
but did censure Goodhue for "not having the best interests of the State
at heart." Thereupon, a bill was introduced in the Legislature to dismiss
the architect, which was defeated by the close margin of 49 to 40.[55] The
high-strung and excitable Goodhue emerged from this sordid confrontation fatigued and disillusioned:

> Now I am completely exonerated . . . but the truth is the experi-
> ence has been horrible. I feel years older than I did and am not
> sure the thing is over. Mr. Johnson is such a power that it is quite

conceivable he may run for, and be elected, Governor next election two years from now . . . [the first section of the building] which will be finished a year from now will impress the people and make them realize that I . . . am doing a good piece of work for them for a reasonable price and that the whole thing has been carried out with absolute honesty. However, there is always the spectre of Johnson as Governor before me.[56]

It is clear that right up until his death, Goodhue always had the fear that it was at least possible to lose control of this, his most important commission.

As the first stage of construction neared completion in 1924, one of the most striking features of the building became apparent: the unusual treatment of the carved figures sculpted by Lawrie. The representational sculpture that adorns the Capitol is an integral part of the fabric of the building.[57] Perhaps most characteristic are the four colossal human figures that flank the arched portal of the main entrance, symbolizing the guardians of the law—wisdom, justice, power, and mercy (Figs. 134, 135). These four figures loom up out of the walls and look down sternly from where the building meets the sky. The fusion of architecture and sculpture was hailed as a new approach to architectural ornament, and became one of the building's most imitated features. This expressive but astylar system integrating architecture and sculpture was used on the exterior in lieu of the more usual orders. When conventional elements like columns were used on the interior of the building, they were designed with stylized, idiosyncratic capitals (Fig. 136). The building's balance of freedom and discipline in the use of the orthodox formulae of classicism is characteristic of Byzantine architecture. It is perhaps for this reason that Hitchcock thought the Capitol to be "vaguely Byzantinesque." But this narrow appellation misrepresents the building's true position within the much broader classical tradition—the fundamental architectural discipline of western civilization—to which the Byzantine as well as the Romanesque and much else belong.[58]

The fusion of architecture and sculpture in the Capitol is not, of course, unique or original. As in other aspects of this building, there are precedents, one of which is the similar handling of the figures on the front of Eliel Saarinen's widely published Helsinki Railroad Station (1906–1914), much admired by Goodhue.[59]

A more obvious precedent is the consistent use of representational sculpture in all of Gothic architecture. In medieval Gothic churches, the figures were usually discrete objects, placed in canopied niches. In Goodhue's churches, this format was varied. For example, in the Chapel of the Intercession, the head and wings of two angels grow out of the stone chancel parapet. In the Church of Saint Vincent Ferrer, the figures on the west turrets emerge out of the stone. And in several other churches by Goodhue, taking inspiration from buildings like Henry Vaughan's

135. *1934 detail view of the statues of Wisdom and Justice on the north
portal of the Nebraska State Capitol, Lincoln, 1920–1932*

chapel at Saint Paul's School in Concord, New Hampshire, there are
numerous figures that grow out of conventional elements like stair newel
posts, pew ends, parclose screens, organ cases, and the like. And in a
sketch by Goodhue for a child's bed, the four Evangelists rise up out of
the structural corner posts to act as guardians (Fig. 137). The originality
in the sculptural effect at Nebraska lies in its monumental scale and its
stripped-down spareness: a sculptural idea which had been expressed as
charming decorative detail in furniture was now embodied in figures of
colossal scale rendered with great severity. Because of his long personal
and professional relationship with Goodhue, Lawrie was obviously sympathetic to the new relationship of wall and sculpture being developed for

200

the Capitol, and was himself able to make a parallel shift from his earlier "Gothic" sculpture to the new style for Nebraska.[60]

The sculpture contributed to the lively appearance of the Capitol, and it was further integrated with the architecture as the vehicle for didactic iconography. The Capitol Commission hired Dr. Hartley Burr Alexander, a poet-philosopher from the University of Nebraska, to collaborate with Goodhue, and together they developed a program for the exterior that expressed the history of law, and one for the interior that expressed the relationship of the natural and the cultural world. The inclusion of representational iconography expressing the purpose and the cultural context of the Capitol allows it to be directly compared with a monument of Gothic architecture like Chartres Cathedral. And, of course, figurative imagery was a prominent feature in most of Goodhue's other buildings. His churches included figures culled from the vast lore of Christian history, and the secular-theme building for the Panama-California Exposition incorporated events from California's past. What was new in the Capitol was the rigorous way the program of art and symbolism was deployed throughout the fabric of the building to enhance both its

136. *Detail view of a column capital in the entrance vestibule of the Nebraska State Capitol, Lincoln, 1920–1932*

201

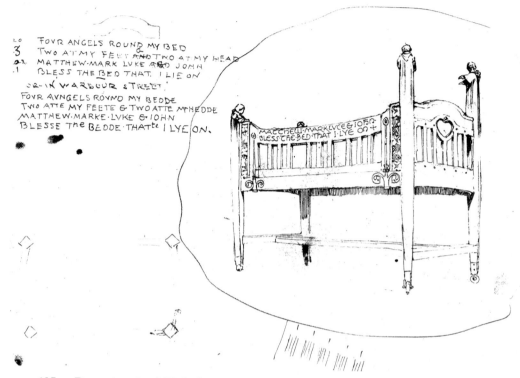

FOVR ANGELS ROUND MY BED
Two AT MY FEET AND TWO AT MY HEAD
MATTHEW·MARK LVKE AND JOHN
BLESS THE BED THAT. I LIE ON
OR IN WARBOUR STREET
FOVR AVNGELS ROVND MY BEDDE
Two ATTE MY FEETE & TWO ATTE ᵐᵀHEDDE
MATTHEW·MARKE·LVKE & IOHN
BLESSE ᵀᴴᵉ BEDDE·THATᵗᵉ I LYE ON.

137.   Perspective of a child's bed

form and its meaning. The sculpture is not placed for purely decorative reasons, but to clarify the viewer's perception of the composition of masses. The most literal subjects are at the base of the building and the most abstract are at the top; the flattest bas-relief expression is at the base and the most fully three-dimensional at the top. The two systems of meaning and expression are correspondingly shaded from bottom to top, so that as the masses pile up to the tower, the ornament reinforces this. The names of the counties of Nebraska form a continuous frieze around the base of the building. The history of the law is allegorically recounted in twenty-one panels placed at the four corner pavilions of the building and on the west, south, and east entrances to reinforce the geometrical order of the plan, beginning with Mosaic law in the northwest corner and proceeding counterclockwise around to Nebraska statehood in the north-east corner (Figs. 138–140). Images of ancient events of cosmic impor-tance and more recent images of nationhood and statehood are woven into one epic panorama, revealed as the beholder circumnavigates the building. On the south facade, just above the Supreme Court chamber, and emerging up from the walls and pilasters surrounding the reading

202

room of the State Library, stand ten great lawgivers of Western culture: Minos, Hammurabi, Moses, Akhnaton, Solon, Solomon, Julius Caesar, Justinian, Charlemagne, and Napoleon. Encircling the base of the tower are figures symbolizing eight ideals of culture protected and nourished by the law: Pentaour (history), Ezekiel (vision), Socrates (reason), Marcus Aurelius (statecraft), St. John (faith), Louis IX (chivalry), Newton (science), and Lincoln (liberty). On the tower is a frieze of thunderbirds, symbol of the rains, and at the very top a bronze figure of "The Sower" casts his seeds (Fig. 141).[61]

On the exterior, the program of symbolism was expressed in sculpture and inscriptions; on the interior, it was expressed in tile decoration, murals, and inscriptions which introduced large areas of color. The major ceremonial spaces have broad surfaces of tile decoration designed by Hildreth Meiere, composed to express the relationship of the natural world and the cultural world as the beholder moves from the monumental

138. View of the west portal of the Nebraska State Capitol, Lincoln, 1920–1932

*139.   Detail view of Moses bringing the law from Mount Sinai, on the
northwest corner of the Nebraska State Capitol, Lincoln, 1920–1932*

*140.   Detail view of Nebraska's entrance into the Union, on the northeast
corner of the Nebraska State Capitol, Lincoln, 1920–1932*

141.   1934 view of the south facade of the Nebraska State Capitol,
Lincoln, 1920–1932

north portal into the aedicular vestibule, along the foyer to the rotunda
and from there to the legislative chambers. The theme of the domed
vestibule is the gifts of nature, and the foyer is divided into three zones
depicting the past, present, and future life of man on the prairies. The
rotunda is devoted to the expression of civic and religious virtues which
sustain society: tiled images of eight Nordic angels—embodying the virtues of hope, charity, magnanimity, justice, faith, wisdom, temperance,

and courage—grace the dome; marble mosaic representations of Mother Earth, and the genii of Earth, Air, Fire, and Water are worked into the floors; the chandelier is emblazoned with the twelve signs of the zodiac; and corn husks, wheat sheaves, and heads of buffalo are employed as motifs in the column capitals and onyx balustrades. The decoration of the Senate chamber is devoted to Indian cultures native to Nebraska, and the House chamber depicts the Spanish, French, and American cultures that later added their imprint to the land. The walls and ceilings of the Governor's reception room and office are covered by murals painted by Augustus Vincent Tack, which reiterate many of the symbolic themes used elsewhere in the building.[62] The placement and composition of the elaborate decoration is disciplined by the classical order of the architecture, so that the exotic splendor of the Indian and Nebraskan themes does not detract from the calm, impressive grandeur of the ceremonial rooms (Figs. 142–146).

Goodhue's artistic intentions at the Capitol were enriched by the work of his able collaborators. Lawrie, Meiere, and Tack were selected by the architect because they were sympathetic to his work, and they were given license to fully develop their own art in the building. As in his earlier ecclesiastical commissions, he understood the importance of the collaborative artist and craftsman to the completed work, and designed a building for Nebraska that allowed his collaborators to play a significant and an integral role in its full realization.

The Capitol was a decade in construction, and was not completed until 1932.[63] By that time, the freshness of its conception and of its stripped classical forms did not seem as remarkable as they had in 1920. During the building boom of the 1920s a number of American skyscrapers had been completed, such as the Chrysler Building in New York (1930), which, while indebted to the Capitol, were even less restrained in their formal conception. However, the influence of the Capitol was recalled in 1931 in an article by the conservative architect and dean of the School of Architecture at Rice University, William Ward Watkin:

> . . . [it gave] lofty structure its meaning in American civilization, as the typical form which has found favor among us, and [gave] to lofty structure at the same time the advantage which it justly deserves of complete and unembarrassed perspective, a quality which it had not enjoyed in Lower Manhattan. Once the beauty of lofty structure pictured itself on the architect's imagination as separated from congestion and confusion, the lofty building became the characteristic monument of our time.[64]

Goodhue's design for the Capitol provided an American vernacular building type—the skyscraper—with monumental form and poetic expression, and influenced the formal composition of the skyscraper in the 1920s. At

142.   *1934 interior view looking toward the rotunda of the Nebraska State Capitol, Lincoln, 1920–1932*

143.   *Interior view of the tooled leather doors to the legislative
chamber of the Nebraska State Capitol, Lincoln, 1920–1932*

the level of pure form, the Louisiana State Capitol at Baton Rouge, the
Bullocks' Wilshire department store in Los Angeles, and the Los Angeles City Hall are among the many buildings influenced by the Capitol.[65]
But Goodhue's design had a fundamental impact upon three significant
projects. The first was Raymond Hood's American Radiator Building
(1924). Of its design, Hood acknowledged:

The exterior is in line with the skyscraper development in America,

208

*144.   1934 detail view of the carved wood doors to the senate chamber
of the Nebraska State Capitol, Lincoln, 1920–1932*

145. Interior view of the senate chamber of the Nebraska State Capitol, Lincoln, 1920–1932

146.   *1934 interior view of the governor's reception room of the
Nebraska State Capitol, Lincoln, 1920–1932*

and I was no more adverse [sic] to studying modern precedent than we have all been to studying ancient precedent. Goodhue, Corbett, Saarinen and the other men who have given an impetus to the study of this problem, and reproductions of whose drawings were scattered over our tables as we worked, gave us a lift over many rough places.[66]

The second was Hugh Ferriss's visionary book *The Metropolis of Tomorrow*, published in 1929.[67] Ferriss eulogized Goodhue as an important American architect, and many of Ferriss's most prophetic drawings seemed inspired by Goodhue's design for Lincoln. The third, and most important project was Rockefeller Center, which drew upon the talents of four key participants who had worked for Goodhue: Hartley Burr Alexander, who composed the initial program of art and symbolism; Lee Lawrie, who was responsible for the lion's share of the sculpture; and Wallace Harrison and Raymond Hood, whose bold, intuitive, and mercurial approach to design seemed closest to that of Goodhue himself. Rockefeller Center was a monumental conception of urban construction which combined tall, mountainous masses, stark and unadorned, a practical approach to design and construction, and a program of art and symbolism which gave a sense of the cultural meaning and purpose of the vast undertaking, all presaged by Goodhue's Capitol.[68]

The Capitol also had a considerable influence in England, where it was published, and especially upon Giles Gilbert Scott's design for the Cambridge University Library. Goodhue's unfulfilled idea for a towered book stack for Lincoln was fully realized in Scott's building, although the brusque brick forms of the English library lack the enriching effect of the Capitol's iconographic sculpture.[69]

At the moment of its conception in 1920, the Capitol was arguably the most compelling design in America. But by a perverse turn of fate, at the time of its completion in 1932, it seemed to belong to a bygone era.[70] The focus of architectural ideas and expression had shifted toward the ascendancy of the Modern Movement, away from the "new tradition" and toward what Hitchcock called the "new pioneers."

CHAPTER EIGHT · A FRESH TRADITIONALISM

THE design for the Nebraska State Capitol heralded changes in American architecture in the 1920s and 1930s. Its wide celebrity transformed Goodhue into an influential leader of his profession in the early 1920s, and it brought a sense of resolution and reintegration to his career. His confidence greatly bolstered and his resistance to classicism behind him, Goodhue addressed a series of new projects with unusual ebullience, producing designs no less distinctive than that for the Capitol. These designs were a significant evolution of his thinking rather than a revolutionary break with his past.

The first of these new projects was a commission for a Convocation Tower to be built in New York City, to house an immense sanctuary in its base and above that the centralized religious offices of all the Protestant denominations in the United States. The large rendering attracted much attention at the Thirty-sixth Annual Exhibition of the Architectural League of New York in early 1921, and at the Thirty-fifth Annual Art Show of Chicago in 1922; it showed an 80-story skyscraper rising 1,000 feet into the air, at a time when the 58-story Woolworth Building was the tallest such structure in the world (Fig. 147).[1] Following its exhibition, the rendering was published in an article in *The New York Times* on July 22, 1923, entitled "No Limit in Sight for Future Skyscrapers."[2]

Four aspects of this unbuilt design contributed to the development of the skyscraper in the 1920s: first, the massing, conceived as a unified, stepped volume rising high into the sky, resembled the generalized form with which architects responded to the requirements of the 1916 New York City Zoning Law; second, the atmospheric rendering by Hugh Ferriss seemed to suggest the awesome scale and raw power of the modern city; third, the siting of the building, not crowded on a narrow city street but spaciously placed on Madison Square, allowed one to see its full height and mountainous shape; and fourth, the timing and prominent display of the sketch in New York City and Chicago came upon the

147. *Perspective drawn by Hugh Ferriss of the proposed Convocational Building, Madison Square, New York City, 1921*

214

eve of an unprecedented skyscraper building boom there and elsewhere across the nation.[3]

Goodhue had always wanted to be more than a church architect, and as early as 1914 he had expressed the desire to design a skyscraper.[4] The rendering of the Convocation Tower, whether or not it was an actual commission, was an attempt to expand the boundaries of his practice by showing not only his desire but his ability to design such a building. Sharing the values and the meaning of Goodhue's late-nineteenth-century drawings of imaginary places, it was an opportunity to pursue issues of architecture beyond the more practical aspects of construction into that realm where the consideration of poetic form is paramount. Although the design was never built, William Ward Watkin subsequently described it in 1931 as

> . . . one of the great imaginative contributions to the dignity of lofty structure as it will be understood in America. The continuity of steel structure in slender ribbed-like treatment between the great corner masses was a poetic story of structural truthfulness controlled with true artistry, and the relation between such ribbed-like structure and the massive corner solids has been repeatedly used in recent buildings, though probably never as successfully as was indicated in Goodhue's dream-like design.[5]

The design incorporated a steel frame as a necessity, but was expressed as a hybrid structure of steel and masonry. The steel was there to enable the creation of an essentially traditional image of a masonry tower. The Convocation Tower embodied the architectural symbolism of the Nebraska State Capitol's slender shaft, enlarged to the proportions of a titanic skyscraper. In its form and its imaginative audacity, it is the child of Saint Kavin's Church (Fig. 20). In the earlier sketch, the tall tower rises above the body of the church; in the later design, the church has been entirely subsumed into the base of the soaring structure.

In 1921, Goodhue was invited to participate in the competition to design the Liberty Memorial, a monument to those who died in World War I, to be built in Kansas City, Missouri. The program, prepared by Thomas R. Kimball, the adviser on the Nebraska competition, included the same principle of selecting a winning entry: "not to buy a plan with the expectation that the proposed Memorial will be built from it, but simply to select an architect through the showings made." The program included the same liberating clauses which freed the Nebraska competitors from the questions of style and tradition:

> . . . as to plan, scope, style, type, or material, the Memorial Association will offer no suggestion . . . even in the matter of tradition it is the desire of this Association that each competitor

215

shall feel free to express what is in his heart, unmindful of what
has been inherited in this regard.[6]

The Association wanted only that the Memorial be

> . . . an inspiring monument worthy of the record of which it is to
> be the messenger—a symbol not of War, but of Peace . . . [and
> a] focal keynote in the great architectural composition embracing
> an art, literary, and musical center, destined some day to occupy
> the whole site.[7]

Beyond the actual programmatic elements, the Association asked the
competitors "to give the widest range to their imagination in all they
submit."[8]

The commanding site was a broad hilltop giving onto "a natural
jutting river promontory, rugged, rocky, and steep in its northern or river
exposure . . . in perhaps the most sightly spot in Kansas City . . .
directly south of the Union Station plaza, which it commands and over-
looks." The program noted that although the site might suggest to the
competitors the Athenian Acropolis, the Association had no particular
form or grouping of buildings in mind for the site.[9]

Eleven entries were received and judged by a jury of five architects:
James Gamble Rogers, Louis Ayres, and Henry Bacon, all from New
York City, Walter R. B. Willcox of Seattle, and John M. Donaldson
of Detroit.[10] They chose for first place the scheme designed by Harold
Van Buren Magonigle of New York. Second place was awarded to Paul
P. Cret and Zantzinger, Borie & Medary of Philadelphia, and third
place to Greenebaum, Hardy & Schumacher, a local firm. Goodhue
placed fourth in the competition and was deeply disappointed at the
result.[11]

The centerpiece of Magonigle's scheme was a tall shaft placed at
the edge of the promontory and rising high into the sky, symbolizing the
Flame of Inspiration, guarded by the Spirits of Courage, Honor, Patri-
otism, and Sacrifice, represented as engaged figures at the top. Flanking
the shaft were two stripped classical pavilions. These three elements sat
on a broad plinth, on the north face of which was inscribed the purpose
of the Memorial, visible from Union Station to the north. Two winged
sphinxes symbolizing Memory and the Future flanked the approach to the
Memorial from the north. A mall, framed in trees, was placed to the
south of the Memorial, allowing the future cultural buildings to be sited
at its edge. The function, size, and number of those future structures
could remain indeterminate and could be added over time without com-
promising the essential features of the Memorial itself.[12] Talbot Hamlin,
the critic and historian, thought the scheme possessed tremendous emo-
tional power, which he attributed to "the boldest uses of plain wall,
cubical composition, and a great shaft rising high to be visible for miles

148. *Plan of Goodhue's competitive design for the Liberty Memorial,*
Kansas City, Missouri, 1921

149. *South elevation of Goodhue's competitive design for the Liberty*
Memorial, Kansas City, Missouri, 1921

217

around."[13]

The focus of Cret's scheme was a Commemorative Center, a big lawn flanked by stepped terraces on which the city would hold ceremonies and pageants. This formal space was placed on the low north end of the site, uniting Union Station with the Peace Statue on top of the promontory, producing an architectural ensemble which Cret likened to the Piazza del Popolo in Rome. The future cultural buildings were to be placed up on the hill to the south of the Memorial itself, to "form the modern acropolis of Kansas City." The formalized lines of the stepped terraces, vast plazas, and grouped buildings entirely subsumed the natural landscape.[14]

The scheme by Greenebaum, Hardy & Schumacher placed a colossal Ionic column in the center of a broad terrace flanked by trees and an asymmetrical grouping of cultural buildings. The composition of memorial, cultural buildings, and stepped terraces minimized the inherent drama of the site, and the classical style of the elements was the most orthodox sort.[15]

Goodhue's scheme occupied the top of the promontory like a fortress (Figs. 148, 149). From the north, the crisp lines of the Memorial contrasted with the rough, natural escarpment below.[16] Goodhue described his intentions in his competition thesis:

> Aiming fittingly to perpetuate the memory of those recently fallen, to express our national love of liberty, and to symbolize the "dawn of a warless age," we are yet constrained to regard such a "dawn" as still hid in the mists of the future, and, in this belief, have endeavored to express its ultimate certainty rather than present triumphant realization.
>
> Stark, almost inaccessible at the north, the monument's southern face is its principal one, sequestered from what lies about it by a forecourt, wherein anniversary services and public gatherings might well be held, and whose arcades would provide space for minor, more personal memorials.
>
> At the end of this court, instead of the traditional arch that signified the enslavement of a defeated enemy, rises a great pylon. At the base, below a relief picturing the august teachers of humanity, is the entrance to a domed chamber, where upon a cenotaph rests a vast sword, fast-sheathed to symbolize the ending, not of the recent conflict only, but of all war, utterly and forever. Above its tile-lined niche, the simply incised inscription makes clear to even the most heedless, the meaning of the whole.
>
> Flanking the great central recess are two seated figures, stony, hieratic, representing the two principles from which all life, and hence all achievement, is derived; the first grasps the Hammer of Toil and the Axe of Force, not lightly to be withdrawn from the

218

Fasces of the Law; the second rests one hand upon the Book of Wisdom, with the other drawing closely to her the Youth, the eternal hope of all the world.

Gigantic as these are, they but serve to buttress the figure standing between them, vast, passionless, serene—Civilization, triumphant above the oblation of the slain.

The materials of which she is made, at first stone like the rest, change and become more precious. Her cloak is bronze, her flesh is creamy marble, her coronal, no mere regal device, but tier upon tier the mark of man's dominion over the elements, is gold.

So exact is the acropolitan analogy, that our design has taken shape along lines, in general effect at least, "classic." Here our endeavor to ape the Greeks ceases, and we have not scrupled to seek inspiration from other lands and periods, and to draw freely upon our own fancy, for we hold that precedent should fade and tradition abdicate whenever and wherever they clash with modern needs and ideals.

Since the use of local material was invariable in all great artistic periods of the past, as witness the Brick of Elam, the Syenite of Egypt, and the Pentelic Marble of Athens, we advocate the use of the same yellowish stone as that underlying the site. Friable and laminated at the surface, this culminates in a hard, almost white, limestone, comparable to marble. With ashlar of this and an infilling of solid concrete, the monument should be as enduring as those of antiquity.[17]

In its siting, Goodhue's scheme recalled both the idealized Mediterranean city of the Panama-California Exposition and the dreamlike castle of the Peterson House. But in its character, the Kansas City Memorial was brooding, stark, and somber, and in its bold, severe, and monumental masses, architecture and sculpture were united into one indivisible whole. Talbot Hamlin thought this scheme, in many ways the finest of Goodhue's entire career, "a climactic point in American architecture; here for the first time was revealed complete freedom and mastery of style," and he discerned:

In its piled majesty there is no dictation of forms by a priori styles. Rather the free classic details flow naturally from the mass. It is the mass composition that dominates; a mass conceived with a tremendous sense of climax, so that the whole has an austere and tragic emotionalism characteristic only of very great art.[18]

The jury may have felt that Goodhue's scheme had too stark a character, too pessimistic a meaning. But it had another flaw: it couldn't easily be built in stages. Its success was too dependent upon the completion of all the future cultural buildings; without them the actual monument

219

might have seemed merely ponderous. In contrast, Magonigle's scheme has, indeed, stood alone in its park setting, heedless of the fact that the cultural buildings were never constructed.

On June 10, 1922, to coincide with its seventy-fifth anniversary, *The Chicago Tribune* announced an international competition to secure for Chicago "the ultimate in civic expression—the world's most beautiful office building," a claim that was later modified to "the most beautiful which could express the ideals of *The Tribune*."[19] The site for the new building was in a felicitous location, able to command a view up and down Michigan Avenue. Chicago was already famous for the development of the skyscraper in the 1880s and 1890s, but, as Colin Rowe observed in 1956 in the article, "Chicago Frame," the early steel-and-glass structures so admired by mid-twentieth-century architects and critics as precursors of the International Style were in fact utilitarian structures created for mercantile clients.[20] In contrast to the early no-nonsense office buildings, the Tribune Tower was to be a monument, "a worthy structure, a home that would be an inspiration to its own workers as well as a model for generations of newspaper publishers."[21] In short, the program called for the design of a private corporate headquarters building that would enact the role usually reserved to public buildings. This was not an entirely new phenomenon. The Woolworth Building (1913) in New York City, known as "The Cathedral of Commerce," had been built as corporate headquarters. What made the *Tribune* competition special was its international importance, the great variety of entries submitted, and the subsequent traveling exhibition of 135 of the entries "for the stimulation and encouragement of better designs in skyscraper architecture, its appreciation by the public, and the consequent achievement of beauty in big buildings."[22]

The competition offered $100,000 in prizes, with $50,000 as first prize, and was open to qualified architects in all parts of the world. In addition, ten architects were invited to compete: Holabird & Roche, Jarvis Hunt, D. H. Burnham & Co., Schmidt, Garden & Martin, and Andrew Rebori of Chicago; Bertram Goodhue, James Gamble Rogers, Benjamin Wistar Morris, and Howells & Hood of New York; and Bliss & Faville of San Francisco. The jury was composed of one architect, Alfred Granger of Chicago, and four members of The Tribune Building Corporation: Colonel Robert R. McCormick, Captain Joseph M. Patterson, Edward S. Beck, and Holmes Onderdonk. The jury's composition ensured that the new building would express the desires of the corporate leaders. From among the designs submitted in response to the general invitation, ten were selected to be judged alongside the ten invited architects, and three of the twenty were awarded cash prizes.[23]

During the period of the competition, *The Tribune* published photographs of important traditional architecture, among them Italian *palazzi* and Gothic churches. With each photograph came the question, "Is this to be the type of architecture embodied in *The Tribune's* new home?" This had a decisive but unfortunate effect of causing a schizophrenic result in many entries. As the architect Irving Pond observed in his article, "High Buildings and Beauty," most of the design effort was focused on "how to effect a transition from the 260-foot base devoted to use to the 140- to 250-foot superstructure so essential to beauty."[24] What most entries failed to achieve was an organic unity of form, use, structure, and symbol.

Pond identified two buildings which were influential examples in the competition, in addition to the images published by *The Tribune:*

> Fortunately, a starting point had been provided, one for the classicist and one for the Gothicist. The Nebraska state house tower, essentially classic in its topping out, had met, seemingly, yes, assuredly, popular and professional favor; while for the Gothicist there were the towers of the Harkness memorial—the best advertised and exploited and admired group of the decade. Here were the necessary elements, height and materialized concepts of beauty, all ready to hand![25]

On December 3, 1922, the unanimous decision of the jury was announced, the first place going to John Mead Howells and Raymond Hood of New York City. The second-place prize was awarded to Eliel Saarinen of Helsinki, and third place was given to Holabird & Roche of Chicago. Howells and Hood had designed a slender shaft resting on a solid base and surmounted by an elaborate Gothic crown. The architects felt that they had designed a unified building:

> . . . our desire has been not so much to secure an archeological expression of any particular style as to express in the exterior the essentially American problem of skyscraper construction, with its continued vertical lines and its inserted horizontal.[26]

Appraisals of the winning scheme were mixed. Irving Pond thought it contradictory, "at first blush, almost of a pure masonry type, but soon scale and mass and dimensions proclaim the presence of steel while dominant forms deny it."[27] Thomas Tallmadge regarded the winning scheme as the work "of such superlative talent" that even close scrutiny of "its proportions, its scale, its detail, its presentation even will not yield a flaw." Yet he thought the design had faults, ones which were "moral, not physical, internal not superficial . . . its style is its raiment, not its flesh and blood . . . the flying buttresses are, of course, stage scenery to the last degree, for they have no structural nor even a useful function." In so criticizing the winning design, Tallmadge was suggesting that the jury had selected a good, conservative design over Saarinen's, which he regarded as "a work of unquestioned genius . . . the best design since Amiens!"[28]

Saarinen's scheme, which received universal praise, stepped back uniformly on all sides as it rose into the sky, giving it a sense of telescopic mass. Above a simplified base, extruded ornament alongside the windows and slightly enriched window spandrels gave the surfaces a strong vertical expression. The crown was not a distinct architectural form but a natural extension and elaboration of the lower massing. The unified massing and the spare surfaces gave the graceful and lithe design its lasting significance and influence, and caused Louis Sullivan to exult that, "rising from the earth . . . it ascends in beauty lofty and serene . . . until its lovely crest seems at one with the sky."[29] In a more restrained appraisal, Talbot Hamlin thought "its silhouette of setbacks and breaks interesting, powerful, and well-proportioned."[30]

Goodhue won an honorable mention with a composition of masses rising to a richly plastic, square lantern surmounted by a pyramidal crown (Fig. 150). Although severe in expression, the lively, stepped massing of the building followed his familiar approach: The building rose from a solid, simplified base and at the top blossomed out into a sculptural skyline enlivened, in this case, with polychromed tilework and a statue of an archetypal newsboy. This building was too severe and even somewhat funereal for its intended role as a corporate headquarters. The sobriety of the scheme was criticized by Tallmadge, who noted that it "speaks of reinforced concrete and inlaid decoration. Such a building, relying on color in its ornamentation and unrelieved by light and shade in its detail, would be doomed to failure in smoky Chicago."[31]

One of the key issues in the evaluations of the Tribune Tower designs was the expression of the requisite steel frame. Irving Pond noted the prevalent avenues of approach:

> Saarinen's forms are steel forms clothed in stone, and not, like those of the design placed first by the jury, stone or masonry forms stayed and stiffened to their task by steel, nor like those of the design unaccountably placed third, whose monumentally massive, crypt-like chapel of masonry crushes the hybrid substructure of masonry and steel.[32]

A fourth approach was "to treat the entire structure as a masonry design, ignoring absolutely the steel skeleton," and of these Pond regarded Goodhue's as "the most refreshing."[33] By calling Goodhue's scheme illogical in terms of structural expression, Pond missed the clearness and the strength of its massing, and the unity which the planar surfaces and the carefully considered setbacks provided. Tallmadge, however, observed the originality of the scheme and noted that, "Mr. Goodhue, who speaks to us ex cathedra, is rapidly becoming the apostle of secessionism or rational-

222

150. Perspective of Goodhue's competitive design for the Chicago Tribune Tower, 1922

ism. He appears to be bending his shoulders for Sullivan's mantle."[34] In so doing, Goodhue was not seeking to use the steel cage as a medium of expression, as Sullivan had previously done. Rather, he continued to rely upon the composition of streamlined masonry mass as the medium through which he could explore the direction of his art.

In 1923, the commission to design the Sterling Memorial Library at Yale University, which had lain dormant since 1920, was revived.

223

Goodhue described his intention for this building in a letter to Giles Gilbert Scott in 1924:

> Of course, it has to be in the "Gothic manner." Anyhow, most of the other buildings at Yale are—or their authors and owners think they are. I've lost my taste for "straight" Gothic, so I am hoping to "put over" something that won't be, although it will look like, Gothic. Burn a candle for me to St. Anthony![35]

The architectural style of the campus of Yale University had been given clear and decisive direction with the design by James Gamble Rogers of the Harkness Memorial Quadrangle in 1916: The style would be English Gothic.[36]

In 1919, John Russell Pope published a privately commissioned proposal, *Yale University, A Plan for its Future Building*.[37] Yale, like many older universities, had not been laid out with a strong, centralized plan, and therefore the goal of Pope's proposal was "the unification of present buildings among themselves and of present buildings with those of the future." Pope was aware that the potential growth of the university did not "appear to warrant the preparation of a plan that would compel radical or destructive measures," and his new plan combined a contextual, evolutionary approach with the usual bold strategy of a City Beautiful scheme. The key to the new grouping of buildings was the conversion of Wall Street into a broad pedestrian walk terminated at one end by an open square linking the campus with the town, and at the other end, by a new gymnasium. A cross axis connected this new portion with the existing campus, and at the intersection of the two axes sat the library.[38]

Pope proposed that the style of the campus should be English Collegiate Gothic, thus conforming to the direction already established. To the extent that he sketched buildings for this plan, they were quite orthodox in effect. The library, for instance, was an iteration of Kings College Chapel, intersected by a tall Perpendicular Gothic tower, a gesture that reaffirmed that the library had replaced the chapel as the dominant building type.[39]

Goodhue's scheme for the Sterling Library was sited where Pope had placed the gymnasium, and it was more severe than what Pope had envisioned (Figs. 151, 152). The plan of Sterling showed Goodhue's customary approach. At the center was a main hall above which were the library stacks, housed in a vast cubical block. Located on the cross axes of this main hall were the entrance, delivery desk, museum, and main reading room. The four smaller corner halls led to the offices, additional reading rooms, and a quadrangle of seminar rooms. From the surrounding streets, the clarity in plan would have been belied by the picturesque quality of the elevations. Rather than a single building, the design resembled a medieval village gathered about a castle of books.

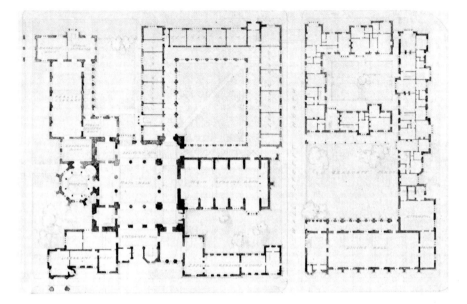

151. Plan of the proposed Sterling Memorial Library, Yale University,
New Haven, Connecticut, 1924

152. Perspective drawn by Hugh Ferriss of the proposed Sterling Memorial
Library, Yale University, New Haven, Connecticut, 1924

225

After Goodhue's death, the Sterling Library commission was given to James Gamble Rogers to complete. His scheme had many similarities to that proposed by Goodhue, and it resulted in a distinguished building characterized by strong massing and somewhat archaeological detail.

In March 1924, Goodhue wrote a long reflective letter to William Lethaby about his newest designs:

> What I want to do more than anything else is to show you some of the stuff that we are turning out here, whether it's good or not, I don't know, but I should not be doing it if I did not think it was better than what I used to do. Next month, I shall be 55, and for almost 35 of those years I have been working at architecture doing all sorts and kinds of dreadful things—Classic, Gothic, and Goodness-Knows-What—and I still do. However, my Gothic is no longer anything like historically correct, and my Classic (my formalistic friends deny me the use of this term) is anything but book Classic . . . [and now] at Los Angeles, I have a Public Library in the same strange style, or lack of style, I have been telling you about.[40]

Goodhue had designed an initial scheme for the Rufus B. Von Kleinsmid Central Library in Los Angeles just after the Panama-California Exposition, and this early design, not built for lack of funds, was Spanish in feeling with a dome and arched openings. In 1921, when the funds became available, the commission was revived. By then Goodhue eschewed the more traditional forms he had used in San Diego, and he redesigned the building, replacing the softer, Spanish forms with severe, cubistic shapes similar to those employed at the Nebraska State Capitol.[41]

The heart of the plan is the domed rotunda flooded with light from four clerestory windows (Fig. 153). Surrounding this majestic room on all sides are the storage areas for books, arranged on seven levels. This great stack of books is, in turn, surrounded by five reading rooms, each suffused with natural light. The reading rooms are linked to the rotunda and to each other by axially controlled vistas. Above the rotunda is a tower, originally designed for an expansion of book stacks that has never materialized, surmounted by a tiled pyramid. The approaches to the building are on axis with the rotunda and the tower above, affirming their centrality at the outset. The north-south symmetry of the central, three-story portion of the building is relieved by a two-story wing of reading rooms arranged around an exterior court at the southeast corner of the main mass, and by elements like stair towers expressed as distinct volumes (Fig. 154).

The structure of the building is a reinforced concrete frame, painted on the interior and covered with stucco on the exterior. The facades are an expression of the structural rhythms and of the spatial composition of

226

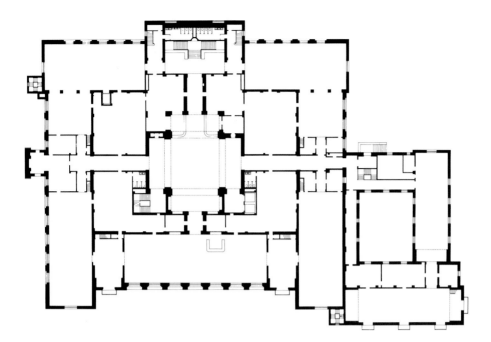

153.   Plan of the Los Angeles Library, 1921–1926

154.   Ca. 1960 view of the west facade of the Los Angeles Library (gardens
not extant), 1921–1926

155.   View of the south facade of the Los Angeles Library, 1921–1926

the building. Goodhue assured the Librarian, Everett Perry, that

> . . . plain masonry and standardized construction are the proper
> things for us to deal with, and ornament that ought to be intelligent
> and isn't should be omitted.[42]

To ensure the appropriateness of the ornament, Goodhue collaborated
once again with Hartley Burr Alexander. Goodhue and Alexander chose
The Light of Learning as the theme for the iconographic program, embodied in heroic inscriptions, in various literary and historical figures, in
interior murals, and in the torch of knowledge atop the pyramid.[43] On
the south facade the thematic elements are fully architectural, creating a
complex composition of structure, sculpture, and symbolism (Figs. 155,
156). A ray-encircled book inscribed with *Lucerna pedibus meis . . .
lumen semitis meis* ("a lamp to my feet . . . a light to my paths") forms
an overdoor, flanked by carved figures of the Thinker (portrayed as a
Greek) and the Writer (portrayed as an Egyptian), symbolizing reflection
and expression. Rising out of the structural columns above are six carved
figures. Three are grouped above the Thinker and symbolize reflective
thought: Herodotus (history), Virgil (letters), and Socrates (philosophy). Three more are grouped above the Writer and symbolize expressive
thought: Justinian (statecraft), Leonardo da Vinci (the arts), and Copernicus (science). These same six figures form three pairs symmetrically

228

disposed about the entrance, symbolizing complementary qualities of civilization. Thus, Socrates (philosophy) is paired with Justinian (statecraft), Virgil with Leonardo da Vinci, and Herodotus with Copernicus. Here, too, all the sculpture in the building was modeled by Lawrie, as were the lighting fixtures, metal grilles, and other architectural elements of an ornamental nature.

On the interior, the ceilings of all five reading rooms and the rotunda are decorated with ornamental motifs, designed by the muralist Julian Ellsworth Garnsey. The polychromed patterns and heralds are painted directly on the concrete surfaces, emphasizing the surface of which they are an integral part, and reiterating the hierarchical relationships of the various reading rooms to the rotunda and to each other (Figs. 157, 158). The walls of the Children's Room are embellished with

156. Detail view of the south facade of the Los Angeles Library, 1921–1926

157.   Interior view of the rotunda of the Los Angeles Library, 1921–1926

murals depicting twelve episodes from Sir Walter Scott's *Ivanhoe*. Thus, in his last building, Goodhue returned again to the romantic image of a knight-errant.

When completed in 1926 under the direction of the associated architect, Carleton Winslow, the Library was considered an impressive achievement. [44] A contemporary critic, Merrill Gage, noted:

> . . . to a public long steeped in the classical orders of architecture, this building comes as a distinct shock . . . it takes from the fundamentals of geometry the cube and the prism, assembles them in a new arrangement, piles them up mass on mass with a convincing strength . . . [and the] Southland sunlight blazing on its walls cuts interesting patterns of light and shade, throwing a bold profile against the sky. [45]

158.   1928 interior view of the Reference Room (now the California Room)
of the Los Angeles Library, 1921–1926

The building seemed at once to have no style and to borrow elements of many styles; to be a regional and at the same time abstract expression; to be a bald statement of rational concrete construction yet with chamfered, battered forms that suggested traditional handlaid masonry; and to be a modern facility with then-advanced techniques of processing, storing, and circulating books that explicitly evoked ancient cultural values. Its gardens recalled those of the Mediterranean world and embodied the aspirations of Southern California. In fact, Goodhue combined the calm discipline of a classical building, the romantic spirit of Persia, a pragmatic approach to construction, and a regional vernacular to create an Arcadian vision of civic order and monumentality. With its stripped-down forms the Library seemed to herald a fresh, astylar approach to architecture, while in its evocation of cultural continuity, its expression of mass and weight, its tectonic rigor, and its integration of iconographic painting, sculpture, and decoration, it remained essentially true to the most traditional aspects of architecture.

Lewis Mumford observed that the Library represented two distinct achievements. One was the success of Goodhue's personal search for a way beyond an archaeologically based traditionalism:

> It must have been hard for anyone who loved subtle and complicated forms, as Mr. Goodhue did from his earliest days as a designer of bookplates, to strip off one by one all these delicate acquisitions and to begin with fresh surfaces and planes, boldly modeled around the plan itself. [46]

The second was the Library's embodiment of a new monumentality and a new symbolism. Mumford observed:

> We live in an age that has still to create or re-create its symbols. Here lies the great difficulty for our monumental architecture; and this is why our utilitarian buildings are fresh and vigorous, expressing with confidence their own functions, whilst our churches and our colleges and our museums and statehouses are, for the greater part, subordinated to stale symbols which no longer work significantly on the beholder. [47]

Mumford felt the success of the Library lay in its unity of architecture and sculpture, and he praised Goodhue and Lawrie "for having the courage to explore together some of the possibilities of a modern symbolic architecture." [48]

The forms of the Library—stark, solid, and monumental—seemed to suggest to Mumford a distinct break from Goodhue's early work. Other critics felt differently. Hitchcock, for instance, claimed in 1929 that "even the later designs of Goodhue, although the result of more conscientious and fundamental study, do not succeed in the attainment of

*159.   Perspective sketch of a "view of the poorer business quarters
of the City of Sarras," 1924*

qualities which were not inherent in his earlier traditional building."[49] The
harshest judgment of Goodhue's late work was offered by the architect
and historian, Fiske Kimball, who in 1927 called it "not a transition but
a tardy compromise" with classicism. Kimball also cast aspersions on
Goodhue himself, claiming "that in the great movements on the stage of
the world he made but a dilatory entrance, and his steps were halting
and uncertain. . . . Supremely impressionable, he veered . . . with every
wind that blew. . . ." Kimball felt that Goodhue, at the time of his
death, was moving "toward the camp of the logicians and modernists."[50]
    But the Los Angeles Library, characteristic of Goodhue's late
work, was neither protomodernist nor a warmed-up traditional scheme.

233

If it seemed strange, enigmatic, and perplexing, at least part of the problem was the lack of a critical framework to understand it. In the 1920s, architectural discourse dealt primarily with the waning of academic eclecticism and the rise of European modernism. As criticism became polarized around fairly rigid conceptions of what was "traditional" and what was "modern," of what was "orthodox" and what was "free," Goodhue's work became more difficult to evaluate: he was too advanced to be a "traditionalist" and too conservative to be a "modernist."

Goodhue's fundamental artistic goal remained constant throughout his career: he always attempted to reconceive traditional forms in a personal and imaginative way, free of the rules of the orthodox styles. The critic Howell Lewis Shay, in "Modern Architecture and Tradition," discerned that Goodhue had "so interpreted and adapted the great traditions of the past and so applied them to modern uses as to produce a truly modern architecture."[51]

This simple assessment of Goodhue's career is confirmed by two of his sketches, one drawn very early in his career and one near the end. The first is that of Saint Kavin's Church, drawn in 1896 (Fig. 20). The second is the last known sketch, drawn on the train in the flyleaf of *The Glorious Mystery*, on April 13, 1924.[52] It shows a "view of the (poorer) business quarters of the city of Sarras," and it resembles the Los Angeles Library (Fig. 159). But with its romantic aura and bold forms, it recalls as well Saint Kavin's Church; indeed, the two sketches suggest those qualities of Goodhue's work which varied and those which remained constant throughout his career. In the earlier sketch, Goodhue immersed himself in the Gothic vocabulary as a way of articulating an architectural image. In the later sketch, Goodhue had evolved what essentially was a language of his own: the willful fusion of elements from disparate sources. While the style of each building is different, they share what is common to the creation of most art, a debt to and at the same time a freedom from the traditions of the past. In a letter to Whitaker, Goodhue himself confirmed that this ideal—embodied in the two sketches—was central to his artistic intentions: "I do believe that architecture should be a 'free' art, always governed by immutable principles, that is, but never by temporary rules."[53]

In 1924, Goodhue was as peripatetic as ever, with major projects in design or construction all across the country, requiring a schedule better suited to a younger, healthier man. Although resentful of his erratic health, he was happy with the state of his work. He wrote ebulliently to Marie Bachman, his former secretary who had married one of his chief assistants, Austin Whittlesey:

> Things are going very well here at the office. The Yale University has signed its contract with me for the library; I have got, I

understand, a new big church to do in Cleveland; and the other day the new president of the University of Chicago came in with his treasurer and put new life into [the chapel] project by indicating he can raise another half a million. Isn't it wonderful how the Lord loves me![54]

In the late works, Goodhue broke his earlier attachment to that balance of discipline and freedom which characterized the looser historical styles such as Gothic, Spanish, and Byzantine. In its place, he embraced the stricter order of the classical mind, and gave free rein to the creative vitality of his own fertile and romantic imagination. In doing so, his work embodied those contradictory qualities of "calm perfection" and "restless mystery" he had envisioned years earlier, becoming in the process more individualistic than ever before. His pursuit of this unique direction entailed a high price. He and his work became increasingly ignored and even quickly forgotten by many in the years after his death.[55]

In April 1924, Goodhue returned to New York from Los Angeles, where the Library bids had been accepted. He focused his attention on the final details of the National Academy of Sciences building, scheduled to be dedicated on April 28, his fifty-fifth birthday. On April 23, without warning, he died of a heart attack. Funeral services were held at the Chapel of the Intercession on April 26, and his remains were buried at Fresh Pond Cemetery in New York City[56].

Goodhue's office was reorganized into the Bertram Grosvenor Goodhue Associates, headed by three senior assistants—Francis S. L. Mayers, Oscar Murray, and Hardie Phillip—who faithfully completed the Nebraska State Capitol, and several other buildings. In 1931, the three men changed the firm name to Mayers, Murray & Phillip, and in 1940, dissolved the firm. Mayers remained in practice in New York City in Goodhue's old office, completing additional work on Saint Thomas's Church among other commissions. Murray moved to Rhinebeck, New York, and Phillip moved to California.[57]

In March 1926, a retrospective exhibition of Goodhue's work opened in London, an appropriate gesture to honor the anglophilic architect. The opening remarks by Giles Scott captured the essence of Goodhue's career:

> Goodhue was in one way unfortunate in his time, in that he formed one of the small opposition to the great wave of architectural thought that ran contrary to his own. The Beaux Arts had a great following in America and the Beaux Arts tradition exerted a great influence on the American architecture of his time. Goodhue was wholly opposed to the whole of the Beaux Arts tradition, and in that he was at variance with the views of by far the greater number of his contemporaries. And his contemporaries although admiring

160.   *View of Goodhue's tomb in the north transept of the*
Chapel of the Intercession, New York City, 1929

the man, were nevertheless out of sympathy with his outlook.[58]

Scott felt that as the influence of the Beaux Arts waned, especially in the years after World War I, there was a movement toward a greater freedom of expression in architecture. In noting this, he discerned the fateful irony of Goodhue's unexpected death:

> It was then that the architects of America began to look with greater sympathy to the work of Goodhue, and it was just then, when he might have been the governing force in a new movement, that death took him away. In that respect his death was a great tragedy for architecture in America.[59]

In 1929, Goodhue's ashes were removed to a tomb adjacent to the baptismal font in the north transept of the Chapel of the Intercession (Fig. 160).[60] In his tomb, sculpted by Lawrie, the architect is depicted as a full-length recumbent figure clad in doctoral robes. At his feet is Pegasus, the winged horse and a symbol of poetic genius. The arch above his body is adorned with bas-relief images of his greatest buildings. Although the forms of the tomb are stylized and modernistic, the format follows the ancient manner used for a medieval knight or gentleman. The tomb is at once a memorial to Goodhue, at rest beneath a crown of his distinguished works, and an embodiment of the fresh traditionalism which was his cardinal achievement.

NOTES

CHAPTER ONE

1. Albert Goodhue to the Author, October 10, 1979. Letter accompanied by pp. 11, 12, 13, 17, 28, 43, 44, 82, 164, 252 of the *History and Genealogy of the Goodhue Family* (1890).

2. The family tree forms part of the Bertram Grosvenor Goodhue private papers (hereafter Goodhue Papers) which are currently in the care of Avery Library, Columbia University, a gift of his son, Hugh Grosvenor Bryant Goodhue. The papers consist of personal correspondence from 1907 to 1924, and miscellaneous professional papers including transcripts of the legislative hearings in Lincoln, Nebraska. A few remnants of his personal library and a very few drawings remain in the care of Hugh G. B. Goodhue. The majority of the extant drawings by Goodhue are held in the care of his great-grandson, John Rivers.

3. Dates before 1890 appear in the *History and Genealogy of the Goodhue Family,* and dates after 1890 are confirmed in the Goodhue Papers, or by members of the Goodhue family.

4. Edward E. Goodhue to Charles H. Whitaker, September 28, 1924, Goodhue Papers. Whitaker was the editor of the memorial volume, *Bertram Grosvenor Goodhue, Architect and Master of Many Arts* (hereafter *Bertram Grosvenor Goodhue*; New York: American Institute of Architects Press, 1925). The volume was reprinted in 1976 by the Da Capo Press, with a new introduction by Paul Goldberger.

5. Ellen D. Larned, *History of Windham County, Connecticut* (Worcester, Mass.: Charles Hamilton, 1874).

6. Ibid. On July 4, 1916, Bertram Grosvenor Goodhue (hereafter BGG) was "duly elected an hereditary member of the Society in right of Colonel Thomas Grosvenor" (Bryce Metcalf to BGG, July 10, 1916, Goodhue Papers). Goodhue was pleased that he inherited his great-grandfather's membership in the Society, which in turn was passed on to his son, Hugh (BGG to Constance Alexander, November 1, 1916, Goodhue Papers).

7. Edward E. Goodhue to Charles H. Whitaker, September 28, 1924, Goodhue Papers.

8. Goodhue's theory of music and architecture was developed in a lecture delivered at a meeting of the Trustees of the Cathedral of the Incarnation at Baltimore in 1912. A draft of the lecture is in the Goodhue Papers.

9. *Emma Willard and Her Pupils* (Troy, N.Y., n.d.), p. 476.

10. Edward E. Goodhue to Charles H. Whitaker, October 14, 1924, Goodhue Papers.

11. Interview with Hugh G. B. Goodhue by the Author, October 19, 1979.

12. Edward E. Goodhue to Charles H. Whitaker, September 28, 1924, Goodhue Papers. See undated reply by Edward E. Goodhue to a letter sent to him by BGG on June 12, 1922, Goodhue Papers.

13. BGG to Constance Alexander, January 8, 1919, Goodhue Papers.

14. Hugh G. B. Goodhue to the Author, February 7, 1981.

15. See Catalogue No. 3, *Books from the Personal Library of Bertram Grosvenor Goodhue* (Los Angeles: Bennett & Marshall Antiquarian Booksellers, 1961), Goodhue Papers. This collection of books was housed in Goodhue's house at Montecito, and consisted mainly of literature, first editions, art, and architecture books. A number of the books were signed by Goodhue, often using the Latin form of his name: Beltrami Grosvenor Goodhue. Item 61, for example, was an 1811 translation of the *Songe de Poliphile* (the Hypnerotomachia), by Fr. Francesco Colonna (see *Heavenly Mansions*, John Summerson, "The Antitheses of the Quattrocento"). Item 106 was a complete set of *The Chap-Book*, a literary periodical of 1894–1898, with which Goodhue was associated. Five early publications of the Kelmscott Press were among the entries, as well as six early publications by the Merrymount Press.

16. "Half a Dozen Pen and Ink Sketches at Pomfret, Connecticut, by Bertram G. Goodhue," *Building* 7 (September 3, 1887).

17. There is some confusion as to the length of Goodhue's stay at Russell's Institute. John Rivers, in "The Architectural Development of Bertram Grosvenor Goodhue" (a senior thesis at Wesleyan University, Middletown, Connecticut, 1972), writes, "He spent one year, when he was ten years old, at Russell's Collegiate and Commercial Institute in New Haven, Connecticut, but returned home, disgusted with all schooling." For other opinions, see Edward E. Goodhue to Lydia Goodhue, 1924; Henry S. Washington, February 15, 1925; and Harry C. Crosby, April 4, 1916, Goodhue Papers.

18. Henry S. Washington to Charles H. Whitaker, February 15, 1925, Goodhue Papers; Sr. Don Jorge Bird y Airias to BGG, 1921, Goodhue Papers.

19. As quoted in Whitaker, *Bertram Grosvenor Goodhue*, p. 15; BGG to Frazier Gibson, January 2, 1913, Goodhue Papers.

20. BGG to Frazier Gibson, January 2, 1913, Goodhue Papers. No other reference to the financial condition of Goodhue's parents as explicit as this is known. However, in much of the correspondence between Goodhue and his brothers there is a concern for money and the lack thereof. The impression gained from the correspondence is that there were no family resources for emergencies. When Helen Goodhue died, she left no will and an estate so small as to make the hiring of a lawyer unnecessary. The single largest inheritance was a small piece of land on the Maine coast given jointly to the three sons.

21. Whitaker, *Bertram Grosvenor Goodhue*, p. 11.

22. BGG to Sr. Don Jorge Bird y Airias, June 22, 1920, Goodhue Papers.

23. At a meeting of the Trustees of Trinity College on April 29, 1911, Goodhue was "appointed to receive the degree of Doctor of Science, in recognition of your distinguished position as an architect" (President F. S. Luther to BGG, May 1, 1911, Goodhue Papers). For the ceremony on June 28, 1911, Goodhue ordered an academic robe. There are two known photographs of Goodhue in this robe: a profile and a three-quarter view. Both are decidedly flattering images;

he appears boyish, debonair, and aristocratic. The profile especially seems to capture a sense of barely contained dynamic energy. In a bemused letter to his half-brother, Wells, he noted "that on and after June 28th you can call me Doctor if you want to, as Trinity is giving me an honorary degree of this sort in Science. I don't care much about the degree but I love the sartorial effect I am going to produce at cornerstone laying and the like" (May 12, 1911, Goodhue Papers).

24. Interview with Hugh G. B. Goodhue by the Author, October 19, 1979.

25. BGG to William A. Boring, January 1920, excerpt in Goodhue Papers. When Goodhue wrote this, he had been a member of the Board of Visitors to the School of Architecture at Columbia University for five years.

26. Donn Barber, "Bertram Grosvenor Goodhue," *Architectural Record* 55 (May 1924), no pagination.

27. For a discussion of New York City at the close of the nineteenth century, see Richard Oliver, ed., *The Making of an Architect: 1881–1981* (New York: Rizzoli International Publications, 1981), pp. 13–85, 127–36. See also, Paul Baker, *Richard Morris Hunt* (Cambridge, Mass.: M.I.T. Press, 1980).

28. There are a number of descriptions of the system of education at the Ecole des Beaux Arts. A selection of them within a century includes: Richard Whiting, "The American Student at the Beaux-Arts," *The Century Illustrated Monthly Magazine* 23 (November 1881–April 1882), pp. 259–72; Ernest Flagg, "The Ecole des Beaux-Arts," *Architectural Record* 3 (January–March 1894), pp. 303–13; 3 (April–June 1894), pp. 419–28; 4 (July–September 1894), pp. 38–43; Paul Cret, "The Ecole des Beaux-Arts and Architectural Education," *Journal of the Society of Architectural Historians* 1 (April 1941), pp. 3–15; James Noffsinger, *The Influence of the Ecole des Beaux-Arts on the Architects of the United States*, (Ph.D. diss., Catholic University, Washington, D.C., 1955); and Richard Chaffee, "The Teaching of Architecture at the Ecole des Beaux-Arts," *The Architecture of the Ecole des Beaux-Arts*, edited by Arthur Drexler (New York: The Museum of Modern Art, 1977).

29. Noffsinger, *The Influence of the Ecole des Beaux-Arts*. See also, Richard Oliver, ed., *The Making of an Architect: 1881–1981* (New York: Rizzoli International Publications, 1981), pp. 13–48, 87–126.

30. *Dictionary of American Biography*, pp. 507–9. In the spring of 1843, at the age of 25, Renwick won the competition for the new Grace Church, New York's wealthiest and most fashionable parish. Thus, his entry into the profession simultaneously made his reputation and secured his future prospects. His practice, naturally enough, consisted largely of designing churches, although he was also the architect of a number of secular buildings. Most notable perhaps, and certainly one of the largest, was the building for the new Smithsonian Institution in Washington, D.C., built in 1846. The crowning achievement of his career, however, was his appointment in 1853 to be the architect of Saint Patrick's Cathedral. See also, Bertram Goodhue, "An Appreciation [of James Renwick]," *The Churchman* 72 (July 20, 1895), p. 77.

31. W. H. Russell to "my dear Billie," April 17, 1885, Goodhue Papers.

32. BGG to his nephew, Wright Goodhue, May 7, 1920, Goodhue Papers.

33. "A Cottage at Tuxedo," *American Architect and Building News* (hereafter *AABN*) 27 (March

29, 1890), plate; "Design for Saint Patrick's Cathedral" (Architect: James Renwick), *Building* 8 (March 17, 1888), plate; "Memorial Hall, Clinton, South Carolina" (Architect: A. Page Brown), *Building* 10 (April 6, 1889), plate; "Residence of Dr. James McCosh, Princeton, N.J." (Architect: A. Page Brown), *Building* 10 (April 27, 1889), plate; "Playroom and Hospital Ward for Saint Christina Home, Saratoga, N.Y." (Architect: A. Page Brown), *Building* 10 (June 8, 1889), plate; "The Country Club of Westchester" (Architect: Renwick, Aspinwall & Russell), *Building* 10 (June 15, 1889), plate; *AABN* 27 (March 29, 1890), plate; "Dining Room with Details," *Architecture and Building* 14 (January 17, 1891), plate. There are three drawings by Goodhue while employed at Renwick, Aspinwall & Russell which pertain to Saint Patrick's Cathedral in the archives at Avery Library, Columbia University, New York City.

34. Whitaker, *Bertram Grosvenor Goodhue*, pp. 16–17.

35. "Sketch of a House and Lodge," *Building* 7 (July 23, 1887). See also: B. G. Goodhue, "An Illustrator's Opinion upon the Architectural Drawing of the Present," *Architecture and Building* 13 (August 16, 1890), p. 75; Bertram G. Goodhue, "The Pen-Drawing of Brick Architecture," *Brickbuilder* 4 (January 1895), pp. 7–8; 4 (November 1895), pp. 228–29.

36. Twenty-one of the designs were published in a special volume on the competition: *Cathedral of St. John the Divine, New York, New York* (Boston: American Architect & Building News Company, 1890). Included were those by Renwick, Aspinwall & Russell, Carrère & Hastings, Peabody & Stearns, Cope & Stewardson, Cram & Wentworth, and Bertram Goodhue. See also *AABN* 26 (October 5, 19, November 2, 23, December 14, 21, 1889).

37. For a discussion of Richardson's career, including both Trinity Church and Richardson's unsuccessful 1882 competition entry for the proposed cathedral at Albany, New York, as well as a general discussion of architecture at the close of the 1880s, see Henry-Russell Hitchcock, *The Architecture of H. H. Richardson and His Times* (New York: The Museum of Modern Art, 1936); Mariana Griswold Van Rensselaer, *Henry Hobson Richardson and His Works* (Boston: Houghton Mifflin and Company, 1888; reprint, New York: Dover Publications Inc., 1969); James F. O'Gorman, *H. H. Richardson and His Office* (Cambridge, Mass.: M.I.T. Press, 1974); Jeffrey Karl Ochsner, *H. H. Richardson: Complete Architectural Works* (Cambridge, Mass.: M.I.T. Press, 1982).

38. "The Late Competition for the Proposed Cathedral of Saint John the Divine," *AABN* 25 (June 1889), pp. 296–97.

39. "The Cathedral of Saint John the Divine, the Second Competition," *AABN* 25 (June 1889), pp. 296–99 *AABN* 32 (May 9, 1891), pp. 81–91, plates. For a retrospective evaluation of the competition, see "The Cathedral of Saint John the Divine, New York City," *Architectural Record* 30 (August 1911), pp. 185–92.

40. Ralph Adams Cram, "Competitive Design for the Cathedral of St. John the Divine, New York," *AABN* 27 (February 15, 1890); Bertram Grosvenor Goodhue, "Competitive Design for the Cathedral of St. John the Divine," *AABN* 27 (February 15, 1890).

41. Goodhue had a history of erratic health, and much of it can be attributed to neurasthenia. He threw himself into his work with such force that he frequently required a breathing spell. He often traveled for rest and relaxation, which happily also expanded his horizons.

42. Donn Barber, "Bertram Grosvenor Goodhue," *Architectural Record* 55 (May 1924), no pagination. See also, E. Donald Robb, "Brief Sketches of Contemporary Members of the Architectural Profession—Bertram G. Goodhue," *Brickbuilder* 24 (April 1915), p. 102.

CHAPTER TWO

1. Cram & Wentworth to BGG, June 24, 1891, Ralph Adams Cram Papers (hereafter Cram Papers), Boston Public Library (hereafter BPL). These papers include letters written by the firms of Cram & Wentworth; Cram, Wentworth & Goodhue; Cram, Goodhue & Ferguson; and Cram & Ferguson. The papers are not a complete history of the various firms, and the remaining papers of Cram are held in the care of his successor firm, Hoyle, Doran & Berry, Boston, Mass.

2. No partnership agreement between Cram, Wentworth & Goodhue is in the Cram Papers. However, the letter files show BGG signing for the firm of Cram, Wentworth & Goodhue after January 1, 1892.

3. See the Revised Partnership Agreement, July 3, 1911, BPL Archives, which is a revision of the 1898 agreement binding Cram, Goodhue & Ferguson.

4. Ralph Adams Cram, *My Life in Architecture* (hereafter *My Life*; Boston: Little, Brown & Co., 1938). Other data on Cram's life and career can be found in the *Dictionary of American Biography*, and the *National Cyclopedia of Biography*. There is no definitive biography of Cram as yet, but the most complete account to date is found in Douglass Shand Tucci, *Ralph Adams Cram: American Medievalist* (Boston: Boston Public Library, 1975), and in Robert Mucci-grosso, *American Gothic: The Mind and Art of Ralph Adams Cram* (Washington, D.C., 1979). Ann Minor Daniel, *The Early Architecture of Ralph Adams Cram, 1889–1902* (Ph.D. diss., University of North Carolina, Chapel Hill, 1978), gives a detailed account of Cram's career up to 1902. For a portfolio of Cram's architectural work, see *The Works of Cram & Ferguson, Architects, including work by Cram, Goodhue & Ferguson*, Introduction by Charles D. Maginnis (New York: The Pencil Points Press, 1929).

5. See Vincent Scully, *The Shingle Style and the Stick Style* (New Haven: Yale University Press, 1955).

6. "Church to be built in Berkshire County," *AABN* 30 (November 29, 1890), plate.

7. "Design for Church of the Messiah," *AABN* 31 (January 10, 1891), plate. See also, Cram, *My Life*, pp. 73–74.

8. Montgomery Schuyler, "The Works of Cram, Goodhue & Ferguson, 1892–1910," *Architectural Record* 29 (January 1911), pp. 1–112. All Saints', Ashmont, is discussed in this article, which is one of the most comprehensive and important evaluations of the firm's work up until that date. See also, Douglass Shand Tucci, *All Saints' Ashmont, A Centennial History* (Boston: All Saints' Church, 1975). This is a history of the parish with lengthy discussion of the present church building, its design, and the professional relationship of its designers. Tucci points out

243

that the rector, the Rev. Charles Whittemore, and the wealthy and pious patrons of the church, Colonel Oliver and Mary Peabody, all were impassioned advocates of the principles of the Oxford Movement. Thus, this church was a particularly apposite commission for the young firm of architects. See also, Cram, Wentworth & Goodhue, *A Decoration of the Proposed Church of All Saints in Dorchester, Massachusetts, Together with various sketches, plans of the same, also a Statement of the Needs of the Parish* (Boston: Elzevir Press, 1892).

9. "All Saints' Church, Dorchester, Mass.," *Architectural Review* (Boston) 12 (September 1905), pp. 268–69. The original site plan of All Saints' showed a landscaped court—or garth—encompassed by the long, narrow church, the Sunday school, a cloister, and the rectory. This would have provided a very complete physical plant for the church, but neither the rectory nor the cloister was built.

10. Ralph Adams Cram, *Church Building, A Study of the Principles of Architecture in their Relation to the Church* (hereafter *Church Building;* Boston: Small, Maynard & Co., 1901), p.6. Cram's book, which reflects the firm's work and theories of the 1890s, outlines a prescriptive view of church architecture that is reminiscent of the architectural edicts of the nineteenth-century English Oxford Movement and Ecclesiological Society.

11. Ralph Adams Cram, "All Saints' Church, Dorchester (Boston), Mass." *The Churchman* 79 (April 15, 1899), pp. 559–64. As an example of the firm's perceptual approach to design, Cram emphasized the visual importance of having an aisle in a church:

> Effects of mystery, shadow, obscurity, of varying light on stone shafts, and sweeping curves of pointed arches . . . tend to create those impressions of awe and majesty that are such potent agencies of worship. These can only be obtained by the use of stone arcades dividing the lighter nave of the church from the darker aisles.

12. Tucci, *All Saints' Ashmont*, p. 24.

13. For a general discussion of the English Gothic Revival, see Henry-Russell Hitchcock, *Early Victorian Architecture in Britain* (New Haven: Yale University Press, 1954); Phoebe Stanton, *The Gothic Revival and American Church Building* (Baltimore: Johns Hopkins Press, 1968); Kenneth Clark, *The Gothic Revival* (New York: Harper & Row, 1962); Nikolaus Pevsner, *Some Architectural Writers of the Nineteenth Century* (Oxford: Clarendon Press, 1972); Peter Ferriday, *Victorian Architecture* (New York: J. P. Lippincott Co., 1964); and George Hersey, *High Victorian Gothic; a study in associationism* (Baltimore: Johns Hopkins Press, 1972). For a general discussion of the American phase of the Gothic Revival, see William H. Pierson, *American Buildings and Their Architects, Technology and the Picturesque, the Corporate and the Early Gothic Styles* (New York: Doubleday & Company, 1978). See also, Beresford Pite, "A Review of the Tendencies of the Modern School of Architecture," *Royal Institute of British Architects' Journal* 8 (1900–1901), pp. 77–91. Pite's article reviews the effect of the Gothic Revival upon subsidiary arts and crafts, the influence of William Morris, the influence of Sedding upon the craft of building, and the influence of William Butterfield, Philip Webb, Richard Norman Shaw, and George Frederick Bodley. See also, Ralph Adams Cram, "John D. Sedding, Some Considerations of his Life and Genius," *Architectural Review* (Boston) 1 (December 14, 1891).

14. Cram, "All Saints' Church," *The Churchman*. See also: "All Saints' Church, Dorchester, Mass.," *AABN* 37 (August 13, 1892), p. 107; "The Nave, All Saints' Ashmont," *AABN* 81 (September 28, 1903), p. 104.

15. Cram, "All Saints' Church," *The Churchman*.

16. Cram Papers, BPL.

17. See the following entries: "The Church of Saint Paul, Brockton, Massachusetts," *AABN* 38 (October 8, 1892), p. 30; "St. Paul's Church, Brockton, Mass.," *The Churchman* 67 (June 17, 1893), pp. 836–37; "Design for the First Congregational Church, Plymouth, Massachusetts," *AABN* 44 (March 10, 1894), p. 118; "All Saints', Brookline, Mass.," *Architectural Review* (Boston) 12 (September 1905), p. 283; "Saint Andrew's Church, Detroit, Michigan," *AABN* 45 (July 7, 1894), p. 11; "Competitive Design for Christ Church, Waltham, Massachusetts," *AABN* 54 (November 28, 1896), p. 74; "Church of Our Saviour, Middleborough, Massachusetts," *The Churchman* 78 (December 17, 1898), pp. 897–98; "Church of Our Saviour, Middleborough, Massachusetts," *Architectural Review* (Boston) 12 (September 1905), pp. 274–75; "Saint Stephen's Church, Cohasset, Massachusetts," *Architectural Review* (Boston) 6 (September 1899), plates; "Competition Design for the First Parish Church, Cambridge, Massachusetts," *Architectural Review* (Boston) 10 (October 1899), plates; "Newton Corner Methodist Episcopal Church, Newton, Mass.," *AABN* 59 (January 15, 1898), p. 24, plate; "Emmanuel Church, Newport, Rhode Island," *AABN* 78 (December 6, 1902), plates; *Christian Art* 1 (January 1908), plates of following completed churches: Church of the New Jerusalem, Newtonville, Massachusetts; Unitarian Church, West Newton, Massachusetts; Congregational Church, Exeter, New Hampshire; and Saint Mary's Church, Walkersville, Ontario. See also, "Design for a proposed church in the suburbs of Boston, Mass.," *AABN* 75 (March 15, 1902), p. 87.

18. Of the several non-Episcopal commissions the firm received, an unbuilt design for a Unitarian church in Somerville, Massachusetts (1894), was a significant variation of the firm's more customary designs: a tall, broad Gothic tower, richly ornamented at the top with spire and corner pinnacles and flanked on three sides by shallow gabled transepts, was placed over an auditorium plan with a semicircular arrangement of seating. With no ritualistic Anglo-Catholic ceremony to prescribe a particular plan and consequent massing, the architects felt free to explore other possibilities. See: Whitaker, *Bertram Grosvenor Goodhue*, plate 5; "Proposed Unitarian Church, Somerville, Ma.," *AABN* 47 (October 6, 1894), plate.

19. Cram, *My Life*, p. 95–96.

20. The firm designed at least four houses. Two are of stone or shingles with a half-timbered second floor, and two are Colonial designs gathered about two tall chimneys. See: "House of Eugene Fellner, Esq., Brookline, Mass.," *AABN* 29 (March 11, 1893), p. 159; "Bushy Hill, The Seat of Walter Phelps Dodge, Esq., Simsbury, Conn.," *AABN* 29 (May 27, 1893), p. 139; and "Proposed House for Joseph Merrill, Esq., Little Boar's Head, N.H.," *AABN* 48 (June 29, 1895), p. 132; and "A House at Athens, Ohio," *Brickbuilder* 8 (July 1899), plate 54.

    Two apartment houses were designed, one of which was constructed. Both were a freely conceived Tudor-style adapted to the needs of a modern, low-rise apartment building. See: "The Richmond Court Apartments, Beacon Street, Boston, Mass.," *AABN* 63 (March 18, 1899), p. 88; "Apartment House Project," *AABN* 69 (July 14, 1900).

    A competition entry for a school showed a well-planned, U-shaped building that employed an unresolved mixture of Dutch and Tudor motifs and plain and patterned brick surfaces. See: "Design for the State Normal School, Jamaica, N.Y.," *AABN* 47 (March 23, 1895), p. 127.

    For an early monumental work, see "Competitive Design for a Memorial Monument at Dorchester Heights, Boston, Mass.," *Brickbuilder* 8 (August 1899), plate 59.

21. "Competitive Design for the Proposed City Hall, New York, New York," *AABN* 52 (May

9, 1896). Plates show a perspective, longitudinal and transverse sections, and two plans.

22. Alastair Service, *Edwardian Architecture* (New York: Oxford University Press, 1977), pp. 140–57.

23. "Public Library, Fall River, Massachusetts," *AABN* 50 (October 26, 1895), plate. The completed building is illustrated in Charles Soule, "Modern Library Buildings," *Architectural Review* (Boston) 9 (January 1902), pp. 1–7, 15.

24. "Public Library, Nashua, N.H.," *Brickbuilder* 10 (November 1901), plate 82. See also, Montgomery Schuyler, "The Works of Cram, Goodhue & Ferguson" (hereafter "The Works of CGF"), *Architectural Record* 29 (January 1911), p. 24.

25. *The Deborah Cook Sayles Public Library, Pawtucket, Rhode Island* (Providence, R.I.: Standard Printing Company, 1902). All three libraries are discussed in "Libraries in the United States," *AABN* 77 (August 23, 1902). See also: "The Deborah Cook Sayles Public Library, Pawtucket, R.I.," *AABN* 78 (October 11, 1902), p. 15, plates; "Successful competitive design for the public library, Pawtucket, R.I.," *AABN* 64 (April 1, 1899), p. 7; Schuyler, "The Works of CGF," p. 20.

26. *Who was Who in America*, vol. 4, p. 559. For Lawrie's recollections about his relationship with Goodhue, see Whitaker, *Bertram Grosvenor Goodhue*, pp. 33–36.

27. Bertram G. Goodhue, *Mexican Memories* (New York: G. M. Allen Company, 1892).

28. Sylvester Baxter, *Spanish Colonial Architecture in Mexico* (Boston: J. B. Millet, 1901), pp. 5, 15–16.

29. Cram, *My Life*, p. 84.

30. Ibid., pp. 90–95.

31. *The Ballad of Saint Kavin* (Boston: 1895). Copies of the limited edition of fifty are in the Boston Public Library and in the care of Hugh G. B. Goodhue.

32. Frank Denman, *The Shaping of Our Alphabet, A Study of Changing Type Styles* (New York: Alfred A. Knopf, 1955); George Parker Winship, *The Merrymount Press of Boston: An Account of the Work of Daniel Berkeley Updike* (Vienna: Herbert Reichner, 1929); *Book Decorations by Bertram Grosvenor Goodhue* (New York: The Grolier Club, 1931); Sheldon Cheney, "The Book Plate and the Architect," *Architectural Record* 32 (August 1912), pp. 149, 151; "Goodhue in the Realm of the Book Arts," *American Institute of Architects' Journal* 34 (August 1960), p. 60; a copy of *The Altar Book of the Episcopal Church*, a gift of Hugh G. B. Goodhue, is in the library of the Cooper-Hewitt Museum.

33. In 1919, Goodhue arranged for an edition of sixty copies of James Russell Lowell's *The Cathedral*, privately printed by T. M. Cleland of New York City. The book, a copy of which is in the Boston Public Library, contained a frontispiece drawing by Goodhue.

34. An example of this phenomenon is *An Appeal for the New Christ Church, Hyde Park, Massachusetts, 1893*, a booklet with three exterior sketches and one interior sketch. Others were produced for Saint Andrew's, Detroit; Saint Bartholomew's Church; and Saint Thomas's Church.

35. *The Knight-Errant* (Boston, 1892–1893). A complete set of four volumes is held in the Boston Public Library and in the library of the Cooper-Hewitt Museum, the latter a gift of Hugh

G.B.Goodhue. Cram and Goodhue also contributed to other similar journals, such as *Moods, A Journal Intime* [sic]. In volume 2 of *Moods*, Goodhue contributed a fable entitled "The Sculptured Stone."

36. *The Knight-Errant* 1 (April 1892), p. 1. The following commentary on *The Knight-Errant* is found in *Architectural Review* (Boston) 1 (June 13, 1892): "We would like to have an affection for *The Knight-Errant*, of which the first number appears in so satisfactory a form . . . but we cannot find it in ourselves to agree with its attitude. There is a prettiness about it, a gentle courtesy, and withal an adolescent courage . . . [but] *The Knight-Errant* seems rather an aesthetic anarchist, and as such must be taken with an allowance for exaggeration."

37. *The Knight Errant* 1 (April 1892), pp. 7–9.

38. Ibid., 1 (January 1893), pp. 106–12.

39. BGG to J.C.M. Keith, February 1, 1915, Goodhue Papers. In that letter, Goodhue expressed his admiration for Lethaby and Giles Gilbert Scott:

> The fact that both Mr. Scott and Dr. Lethaby are friends of mine does not, believe me, affect my opinion that they are, the one, the greatest living ecclesiastical architect, and the other the greatest living theorist on matters architectural; for the already completed Lady Chapel at Liverpool proves the first, and the fact that Dr. Lethaby has . . . written such books as "Architecture, Mysticism, and Myth" and the little primer for the Home University Library entitled "Architecture," proves the second.

In another letter, Goodhue exclaimed that "I wish there were more Lethabys in the world . . . I quote him on every possible occasion" (BGG to Cecil C. Brewer, November 23, 1917, Goodhue Papers). See also, Robert MacLeod, *Style and Society: Architectural Ideology in Britain, 1835–1914* (London: R.I.B.A. Publications Ltd., 1971), pp. 55–67.

40. William R. Lethaby, *Architecture, Mysticism & Myth* (London: 1891; reprint, New York: George Braziller, Inc., 1975), pp. v–viii. See also, John Brandon-Jones, "W. R. Lethaby: 1857–1931," *Architectural Association Journal* 64 (March–April 1949), pp. 167–71, 194–97. For a complete listing of his writings, see *William Richard Lethaby: A Bibliography of his Literary Works* (London: The Royal Institute of British Architects Library, 1950).

41. Lethaby, *Architecture, Mysticism & Myth*, p. 3.

42. Lethaby, *The Church of Sancta Sophia, Constantinople; a study of Byzantine building* (New York: Macmillan & Co., 1894), p. vi.

43. Lethaby, *Mediaeval art, from the peace of the Church to the eve of the Renaissance, 312–1350* (New York: Charles Scribner's Sons, 1904), p. 4. See also, Lethaby, *Architecture; an introduction to the history and theory of the art of building* (New York: Henry Holt & Co., 1912), p. 18.

44. Cram, *My Life*, p. 96.

45. BGG to Rev. William N. Guthrie, April 17, 1916, Goodhue Papers. In response to an invitation to speak, Goodhue declined, being the "most ineffective public speaker alive." He observed that "the only language an architect can and should use is architecture, and it seems to me, though [Cram] is an exception to this rule, that the glib after dinner speaker is usually glib at nothing else." For a discussion of the relationship of Goodhue's drawings to his artistic intentions, see William Hubbard, *Complicity and Conviction* (Cambridge, Mass.: M.I.T. Press, 1980). See also, Schuyler, "The Works of CGF," p. 10.

46. The public attribution of design credit was often blurred and confused, as is often the case in firms with more than one designing partner, and this was a source of tension between Cram and Goodhue. Because Cram was the more visible spokesman for the firm, he often was credited singularly for work completed by the firm, and this distressed Goodhue. Between 1903 and 1913, when there were two branches of the office, design credit became more difficult to attribute correctly, which distressed both men. After the firm was dissolved in 1914, a true picture of the early collaborative relationship between Cram and Goodhue became even more difficult to envision, clouded by enduring ill-will between the two offices and their successor firms.

47. Cram, *My Life*, pp. 77–78.

48. The financial arrangements of the firm were such that each partner received 15 percent of each commission check, leaving the remaining 55 percent to be applied to the expense of running the office (BGG to Harry Goodhue, March 24, 1911, Goodhue Papers). This, together with the original terms of the association, suggests a more equal balance among the three partners.

49. See Cram, *My Life*. Cram's viewpoint is reiterated in subsequent descriptions. See: Tucci, *American Medievalist;* Daniels, *The Early Architecture of Ralph Adams Cram, 1889–1902*.

50. All of the drawings of imaginary places were reproduced in *A Book of Architectural and Decorative Drawings by Bertram Grosvenor Goodhue* (hereafter *1914 Drawing Book;* New York: The Architectural Book Publishing Company, 1914). Goodhue referred to this publication as "the ME Book." In addition, the drawings were published in the professional press: BGG, "Traumburg," *Architectural Review* (Boston) 4 (1897), pp. 27–30, 35–37; BGG, "The Villa Fosca and its Garden," *Architectural Review* (Boston) 5 (1898), pp. 1–3, 5, 35–37; BGG, "Monteventoso," *Brickbuilder* 8 (1899), pp. 129–33, 151–53. See also: Birch Burdette Long, "Individual Styles of Rendering," *Architectural Review* (Boston) 12 (May 1905), pp. 133–37; Arthur Leighton Guptill, *Drawing with Pen and Ink* (New York: Watson Guptill, 1977); Richard Oliver, "Voyages of the Imagination," *Architectural Record* 162 (September 1978) pp. 101–8.

51. Constance Alexander to BGG, December 29, 1914, Goodhue Papers.

52. *1914 Drawing Book*, p. 15. See also, "A Competitive Design for the Lady Chapel at St. Patrick's Cathedral, New York, N.Y.," *AABN* 69 (August 18, 1900). The competition called for a plan, elevations, sections, and a perspective. The other competitors were George B. Post; N. LeBrun & Sons; William Schickel; Heins & LaFarge; Charles C. Haight; and Renwick, Aspinwall & Owen.

53. *1914 Drawing Book, p. 15*.

54. Ibid., pp. 31–32.

55. Ibid, p. 36.

56. Ibid., pp. 49–63.

57. In drawing this conclusion, I was encouraged by a similar evaluation of Frank Lloyd Wright by Hitchcock, and of Henry Hobson Richardson by Van Rensselaer. See: Henry-Russell Hitchcock, "Frank Lloyd Wright and the 'Academic Tradition' of the early eighteen-nineties," *Journal of the Warburg and Courtauld Institutes* 7 (1944), p. 62; Mariana Griswold Van Rensselaer, *Henry Hobson Richardson and His Works* (Boston: Houghton Mifflin and Company, 1888; reprint, New York: Dover Publications Inc., 1969), p. 89.

58. Schuyler, "The Works of CGF," p. 11. The first instance of this phenomenon seems to have been the design for St. Paul's Church, Rochester, New York. For Cram's scheme, see: "Unsuccessful competitive design for Saint Paul's Church, Rochester, N.Y.," *AABN* 53 (September 12, 1896), p. 88; and "Proposed St. Paul's Church, Rochester, N.Y.," *Architecture and Building* 26 (May 29, 1897). For Goodhue's scheme, see: "Competitive design, St. Paul's Church, Rochester, N.Y.," *Brickbuilder* 5 (August 1896), plates 39, 40. Multiple schemes also were designed for Calvary Church in Pittsburgh, and they are published in *Architectural Review* (Boston) 12 (September 1905), pp. 234–36. Cram's scheme was built and has a very fine tower. See also two competitive entries for the Cathedral of Saint John in the Wilderness in Denver, published in *Architectural Review* (Boston) 12 (September 1905), pp. 288–89. For multiple site plans for The Rice Institute in Houston, Texas, see Stephen Fox, *The General Plan of the William M. Rice Institute and Its Architectural Development* (Houston: School of Architecture, Rice University, 1980).

59. For BGG's drawings of Persian gardens, see *1914 Drawing Book*, pp. 89–97.

60. *Architectural Review* (Boston) 10 (September 1903), pp. 139–40. See also: *American Country Houses of Today* (New York: The Architectural Book Publishing Co., 1912), Preface by Frank Miles Day, pp. 52–58; "El Fureidis, Montecito, California," *House and Garden* 4 (September 1903), pp. 97–103; Schuyler, "Works of CGF," pp. 14–16. The meaning of the Arabic name was provided by Hugh G. B. Goodhue (Hugh G. B. Goodhue to Author, February 7, 1981).

61. Hugh G. B. Goodhue to Author, February 7, 1981.

62. Martha Lou Lemmon Stohlman, *The Story of Sweet Briar College* (Princeton: Princeton University Press, 1956). "Sweet Briar Institute, Virginia," *AABN* 77 (August 23 and August 30, 1902), p. 64, plates of eleven perspective drawings. See also, Alfred Morton Githens, "The Group Plan: Universities, Colleges and Schools," *Brickbuilder* 16 (December 1907), pp. 219–25. For photographs and commentary on completed buildings, see *Architectural Review* (London) 30 (September 1911), pp. 148–50.

63. *Annual Report of the Superintendent of the United States Military Academy, 1903* (hereafter *1903 Report;* Washington, D.C.: Government Printing Office, 1903), Appendix I: Rules Governing Architectural Competition, p. 57, United States Military Academy Archives (hereafter USMA Archives).

64. Colonel David W. Gray, *The Architectural Development of West Point* (West Point, 1951), USMA Archives, pp. 10–11.

65. *Report of Professor Charles W. Larned upon the Reorganization of the Plant of the United States Military Academy, Accompanied by Estimates, Maps, and Drawings*, West Point, New York, December 21, 1901, pp. 4–5, USMA Archives.

66. *1903 Report*. Also see Charles Moore, *Daniel H. Burnham, Architect, Planner of Cities* (New York: Da Capo Press, 1968, reprinted from original), "The West Point Plan, 1902–3," pp. 189–96. In his biography of Burnham, Moore lists the nine invited competitors. Of the firms invited, Cram, Goodhue & Ferguson was probably the least known outside of ecclesiastical circles, and Cram in his autobiography could not recall why the firm had been invited. However, the Honorable Charles H. Grosvenor, a cousin of Goodhue's, had been appointed by the Speaker of the House of Representatives to the Academy's Board of Visitors in 1900, and it is possible that he put in a good word for his cousin's abilities. See *Annual Report of the Board of*

Visitors to the United States Military Academy, 1900 (Washington, D.C.: Government Printing Office, September 28, 1900), USMA Archives.

67. Moore, *Burnham*, p. 190. Schuyler, however, noted that the architects on the jury—Post, Cook, and Gilbert—were "all known as practitioners of the prevailing modes of classical architecture," suggesting that the jury did not succumb to personal feelings about style and chose the most appropriate scheme (Montgomery Schuyler, "The Architecture of West Point," *Architectural Record* 14 [December 1903], p. 478.)

68. Montgomery Schuyler, "The Architecture of West Point," *Architectural Record* 14 (December 1903), pp. 476–77.

69. Moore, *Burnham*, p. 190. For Burnham's scheme, see *AABN* 81 (September 19, 1903).

70. Schuyler, "The Architecture of West Point," pp. 463–92.

71. *1903 Report.* CGF's scheme was published in *AABN* 82 (November 14, 1903), and in *The [Boston] Sunday Herald* on June 7, 1903.

72. Schuyler, "The Architecture of West Point," p. 490.

73. *The American Renaissance, 1876–1917* (New York: The Brooklyn Museum, 1979); Thomas S. Hines, *Burnham of Chicago, Architect and Planner* (New York: Oxford University Press, 1974).

74. BGG to A. L. Frothingham, March 11, 1910, Goodhue Papers. The design of all the new buildings at West Point is credited to Cram, Goodhue & Ferguson as a whole, but in fact the design responsibilities for various buildings were divided between the two offices and subsequent credit has been ascribed to one or the other partner. Goodhue was responsible for the cadet chapel and many smaller buildings, and Cram was responsible for the post headquarters, the riding hall, and several lesser buildings. However, the working drawings and almost all the supervision of construction were completed by the New York office of the firm.

75. "The United States Military Academy at West Point," *American Institute of Architects' Journal* 1 (March 1913), pp. 113–23. See also, *Brickbuilder* 18 (October 1909), plates 128–30.

76. Schuyler, "Works of CGF," p. 98. While the West Point work was in general a great success artistically, the firm incurred financial losses as a result of a contract written in favor of the government. See Cram, *My Life*, pp. 110–13. See also "Report to the Superintendent, USMA, from The Office in Charge of Construction, USMA," May 14, 1913, Goodhue Papers. For a discussion of Mont St. Michel, see Henry Adams, *Mont St. Michel and Chartres* (Boston: Houghton Mifflin Company, 1905), Introduction by Ralph Adams Cram.

CHAPTER THREE

1. These two ideas have usually been combined under the same title. Henry-Russell Hitchcock has used the term "academic reaction"; Richard Guy Wilson has used "scientific eclecticism"; Carroll L. V. Meeks has used "creative eclecticism"; and Richard W. Longstreth has used "academic eclecticism." See: Henry-Russell Hitchcock, *The Architecture of H. H. Richardson and His Times* (New York: The Museum of Modern Art, 1936), pp. 290–304; Hitchcock, *Architecture: Nineteenth and Twentieth Centuries* (New York: Penguin, 1958), chapter 13; Hitchcock, "Frank Lloyd Wright and the 'Academic Tradition' of the early eighteen-nineties," *Journal of the Warburg and Courtauld Institutes* 7 (1944), pp. 46–63; *The American Renaissance, 1876–1917* (New York: The Brooklyn Museum, 1979), pp. 57–61; Carroll L. V. Meeks, "Creative Eclecticism," *Journal of the Society of Architectural Historians* 12 (December 1953), pp. 15–18; Richard W. Longstreth, "Academic Eclecticism in American Architecture," *Winterthur Portfolio* 17 (Spring 1982), pp. 55–82. For a contemporary account, see Ralph Adams Cram, "Style in American Architecture," *Architectural Record* 34 (September 1913), pp. 232–39.

2. Charles Herbert Reilly, *The Architecture of McKim, Mead & White* (London: Architectural Book Publishing Co., 1924; reissued, New York: Benjamin Blom, 1973), pp. 15, 23. See also: *A Monograph of the Work of McKim, Mead & White* (New York: 1915–1925; reissued, New York: 1973, with an essay by Leland Roth); Alfred Hoyt Granger, *Charles Follen McKim* (Boston: Houghton Mifflin Co., 1913); Charles C. Baldwin, *Stanford White* (New York: Dodd Mead, 1931; reissued, New York: Da Capo Press, 1976, new introduction by Paul Goldberger); Henry Desmond and Herbert Croly, "The Work of Messrs. McKim, Mead & White," *Architectural Record* 20 (September 1906), pp. 153–246.

3. Montgomery Schuyler, "Last Words about the World's Fair," *Architectural Record* 3 (January–March 1894), pp. 291–301. See also, Thomas S. Hines, *Burnham of Chicago, Architect and Planner* (New York: Oxford University Press, 1974), pp. 92–124.

4. Reginald Theodore Blomfield, *Richard Norman Shaw* (London: 1940); William R. Lethaby, *Philip Webb and His Work* (London, 1935).

5. William Morgan, *The Almighty Wall: The Architecture of Henry Vaughan* (New York: The Architectural History Foundation, 1983); Morgan, "Henry Vaughan: An English Architect in New Hampshire," *Historical New Hampshire* 28 (Summer, 1973), pp. 120–40; Basil F. L. Clark, *Church Builders of the Nineteenth Century* (New York: Augustus M. Kelley, Publisher, 1969); Henry Vaughan, "The Late G. F. Bodley—an appreciation," *Architectural*

Review (Boston) 14 (1907), pp. 213–15; Ralph Adams Cram, "John D. Sedding, Some Considerations of his Life and Genius," *Architectural Review* (Boston) 1 (December 14, 1891).

6. Henry-Russell Hitchcock, *In the Nature of Materials* (New York: Hawthorn Books, Inc., 1942; reissued, New York: Da Capo Press, 1975); Hugh Morrison, *Louis Sullivan, Prophet of Modern Architecture* (New York: Norton, 1935); Willard Connely, *Louis Sullivan* (New York: Horizon Press, 1960); Esther McCoy, *Five California Architects* (New York: Reinhold Publishing Co., 1960); Richard W. Longstreth, *On the Edge of the World, Four Architects in San Francisco at the Turn of the Century* (New York: The Architectural History Foundation, 1983); Kenneth Cardwell, *Bernard Maybeck: Artisan, Architect, Artist* (Santa Barbara: Peregrine Smith, 1977); Randall L. Makinson, *Greene & Greene: Architecture as Fine Art* (Santa Barbara: Peregrine Smith, 1977); Christopher Hussey, *The Life of Sir Edwin Lutyens* (New York: Charles Scribner's Sons, 1950); Lawrence Weaver, *Houses and Gardens by E. L. Lutyens* (London: Country Life, 1914); Albert Christ-Janer, *Eliel Saarinen* (Chicago: University of Chicago Press, 1948); Peter Collins, *Concrete: the vision of a new architecture; a study of Auguste Perret and his precursors* (London: 1959); William H. Jordy, *American Buildings and their Architects: Progressive and Academic Ideals at the Turn of the Twentieth Century* (New York: Doubleday and Company, 1972).

7. Henry-Russell Hitchcock, *Modern Architecture: Romanticism and Reintegration* (New York: 1929).

8. The distinctions between associational and intrinsic values in architecture have been developed in two books. See: Geoffrey Scott, *The Architecture of Humanism* (London: Constable & Company, Ltd., 1914; reissued, New York: W. W. Norton & Co, 1974); Roger Scruton, *The Aesthetics of Architecture* (Princeton, New Jersey: Princeton University Press, 1979).

9. BGG to Oswald G. Villard, January 23, 1909, Goodhue Papers.

10. Ralph Adams Cram, *The Ruined Abbeys of Great Britain* (New York: The Churchman Co., 1905).

11. Hitchcock, *Modern Architecture*, p. 59. See also, George H. Allen, "Cram—the Yankee Medievalist," *Architectural Forum* 55 (July 1931), pp. 79–80. See the following books by Cram, in the order of their publication: *English Country Churches* (Boston: Bates and Guild, 1898); *The Gothic Quest* (New York: The Baker and Taylor Company, 1907); *The Ministry of Art* (Boston: Houghton Mifflin Company, 1914); *Heart of Europe* (New York: Charles Scribner's Sons, 1915); *The Substance of Gothic* (Boston: Marshall Jones Company, 1917); *The Great Thousand Years* (Boston: Marshall Jones Company, 1918); *The Sins of the Fathers* (Boston: Marshall Jones Company, 1919); *Walled Towns* (Boston: Marshall Jones Company, 1919); *The Catholic Church and Art* (New York: Macmillan & Company, 1930); *The Cathedral of Palma de Mallorca* (Cambridge, Mass.: The Medieval Academy of America, 1932); and *Convictions and Controversies* (Boston: Marshall Jones Company, 1935).

12. Bertram G. Goodhue, "Some English Parish Churches," *Architectural Review* (Boston) 1 (April 1912), pp. 41–42. A year later, in 1913, Goodhue offered a sharper criticism of Bodley's churches at Clumber and Hoar Cross, asserting that they were

> . . . not *modern* Gothic, at least in so far as the fabric is concerned; but merely examples of that very able imitation of Medieval work of which I have already spoken . . . quite different in the spirit that inspired them—in the effect they produce upon the beholder, and quite inferior as art—since they *are* mere imitations. (Lecture delivered in Baltimore, 1913,

Goodhue Papers).

13. BGG to Percy E. Nobbs, March 10, 1910, Goodhue Papers.

14. At All Saints', Ashmont, Cram and Goodhue had a splendid opportunity to work with collaborators for the first time, and these initial relationships often lasted for years. Irving & Casson completed the woodcarving and joinery of the choir stalls, paneling, and lectern, retaining Kirschmayer to carve the figures; John Evans, the Welsh sculptor who had worked for Vaughan, Richardson, and McKim, Mead & White, modeled the stone reredos, which was carved by Domingo Mora; and much of the stained glass was designed by Charles Connick and Harry Eldredge Goodhue, Bertram's brother (Tucci, *All Saints', Ashmont*).

    Later, as Goodhue turned more and more to tilework, painting, and other forms of integral ornament, new collaborators were found, like Hildreth Meiere, Augustus Vincent Tack, and Julian Garnsey. What was essential to the success of these collaborative efforts was Goodhue's own ability to design decorative work, as well as his sympathy with the skills brought to bear in this regard by others.

15. BGG to Percy E. Nobbs, March 10, 1910, Goodhue Papers.

16. James McFarlan Baker, *American Churches* (New York: The American Architect, 1915), vol. 2. Goodhue's churches of the period were reviewed retrospectively in the second of a two-volume set entitled *American Churches*. Volume 2 was illustrated only by work of the New York office of Cram, Goodhue & Ferguson, while volume 1 was illustrated by the work of the Boston office and many other firms. These books thus provide a clear indication of the attribution of credit to the firm's many designs during the period of 1903–1913, when there were separate offices.

17. Montgomery Schuyler was effusive, exclaiming, "that the chapel is worthy of its acropolitan preeminence is indisputable. Architecturally, it 'belongs' as distinctly to the landscape as to the architecture underneath" (Schuyler, "Works of CGF," p. 106). See also: Schuyler, "Works of CGF," pp. 95–109; Baker, *American Churches*, plates 1–6; "Architectural Criticism," *Architecture* 21 (May 15, 1910), pp. 65–67, plates 41–45; Egerton Swartwout to BGG, January 28, 1911, Goodhue Papers; "The Chapel of the United States Military Academy," *American Architect* 98 (September 21, 1910), p. 98.

18. George R. Collins, "The Transfer of Thin Masonry Vaulting From Spain to America," *Journal of the Society of Architectural Historians* 27 (October 1968), pp. 176–201; Peter B. Wight, "The Works of Raphael Guastavino," *Brickbuilder* 10, pp. 79–81, 100–2, 184–88, 211–14.

19. George S. Pappas, *The Cadet Chapel, United States Military Academy* (West Point: 1953).

20. Vestry Minutes, Saint Thomas's Church, vol. 5, pp. 217–36, Saint Thomas's Archives. Post concluded that the old church could be rebuilt for $300,000, but that a new church could be built of a simpler ground plan and a more durable material—and fireproof—for about $600,000. In the event, the parish began to solicit subscriptions to the amount of $1 million to build a new design.

21. Before the turn of the century, Fifth Avenue near Saint Thomas's Church was primarily a residential street for wealthy families. Beginning in 1899, with the completion of McKim, Mead & White's University Club at 54th Street and Fifth Avenue, the street began to undergo a transformation. The completion of the St. Regis Hotel in 1904 to the designs of Trowbridge & Livingston, the Gotham Hotel in 1905 to the designs of Hiss & Weeks, and the Plaza Hotel in 1907 by Henry Hardenbergh, confirmed the evolution of the city and of Fifth Avenue. See:

"Club-house of the University Club," *AABN* 65 (August 26, 1899), p. 71; Arthur C. Davis, "The St. Regis—the best type of metropolitan hotel," *Architectural Record* 15 (June 1904), pp. 552–623; "Hotel Gotham, New York," *Architects' and Builders' Magazine* 7 (1905–1906), pp. 45–56, 81–84; H. W. Frohne, "Designing a metropolitan hotel, The Plaza," *Architectural Record* 22 (September 1907), pp. 349–64.

22. "Preliminary Report of Plan and Scope Committee, November 15, 1905," Vestry Minutes, Saint Thomas's Church, vol. 5, pp. 242–52. See also, "Report of Plan and Scope Committee, April 9, 1906," Vestry Minutes, Saint Thomas's Church, vol. 5, pp. 276–82, Saint Thomas's Archives.

23. "St. Thomas' Church Competition," *Architecture* 13 (May 15, 1906), p. 65. The ten invited competitors were: Cram, Goodhue & Ferguson; Henry Vaughan; George B. Post & Sons; Allen & Collins; Parish & Schroeder; Charles C. Haight; Carpenter & Blair; Lord & Hewlett; R. W. Gibson; and Barney & Chapin. Cram, Goodhue & Ferguson probably were added to the list by the Rector, Ernest M. Stires, who had been a member of the Board of Visitors to West Point in 1903, and who would have had the opportunity to inspect the firm's designs for the major additions there. Nine of the schemes, all excepting that by CGF, were published in *Architecture* 13 (May 15, 1906), pp. 68–70, 72–74, 76–78, 80–82, 84–86, 88–90, 92–94, 96–98. CGF's scheme was revised before publication.

24. "Report of Plan and Scope Committee, April 9, 1906," Vestry Minutes, Saint Thomas's Church.

25. BGG to D. B. Updike, May 7, 1913, Goodhue Papers; BGG to Ralph Adams Cram, April 15, 1907, Goodhue Papers.

26. Vestry Minutes, Saint Thomas's Church. See also, BGG to Colonel J. M. Carson, Jr., August 20, 1913, Goodhue Papers.

27. Ernest Peixotto, "Saint Thomas's and its Reredos," *Architecture* 42 (July 1920), pp. 193–202. This gives a complete listing of the statues, symbolism, and heraldry for the reredos, plus the subjects of carving on all the chancel fittings.

28. H. L. Bottomley, "The Story of Saint Thomas's Church," *Architectural Record* 35 (February 1914), pp. 101–31.

29. Harold E. Grove, *Saint Thomas Church* (New York: Saint Thomas Church, 1965). A descriptive guide and history.

30. BGG to E. M. Camp, January 23, 1914, Goodhue Papers. In the same letter, Goodhue asserted:

> I see no reason why you should consider seriously Mr. Cram's demand that "in the case of anything coming up with regard to the work of Cram, Goodhue & Ferguson, Goodhue & Ferguson, Bertram Grosvenor Goodhue, Cram & Ferguson, or Ralph Adams Cram, Consulting Architect," you should immediately communicate with "him" by telephone for the purpose of obtaining exact and definitive information. This because I unfortunately cannot regard the information he has given you in his statement as either exact or definitive, and also because I claim for Mr. Ferguson and myself as much right to determine such matters as he.

31. Gerald Allen, "Saint Thomas Church: Serving Two Spaces," *Dimensions* (New York: Architectural Record Books, 1976), pp. 25–40.

32. The vaults were made of a new material called Rumford tile, which had just been invented to

aid in the acoustic problems inherent in a space intended both for speaking and for music. The tile was used on the one layer of a three-layer vault which faced into the space in question, and it was designed with a degree of porosity to absorb sound. Goodhue had introduced its inventor, the famous acoustician, Dr. Wallace C. Sabine, Professor of Physics at Harvard University, to Raphael Guastavino, the manufacturer of clay products who had for some time been producing thin tiles used by many architects for large interior vaults, and so Goodhue took special proprietary interest in the new material.

33. Peixotto, "Saint Thomas's and its Reredos." See also, "Mosaic Parapet Rail in St. Thomas' Church, New York City," *Architectural Record* 47 (February 1920), pp. 128–29.

34. Truman H. Talley, "Satire in Church Decoration," *The New York Times*, August 28, 1921, p. 3:18.

35. "Japing in Stone," *The New York Times*, August 14, 1921, p. 2:4.

36. Montgomery Schuyler, "The New Saint Thomas's Church," *Brickbuilder* 23 (January 1914), pp. 15–20; Baker, *American Churches*, plates 7–21, 74.

37. Cram, Goodhue & Ferguson, *The Plans for Saint Thomas's Church, New York City* (Boston: The Merrymount Press, 1908), Saint Thomas's Archives. See also, Gerald Allen, "Saint Thomas Church: Serving Two Spaces," *Dimensions* (New York: Architectural Record Books, 1976), pp. 25–40, in which Allen observes that Saint Thomas's Church has indeed continued to have a dominant place on Fifth Avenue despite the fact that all of its neighbors have changed since its construction.

38. For Unity Temple, see Henry-Russell Hitchcock, *In the Nature of Materials*, pp. 53–54, plates 118–21, 123.

39. Schuyler, "Works of CGF," p. 69. For Christ Church, see: Baker, *American Churches*, pp. 1, 4, 5, plate 57; Schuyler, "Works of CGF," pp. 24–25, 69. For Saint John's Church, see: *A History of Saint John's Church, 1841–1941*, Saint John's Archives; Whitaker, *Bertram Grosvenor Goodhue*, plates 48–50; *1914 Drawing Book*, plate 24; Baker, *American Churches*, plates 54–57; Schuyler, "Works of CGF," pp. 50–53. For Saint Mark's Church, see: Whitaker, *Bertram Grosvenor Goodhue*, plates 147–51; Baker, *American Churches*, plates 61–63; Schuyler, "Works of CGF," pp. 60–62.

40. BGG to Montgomery Schuyler, October 24, 1910, Goodhue Papers.

41. Ernest Peixotto, "Saint Mark's," *Architecture* 42 (December 1920), pp. 356–58.

42. There were other examples. For Goodhue's Russell Sage Memorial Presbyterian Church in New York City, see: Baker, *American Churches*, plates 50–53, 64; Schuyler, "Works of CGF," pp. 65–69. For the "Old South" Dutch Reformed Church in New York City, see: "The South Church, New York," *Architectural Review* (Boston) 17 (April 1910), plates 29–33; "The South Church, New York," *Architecture* 24 (September 15, 1911), p. 134, plates 92–96; Baker, *American Churches*, plates 45–49; Schuyler, "Works of CGF," pp. 56–57.

43. *The First Baptist Church of Pittsburgh* (Pittsburgh: The First Baptist Church, 1924), pp. 14–18.

44. The five invited architects were Coolidge & Carlson, Boston; Cram, Goodhue & Ferguson, New York; Edgar V. Seeler, Philadelphia; John T. Comes, Pittsburgh; and Janssen & Abbott, Pittsburgh (Competition Program, Archives, First Baptist Church).

45. "First Baptist Church," *Architectural Review* (Boston) 17 (February 1910), pp. 17–21, plates 9–20.

46. Arthur Byne, "First Baptist Church," *Architectural Record* 32 (September 1912), pp. 193–208. Arthur Byne noted several precedents for the broad, open plan of this church: the Romanesque Benedictine hall churches of southern France; the early Gothic chapels at English universities; and the typical New England Meeting House. An editorial in *Architecture* 26 (October 1912), stated that this church is

> . . . genuine modern architecture, impossible of course without knowledge of traditional forms, but a building which could not conceivably have been designed by either French or English Gothic architects, or by a collaboration between them.

Similarly, George Edgell, in *The American Architecture of Today*, observed:

> . . . as one studies this monumental work, one feels more and more that American Gothic has originality and beauty and that the modern work shows an *understanding* and deliberate deviation from historic form thoroughly assimilated (p. 205).

See also: Baker, *American Churches*, plates 21–25; Schuyler, "Works of CGF," pp. 73, 74; E. Donald Robb, "The Small Church," *Brickbuilder* 22 (October 1914), pp. 233–38.

47. Bertram G. Goodhue, "Book Review of *The Medieval Church Architecture of England*, by Charles Herbert Moore," *American Institute of Architects' Journal* 2 (April 1914), pp. 219–20. A draft of this review forms part of the Goodhue Papers. Charles H. Moore sent a letter to the magazine in response to what he regarded as a review which inadequately addressed the issues of his book: *American Institute of Architects' Journal* 2 (July 1914), p. 330. Goodhue responded in turn: *American Institute of Architects' Journal* 2 (August 1914), p. 398. See also: Goodhue, "Book Review of *Perspective*, by Ben J. Lubschez," *American Institute of Architects' Journal* 1 (September 1913), p. 416; Goodhue, "Book Review of *Stained Glass of the Middle Ages in England and France*, by Hugh Arnold," *American Institute of Architects' Journal* 2 (June 1914), p. 324.

48. Goodhue, "Book Review of *The Medieval Church Architecture of England*."

49. Ibid.

50. "La Santisima Trinidad, Havana," *AABN* 91 (May 4, 1907), plate; Schuyler, "Works of CGF," pp. 20–22, 41; Baker, *American Churches*, plate 66. For a description of the church, see George Edgell, *The American Architecture of Today* (London: Charles Scribner's Sons, 1928), p. 217. See also: *1914 Drawing Book*, p. 43; Whitaker, *Bertram Grosvenor Goodhue*, plates 33–34; "Los Todos Santos, Guantanamo," *AABN* 93 (June 17, 1908); *1914 Drawing Book*, pp. 41–42.

51. Vestry Minutes, Chapel of the Intercession, Trinity Parish Archives.

52. BGG to Nevil Jodrell, August 12, 1914, Goodhue Papers. The ceiling decorations, designed by Thomas Watson Ball, caused controversy and were criticized as a departure from Gothic precedent. A review of the completed church in *Architecture* observed:

> Certain it is that elaborate polychrome work of this nature has been hitherto unknown in the new world north of Spanish America. Nevertheless, there is positive proof that nearly if not quite, all of the Medieval roofs were so treated; and not only the roof but also the whole of

the structure, inside and out, of which it formed a part ("Chapel of the Intercession," *Architecture* 29 [January 1913], pp. 34–36).

Thus the ceiling design seemed "new," although it was based upon a scholarly knowledge of Gothic tradition. Similarly, George Edgell, in *The American Architecture of Today* (London: Charles Scribner's Sons, 1928), observed that:

> Mr. Goodhue probably made archeological researches, but he designed his colour not to be correct so much as to be brilliant, rich, and harmonious. He thus got it correct in spirit, though whether it be correct in fact the writer does not know, nor care (p. 205).

53. C. Matlack Price, "The Chapel of the Intercession," *Architectural Record* 35 (June 1914), pp. 526–43. See also: Montgomery Schuyler, "Chapel of the Intercession," *Brickbuilder* 23 (April 1914), pp. 85–90; "Chapel of the Intercession," *Architecture* 29 (January 1913), pp. 34–36, plates 14–23; Baker, *American Churches*, plates 26–41; Caryl Coleman, "The Jesse Tree," *Architectural Review* (Boston) 21 (May 1907), pp. 360–70.

CHAPTER FOUR

1. For two examples, see "Proposed Community House for the Paulist Fathers, New York," and "Proposed House of Studies for the Paulist Fathers, Washington, D.C.," *Christian Art* 3 (September 1908), pp. 271–75; Schuyler, "Works of CGF," pp. 42–45.

2. "The Taft School," *Architectural Forum* 26 (January 1917), p. 25, plates 1–3; Schuyler, "Works of CGF," pp. 58, 59.

3. "Kitchi Gammi Club, Duluth," *Architectural Forum* 26 (March 1917), p. 79, plates 37–39. See BGG to Edgar Guy, November 4, 1911, Goodhue Papers.

4. *1914 Drawing Book*, p. 85; Schuyler, "Works of CGF," p. 19.

5. For Lutyens's scheme for the Harriman House, see Peter Inskip, *Edwin Lutyens* (New York: Rizzoli International Publications, 1979), pp. 60–61. See also, "The Works of Carrère and Hastings," *Architectural Record* 27 (January 1910), pp. 1–120.

6. Henry-Russell Hitchcock, *In the Nature of Materials* (New York: Hawthorn Books, Inc., 1942; reissued, New York: Da Capo Press, 1975), pp. 39–48, plates 100–4, 139–41, 181–82.

7. Jacques Gréber, *L'Architecture aux Etats-Unis* (Paris: Payot & Cie, 1920), pp. 79, 80, plate 9.

8. BGG to Cecil C. Brewer, November 23, 1917, Goodhue Papers.

9. George H. Edgell, *The American Architecture of Today* (London: Charles Scribner's Sons, 1928), p. 129.

10. For an account of the Edwardian free-style houses of Lutyens, see: Alastair Service, *Edwardian Architecture* (New York: Oxford University Press, 1977); Daniel O'Neill, *Lutyens: Country Houses* (New York: Whitney Library of Design, 1981).

11. Robert Craighead, "Homes of Well-known Architects: The Home of Mr. Bertram Grosvenor Goodhue, New York City," *House Beautiful* 39 (February 1916), pp. 65–68, xxv. Goodhue's house is now demolished. See also, Robert S. Bowen, "The Designing of Piano Cases," *Architectural Review* (Boston) 12 (June 1905), pp. 145–49.

12. Alfred Morton Githens, "Recent American Group Plans: Fairs and Expositions," *Brickbuilder* 21 (October 1912), pp. 257–60.

13. The development of the campus of The Rice Institute, now Rice University, is fully documented: Stephen Fox, *The General Plan of the William M. Rice Institute and Its Architectural Develop-

ment (Houston: School of Architecture, Rice University, 1980).

14. Alfred Morton Githens, "Recent American Group Plans: Colleges and Universities," *Brickbuilder* 22 (January 1913), pp. 11–14.

15. Francesco Passanti, "The Design of Columbia in the 1890's, McKim and His Client," *Journal of the Society of Architectural Historians* 36 (May 1977), pp. 69–84.

16. BGG to Henry Gennert, March 11, 1915, Goodhue Papers. See also: "The Administration Building of the Rice Institute," *Brickbuilder* 21 (December 1912), pp. 321–24, plates 165–68; "The Administration Building of the Rice Institute," *Western Architect* 19 (February 1913), pp. 20–22.

17. Schuyler, "Works of CGF," pp. 30, 76–78. The drawing of the Byzantine-style auditorium was seen at the Annual Exhibition of the Architectural League of New York in 1911. See *Yearbook of the Architectural League of New York* (New York: Kalkhoff Co., 1911).

18. *1914 Drawing Book*, pp. 89–97; Whitaker, *Bertram Grosvenor Goodhue*, plates 115–18.

19. For Lutyens's work at Delhi, see Robert Grant Irving, *Indian Summer: Lutyens, Baker, and Imperial Delhi* (New Haven: Yale University Press, 1982).

20. "Washington Hotel, Colón, Panama," *Architectural Record* 32 (July 1912), pp. 65–70; BGG to Waldron Gillespie, March 31, 1911; Charles D. Norton to Frederick Law Olmsted, Jr., January 7, 1911; Olmsted to Norton, January 10, 1911; BGG to Olmsted, March 24, 1911, Goodhue Papers.

21. BGG to J. M. F. Baker, April 16, 1911, Goodhue Papers.

22. Ibid.

23. This was not the first instance of the city's concern for its future development. In 1908, John Nolen, the noted city planner and landscape architect from Cambridge, Massachusetts, was hired by the local Civic Improvement Committee to prepare a comprehensive urban plan. Nolen proposed a spacious, idealized Mediterranean city that responded to the dramatic landscape, benign climate, and Latin heritage. See John Nolen, *San Diego, A Comprehensive Plan for Its Development* (Boston: 1908).

24. Kevin Starr, *Americans and the California Dream* (New York: Oxford University Press, 1973), p. 404.

25. Esther McCoy, *Five California Architects* (New York: Reinhold Publishing Co., 1960). See also, "Creating an American Style of Architecture," *House and Garden* 26 (July 1914), pp. 17–20.

26. BGG to F. L. Olmsted, December 24, 1910, Goodhue Papers.

27. McCoy, *Five California Architects*, p. 88. The book Goodhue referred to was probably the one on which he had collaborated with Sylvester Baxter and Henry Greenwood Peabody: *Spanish Colonial Architecture in Mexico* (Boston: J. B. Millet, 1901). Baxter is listed as the author of record.

28. Elmer Grey to BGG, January 4, 1911, Goodhue Papers.

29. Bishop Joseph Johnson to BGG, January 2, 1911, Goodhue Papers.

30. *The San Diego Union*, January 28, 1911. The article also reported that the "Olmsted Brothers

259

will lay out the grounds, plant trees, shrubs and flowers and make the general ground plan for the exposition," and that "Mr. [Frank P.] Allen of Seattle has been engaged to manage and direct all the work on the exposition buildings. He will act as engineer, constructing architect and general contractor." The article reported that Director-General D. C. Collier was pleased with the selection of Goodhue, noting that his "work will be the most important of all, perhaps, for it will be the effect of the first sight of the exposition in Balboa Park that will remain longest with the visitor to San Diego in 1915. The 'Mission City' of the Panama-California Exposition will become more famous, I can now imagine, than the 'White City' of Chicago's fair, and it will carry the fame of San Diego and her exposition in 1915 to the far ends of the earth."

While Goodhue was at work on the San Diego fair, Willis Polk was organizing a much grander fair in San Francisco—the Panama-Pacific Exposition. It was Polk's intention to have a large number of different architects design the various buildings and have all the designs drawn up in one drafting room. Goodhue was invited to be one of that group, which included Henry Bacon, Thomas Hastings, and William Kendall, but D. C. Collier, the director of the San Diego fair, worked against this. In the end, Goodhue did design the New York State Building, a modest structure that received little attention.

31. Starr, *Americans and the California Dream*, p. 405.

32. BGG to Frederick Law Olmsted [Jr.], September 14, 1911, Goodhue Papers.

33. Alfred Morton Githens, "Recent American Group Plans: Fairs and Expositions," *Brickbuilder* 21 (October 1912), pp. 257–60.

34. Bertram G. Goodhue, *The Architecture and the Gardens of the San Diego Exposition* (San Francisco: Paul Elder & Co., 1916), p. 4. The book, subtitled "A Pictorial Survey of the Aesthetic Features of the Panama-California International Exposition," has an essay by Goodhue, another essay, "A Triumph of the Spanish-Colonial Style," by Clarence Stein, and descriptive notes by Carleton Monroe Winslow. Winslow was Goodhue's site architect, and he remained in California and built a sizable and distinguished practice of his own. He later was the site architect for the Los Angeles Library.

35. Ibid., p. 6.

36. C. Matlack Price, "The Panama-California Exposition, San Diego, California; Bertram G. Goodhue and the Renaissance of Spanish-Colonial Architecture," *Architectural Record* 37 (March 1915), pp. 228–51. See also, "Panama-California Exposition, San Diego, California," *Construction Details* 6 (1914), pp. 142–59. The inscription on the dome is taken from the Book of Deuteronomy 8:8.

37. Goodhue, *The Architecture and the Gardens of the San Diego Exposition*, p. 7.

38. *1914 Drawing Book*, p. 37.

39. BGG to Mrs. Robert Cameron Rogers, November 18, 1915, Goodhue Papers.

40. George H. Edgell, *The American Architecture of Today* (London: Charles Scribner's Sons, 1928), p. 66. See also, W. B. Faville, "The Panama-California Exposition, San Diego, California," *American Architect* 107 (March 17, 1915), pp. 177–80, plates; Walter V. Woehlke, "Nueva España by the Silver Gate," *Sunset* 33 (1914), pp. 1119–32; Woehlke, "Magic Spanish City at San Diego," *Out West* 8 (1914), pp. 291–306.

41. Henry-Russell Hitchcock, *Architecture: Nineteenth and Twentieth Centuries* (New York: Penguin Books, 1958), p. 450.

42. Starr, *Americans and the California Dream*, p. 409.

43. Goodhue, *The Architecture and the Gardens of the San Diego Exposition*, pp. 6–9. See also, BGG to Charles A. Edsall, June 2, 1916, BGG to Wallace Gillpatrick, March 18, 1919, Goodhue Papers. Goodhue was angered by an attempt by the director of the works, Frank Allen, to claim undue credit for the design of the fair; see, BGG to Christian Brinton, August 17, 1915, Goodhue Papers.

44. William Winthrop Kent, "The Modern Country House in California," *Country Life* 37 (April 1920), p. 122. For Goodhue's house for Herbert Coppell, see Edgell, *The American Architecture of Today*, p. 103.

45. Myron Hunt, an accomplished regional architect, designed the First Congregational Church (1912–1914) in Riverside, California, in a Spanish style as scholarly as Goodhue's work at the fair; the planning, however, is not as clear, nor is the ornamentation as vividly modeled. See "First Congregational Church," *American Architect* 105 (May 27, 1914), pp. 267–68.

46. David Gebhard, *George Washington Smith* (Santa Barbara: University of California, 1968); Gebhard, "The Spanish Colonial Revival in Southern California (1895–1930)," *Journal of the Society of Architectural Historians* 26 (May 1967), pp. 131–47; Rexford Newcomb, "Some Spanish Residences in Southern California by George Washington Smith, Architect," *Western Architect* 31 (1922), pp. 58–61; William Winthrop Kent, "Domestic Architecture of California," *Architectural Forum* 32 (March 1920), pp. 95–100, 151–56; Kent, "Some Work of George Washington Smith," *Architectural Forum* 35 (August 1921), p. 45; Dwight James Baum, "An Eastern Architect's Impression of Recent Work in Southern California," *Architecture* 38 (1918), pp. 177–80, 217–21; Baum, "Architectural Impressions of Southern California," *American Architect* 133 (1928), pp. 71–80; Elmer Grey, "Southern California's New Architecture," *Architecture* 39 (1919), pp. 57–61, 103–7; Henry F. Withey, "A Revival of True Andalusian Spanish Architecture," *Architect and Engineering* 55 (1918), pp. 65–79; I. F. Morrow, "A Revival of Adobe Buildings," *Architect and Engineer* 69 (1922), pp. 47–57; Morrow, "A Step in California's Architecture," *Architect and Engineer* 70 (1922), pp. 47–103; H. Phillip Staats, *Californian Architecture in Santa Barbara* (New York: 1929).

47. BGG to Elmer Grey, December 29, 1914, Goodhue Papers.

48. Elmer Grey to BGG, January 4, 1915, Goodhue Papers.

49. Lewis Mumford, "Bertram G. Goodhue," *The New Republic* 44 (October 28, 1925).

50. BGG to Ralph Adams Cram and Frank Ferguson, February 11, 1910. I am grateful to Douglass Shand Tucci for providing this letter.

51. Schuyler, "The Works of CGF."

52. BGG to Silas McBee, January 4, 1911, Goodhue Papers.

53. See the Revised Partnership Agreement, Cram Papers, BPL Archives.

54. "The Cathedral of Saint John the Divine, New York City," *Architectural Record* 30 (August 1911), pp. 185–92; editorial on Saint John the Divine, *Architecture* 24 (July 15, 1911), pp. 97–99. See also, "Bishop's House and Deanery at St. John the Divine," *Architectural Record* 36 (1913), pp. 137–42.

55. BGG to William Rutherford Mead, June 30, 1911, Goodhue Papers. Goodhue mentioned

one such letter: "One of my greatest friends at the Century Club . . . writes me that unless I publicly break with my partner, my chances of getting into the Century when my name comes up this autumn are exceedingly remote." See also, BGG to Samuel W. Lambert, M.D., June 30, 1911.

56. BGG to Cecil C. Brewer, April 18, 1912, Goodhue Papers.

57. BGG to E. M. Camp, January 23, 1914, Goodhue Papers.

58. "The Cathedral Builders," *The Churchman* 108 (August 30, 1913), p. 279.

59. BGG to Sturdivant J. Read, M.D., August 20, 1913, Goodhue Papers.

60. Charles D. Maginnis, *The Work of Cram & Ferguson, Architects, Including Work by Cram, Goodhue & Ferguson* (New York: Pencil Points Press, 1929).

61. BGG to Cecil C. Brewer, February 5, 1914, Goodhue Papers.

62. Charles D. Maginnis to BGG, January 12, 1916, Goodhue Papers.

63. BGG to Ralph Adams Cram, December 31, 1914, Goodhue Papers.

64. A particularly touchy matter was the credit for the design of the reredos at Saint Thomas's Church. Goodhue designed it and, perhaps inappropriately, claimed sole credit. Under the partnership agreement, even in the case of the dissolution of the firm, the completion of all aspects of Saint Thomas's Church and West Point were to be credited to the firm of Cram, Goodhue & Ferguson. There were also questions about Saint John the Divine. Each of the partners could act independently as a consulting architect, but actual working drawings were to be credited solely to the firm. The full details of the dissolution of CGF, however, must wait until files currently in the care of Hoyle, Doran & Berry in Boston are released for public review. See BGG to Henry G. Gennert, March 11, 1915, and March 7, 1916, Goodhue Papers. See also: Cram and Ferguson to BGG, November 8, 1915, and March 3, March 10, May 3, 1916, Goodhue Papers; BGG to Cram and Ferguson, November 9, 1915, and March 9, March 17, April 26, 1916, Goodhue Papers.

65. BGG to Edward E. Goodhue, October 4, 1921, Goodhue Papers.

CHAPTER FIVE

1. Goodhue had designed two cathedrals previously: one Gothic in Halifax, Nova Scotia (1907) and one Spanish/Romanesque in Los Angeles (1910). The latter was never built. For the Episcopal cathedral in Halifax, see Whitaker, *Bertram Grosvenor Goodhue*, pp. 52, 53; Baker, *American Churches*, plates 64, 67; Schuyler, "Works of CGF," pp. 26–28. For the Episcopal pro-cathedral and hospital in Los Angeles, see: Whitaker, *Bertram Grosvenor Goodhue*, plate 78; *1914 Drawing Book*, plates 47, 70; Baker, *American Churches*, plate 68; Schuyler, "Works of CGF," pp. 80, 81.

2. Rev. John Newton Peabody, *Cathedral of the Incarnation* (Baltimore: Diocese of Maryland, 1976), pp. 72, 83, 89–90. See also, BGG to Percy E. Nobbs, June 2, 1911, Goodhue Papers.

3. "The Cathedral of the Incarnation," *Architectural Record* 33 (June 1913), pp. 477–91. See also, "Mr. Goodhue's Agreement for the Designing of the Baltimore Cathedral," *American Institute of Architects' Journal* 2 (March 1914), pp. 124–28.

4. BGG to James Waldron Gillespie, March 15, 1911; BGG to Percy Newton, May 1, 1913, Goodhue Papers.

5. Vere E. Cotton, *The Liverpool Cathedral Official Handbook* (Liverpool: Liverpool University Press, 1926); Hope Bagenal, "The Cathedral Church of Christ, Liverpool," *Architectural Review* (London) 50 (July 1921), pp. 13–26. For smaller churches by Scott, see Randall Phillips, "Some Lesser English Churches," *Architectural Forum* 33 (October 1920), pp. 115–20. See also: Charles Herbert Reilly, "The Work of Sir Giles Gilbert Scott, R.A.," *Architects' Journal* 61 (January 7, 1925), pp. 13–35; Gavin Stamp, "Giles Gilbert Scott, The Problem of Modernism," *AD Profiles 24: Britain in the Thirties* (London: Architectural Design, 1979), pp. 72–83. For an account of Liverpool Cathedral by one of Goodhue's employees, see Wilberforce Horsfield, "The Cathedral Church of Liverpool," *Architectural Record* 31 (January 1912), pp. 27–43.

6. F. M. Simpson, "Liverpool Cathedral Competition," *Architectural Review* (London) 13 (June 1903), pp. 224–28. For a retrospective analysis of the Liverpool Cathedral competition, see John Thomas, "The Style Shall be Gothic," *Architectural Review* (London) 158 (September 1975), pp. 155–62. In addition to Scott's scheme, Beresford Pite's Byzantine scheme and William Lethaby's free and expressionistic scheme are illustrated. See also, Gavin Stamp, *The Great Perspectivists* (New York: Rizzoli International Publications, Inc., 1982), pp. 92–95.

7. BGG to Archdeacon Madden, January 17, 1911, Goodhue Papers.

8. Giles Gilbert Scott to Archdeacon Madden, January 26, 1911, Goodhue Papers.

9. BGG to Percy E. Nobbs, February 28, 1913, Goodhue Papers.

10. Charles Herbert Reilly, *Representative British Architects of the Present Day* (Freeport, New York: 1931), pp. 142–56.

11. BGG to Percy S. Newton, May 1, 1913, Goodhue Papers. See also, "Finest Modern Church Building," an interview of Goodhue by *The [Liverpool] Daily Courier*, September 5, 1922. This interview, made on a subsequent visit to Liverpool in 1922, reiterates Goodhue's enthusiasm for Scott's design. I am indebted to Gavin Stamp for this reference.

12. Whitaker, *Bertram Grosvenor Goodhue*, plates 100–106.

13. Ibid., plates 95 and 105.

14. BGG to George W. Horsefield, February 6, 1919, Goodhue Papers.

15. Peabody, *Cathedral of the Incarnation*, p. 90. See also, John Dorsey and James D. Dilts, *A Guide to Baltimore Architecture* (Centerville, Md.: Tidewater Publications, 1973).

16. Whitaker, *Bertram Grosvenor Goodhue*, plates 58–60.

17. BGG to Frederick Peterson, April 18, 1916, Goodhue Papers.

18. For Keely's design, see Church of Saint Vincent Ferrer Dedication Book (1940), p. 17. For the proposed remodeling by Allen & Collens and O'Conner, see "Reconstruction of the Church of St. Vincent Ferrer," *American Architect* 96 (August 25, 1909), p. 76.

19. BGG to Henry Gennert, November 3, 1916, Goodhue Papers.

20. Church of Saint Vincent Ferrer Dedication Book (1940), pp. 17, 22, 31. See *Catholic News*, May 11, 1918. For illustrations of Goodhue's design, see "Church of Saint Vincent Ferrer, New York," *Architecture* 31 (March 1915), pp. 84, 86, 88; "St. Vincent Ferrer," *Architecture and Building* 51 (1919), pp. 55–57. See also, *The New York Times*, August 16, 1915, p. 9:4, which observed that "everywhere throughout the design is evidenced the historic and ritual requirements of the Dominican Order for which it is to be erected." Part of Goodhue's task was to design a new, temporary brick church with 1,000 seats, which was ready for services in July 1915; see *The New York Times*, June 27, 1915. See also, transcription of comments by Sister Mary McElroy, Saint Vincent Ferrer Archives.

21. Talbot Hamlin, *The American Spirit in Architecture* (New Haven: Yale University Press, 1926), p. 314. See also: C. Matlack Price, "Two Recent New York Churches," *Architectural Forum* 32 (March 1920), pp. 107–10, plates 33–42; "Church of Saint Vincent Ferrer, New York City," *Architectural Record* 50 (December 1921), pp. 454–58; Whitaker, *Bertram Grosvenor Goodhue*, plates 155–62; Edward Hoak and Willis Church, *Masterpieces of Architecture in the United States* (New York: Charles Scribner's Sons, 1930); Oliver Reagan, *American Architecture of the 20th Century* (New York: Architectural Book Publishing Co., 1929).

22. For a review of Sabine's career see: Wallace C. Sabine, "Architectural Acoustics, Building Material, and Musical Pitch," *Brickbuilder* 23 (January 1914), pp. 1–6; "Architectural Acoustics," *AABN* 62 (November 26, 1898), pp. 71–73; "Architectural Acoustics," *AABN* 68 (1900), pp. 3–5, 19–22, 35–37, 43–45, 59–61, 75–76, 83–84; "Architectural Acoustics," *AABN* 98 (1910), pp. 41–45; Charles O. Cornelius, "Wallace Sabine," *Archi-*

tectural Record 46 (September 1919), pp. 286–87; Paul E. Sabine, "Wallace Sabine," *American Architect* 116 (January 1919), pp. 1–3.

23. Saint Vincent Ferrer Dedication Book.

24. Calvert W. Audrain, William B. Cannon, and Harold T. Wolff, *A Review of Planning at the University of Chicago, 1891–1978* (Chicago: The University of Chicago Press, 1978).

25. John D. Rockefeller to President and Trustees, December 13, 1910, University of Chicago Archives.

26. BGG to Wallace Heckman, April 5, 1918; BGG to Wallace Heckman, October 14, 1918, University of Chicago Archives.

27. BGG to George W. Horsefield, February 6, 1919, Goodhue Papers. See also, Whitaker, *Bertram Grosvenor Goodhue*, plates 130–33.

28. BGG to Harry Pratt Judson, March 24, 1919, University of Chicago Archives.

29. The University asked Rockefeller to cover the additional expense, having already spent all but $1,500,000 of the "Final Gift." Rockefeller declined, suggesting that the funds available be left to accrue such interest as would allow resumption of the project.

30. Edgar Goodspeed, *The University of Chicago Chapel* (Chicago: The University of Chicago Press, 1928).

31. Bertram Goodhue, "The Modern Architectural Problem Discussed from the Romanticist Point of View," *The Craftsman* 8 (June 1905), pp. 332–33.

CHAPTER SIX

1. Bertram Goodhue, "The Home of the Future: A Study of America in relation to the Architect," *The Craftsman* 29 (February 1916), pp. 449–55, 543–44.

2. Eugene B. Howland, "The New Virginia Military Institute," *Architectural Record* 36 (September 1914), pp. 231–40; Royster Lyle, Jr., and Pamela Hemenway Simpson, *The Architecture of Historic Lexington* (Charlottesville: The University Press of Virginia, 1977), pp. 211–76; David Coffey, *Bertram Grosvenor Goodhue, the Gothic Tradition, and the Virginia Military Institute* (Lexington, 1976, unpublished paper). See also, BGG to Wells Goodhue, September 29, 1914, Goodhue Papers.

3. BGG to Mrs. Arthur Molesworth, May 17, 1915, Goodhue Papers.

4. Minutes of the Vestry of St. Bartholomew's Church (hereafter St. Bart's Minutes), June 4, 1914, St. Bartholomew's Church Archives (hereafter St. Bart's Archives). I am indebted to Gregory Gilmartin for the information on Park Avenue.

5. BGG to Arthur C. Jackson, April 29, 1914, Goodhue Papers.

6. Goodhue was instructed to prepare two drawings, "one showing the church occupying the entire Park Avenue front and the other showing the church occupying one hundred and twenty-five feet on Park Avenue and Fiftieth Street," St. Bart's Minutes.

7. *A Description of the Proposed New St. Bartholomew's Church, by The Architect* (appeal booklet written by BGG; hereafter St. Bart's Description), St. Bart's Archives.

8. BGG to Dr. Leighton Parks, December 19, 1914, St. Bart's Archives. Conventional wisdom as well as liturgical convention dictated that the major axis of the church run east and west with the narthex facing Park Avenue. However, Goodhue described a freely conceived variation, "wherein I have . . . run the axis of the church north and south; in other words, made the *side* the Park Avenue *front*, but here instead of making the transept entrance the secondary one, I have used your present doorway. Of course, the scheme is almost unprecedented but I don't know why it should not be regarded as justified by circumstances."

9. BGG to Dr. Leighton Parks, August 12, 1914, St. Bart's Archives. The churches which Goodhue suggested that Parks see were: San Zeno, Verona; St. Ambrose, Milan; Church of St. Michael, Pavia; the cathedrals at Borgo San Donnino, Parma, Placentia, Cremona, Ferrara, and Modena; and churches at Bari and Bitorto.

10. Charles Hadfield, "The Late John Francis Bentley, A Retrospect," *Architectural Review*

(London) 11 (1902), pp. 115–17; Halsey Ricardo, "John Francis Bentley," *Architectural Review* (London) 11 (May 1902), pp. 155–64; 12 (July 1902), pp. 18–31; T. J. Willson, "John Francis Bentley, a Memoir," *Royal Institute of British Architects Journal* 9 (1901–1902), pp. 437–41.

11. Winefride de L'Hopital, *Westminster Cathedral and its Architect* (New York: Dodd, Mead and Co., 1919), Introduction by W. R. Lethaby, p. 35.

12. Charles Hadfield, "Westminster Cathedral," *Royal Institute of British Architects Journal* 10 (1902–1903), pp. 248–76. See also: W. R. Lethaby, "Westminster Cathedral," *Architectural Review* (London) 11 (January 1902), pp. 3–19; Herbert F. Mansford, "The New Cathedral at Westminster," *Architectural Record* 12 (August 1902), pp. 317–37 ; Gavin Stamp, "London 1900," *Architectural Design* 48 (1978), p. 316. Stamp describes the appeal of the Byzantine style to church architects:

> Like Gothic, it was irreproachably "Christian," but it permitted spaces of Classical grandeur and proportion while not being tied to the Orders . . . and demonstrated an attitude to the "rules" which squared with the Gothic Revival conscience.

13. *The New York Times*, January 18, 1916, p. 22:6.

14. BGG to Cecil C. Brewer, January 27, 1916, Goodhue Papers.

15. William Mitchell Kendall to BGG, February 18, 1916, Goodhue Papers.

16. "A Comparison Between the Schemes Submitted for the Proposed New St. Bartholomew's Church and Appurtenant Buildings by the Architect," St. Bart's Archives. The church was originally designed to be placed in the center of the Park Avenue frontage, with the income-producing tower on the north side, and as a result, the north transept was designed as a blank party wall. On the interior of it, Goodhue placed a large painting by Francis Lathrop brought from the old church. When the site plan was revised, Goodhue apparently chose not to redesign the north transept to include a rose window.

17. St. Bart's Description.

18. Ibid. George Edgell, in *The American Architecture of Today*, observed that, "by unerringly skillful composition of material [Goodhue] got one of the finest effects in color and texture which American architecture has attained" (p. 211).

19. Dr. Leighton Parks to BGG, April 13, 1916, St. Bart's Archives; BGG to Dr. Parks, April 14, 1916, St. Bart's Archives; Dr. Parks to BGG, April 18, 1916, St. Bart's Archives; BGG to Dr. Parks, April 29, 1916, Goodhue Papers; Dr. Parks to Mr. David Howard, Rector of St. Luke's Church, Norfolk, Virginia, May 27, 1919, St. Bart's Archives. Several years later, when asked for an opinion of him, Parks replied unfavorably: "I regret to say that my personal relations with Mr. Goodhue were so unhappy that even for the advantage of his artistic gifts I should be unwilling to enter into any undertaking again of which he was to be the architect." Goodhue apparently lost the Los Angeles Cathedral commission in 1910, even after working drawings were essentially complete, because of an offhand remark about budget; he noted that the Vestry "seemed to resent a statement made in one of my letters that to obtain everything they wanted would probably necessitate a 'jerry-built' structure to which, of course, I could not bring myself" (BGG to Carleton Winslow, February 18, 1914, Goodhue Papers).

20. BGG to George W. Horsefield, February 6, 1919, Goodhue Papers. See also, C. Matlack Price, "Two Recent New York Churches," *Architectural Forum* 32 (March 1920), pp. 107–10, plates 33–42.

21. BGG to Frank A. Miller, August 17, 1915, Goodhue Papers.

22. BGG to John D. Moore, December 29, 1915, Goodhue Papers. See also: "The New Mining Community of Tyrone, New Mexico," *Architectural Review* (Boston) 6 (March 1918), pp. 59–62; *Architectural Review* (Boston) 6 (April 1918), plates LII–LVI, p. 60; "Workers' Village for Phelps Dodge Co., Tyrone, New Mexico," *Architectural Record* 46 (October 1918), pp. 314–16; Whitaker, *Bertram Grosvenor Goodhue*, plates 170–71; Robert B. Riley, "Gone Forever: Goodhue's Beaux Arts Ghost Town," *American Institute of Architects' Journal* 50 (August 1968), pp. 67–70; Christopher Tunnard and Henry Hope Reed, *American Skyline* (Boston: Houghton Mifflin and Company, 1955), pp. 221–22.

23. Marcia Mead, "The Architecture of the Small House," *Architecture* 37 (June 1918), pp. 145–54.

24. BGG to George W. Horsefield, February 6, 1919, Goodhue Papers.

25. Bertram Goodhue, "The Home of the Future," p. 543.

26. Goodhue was attempting to achieve the qualities that Gill admired in his own work, which Gill described in *The Craftsman* 30 (May 1916), pp. 147–48:

    There is something very restful and satisfying to my mind in the simple cube house with creamy walls, sheer and plain, rising boldly into the sky, unrelieved by cornices or overhang of roof, unornamented save for the vines that soften a line or creepers that wreathe a pillar or flowers that inlay color more sentiently than any tile could do. I like the bare honesty of these houses, the childlike frankness, and the chaste simplicity of them.

    For Stein's work, see: Richard Pommer, "The Architecture of Urban Housing in the United States during the early 1930s," *Journal of the Society of Architectural Historians* 37 (December 1978), pp. 235–64; "Proposed Museum for Pasadena Art Institute," *Architectural Record* 66 (December 1929), plate; "Proposed Pasadena Art Institute," *Western Architect* 37 (March 1928), p. 63.

27. BGG to James Waldron Gillespie, March 20, 1918, Goodhue Papers.

28. BGG to C. Peake Anderson, November 12, 1918, Goodhue Papers.

29. Trustees' Minutes, July 6 and August 20, 1915; BGG to James Scherer, July 28 and August 13, 1915, California Institute of Technology Archives. See also: *Dictionary of American Biography*, pp. 270–71; Whitaker, *Bertram Grosvenor Goodhue*, pp. 45–46.

30. Trustees' Minutes, May 15, 1916; BGG to James Scherer, January 24, February 19, and April 27, 1916; *Bulletin, Throop College of Technology;* interview with Elmer Grey by Roger Stanton, August 23, 1957, California Institute of Technology Archives; *Pasadena Star News*, March 17, 1917; Stefanos Polyzoides to Author, July 17, 1982.

31. Trustees' Minutes, February 5, 1908; Myron Hunt to James Scherer, August 10, 1908, California Institute of Technology Archives; *Pasadena Star News*, February 29, 1908, p. 8. See also, "Two California Colleges," *American Architect* 97 (June 22, 1910), pp. 233–36.

32. BGG to James Scherer, September 27 and November 15, 1915; June 8 and December 9,

1916; Scherer to BGG, October 5 and October 12, 1915; Goodhue, "A Report to accompany the general Block Plan showing the disposition of present and proposed buildings, a bird's eye view based upon the Plot Plan and sundry sketches of various individual buildings," California Institute of Technology Archives.

33. George Ellery Hale to Arthur Fleming, October 28, 1927, California Institute of Technology Archives. See also, Whitaker, *Bertram Grosvenor Goodhue*, plates 174–80. I am indebted to Alice Stone for the references on the California Institute of Technology.

34. BGG to John D. Moore, April 21, 1917, Goodhue Papers. See also, BGG to Cecil C. Brewer, November 23, 1917, Goodhue Papers.

35. BGG to Cecil C. Brewer, May 6, 1918, Goodhue Papers.

36. Sister Grace Marian, *The Honolulu Academy of Arts, Its Origin and Founder* (Honolulu: Honolulu Academy of Arts, 1967); "The Honolulu Academy of Art," *Magazine of Arts* 30 (February 1937), pp. 84–87; "The Honolulu Academy of Art and its part in contemporary American art," *London Studio* 15 (March 1938), pp. 143–45; James Shipsky, "Goodhue's Serene and Rewarding Museum," *AIA Journal* 71 (March 1982), pp. 64–71.

37. Bertram Goodhue, "The Home of the Future," pp. 449–55, 543–44.

38. BGG to Percy Nobbs, November 11, 1918, Goodhue Papers.

39. William Winthrop Kent, "The Modern Country House in California," *Country Life* 37 (April 1920), p. 126.

40. BGG to Cecil C. Brewer, September 24, 1917, Goodhue Papers. See also: "House of Philip W. Henry, Scarboro, N.Y.," *American Architect* 120 (December 21, 1921) and 121 (January 18, 1922), which was included in a portfolio of houses which have severe, stripped forms and simplified massing; Whitaker, *Bertram Grosvenor Goodhue*, plates 210–12.

41. BGG to John D. Moore, February 6, 1919, Goodhue Papers. For similar work, see Harold Eberlein, "Modern Cotswold at St. Martins, Pa.," *Architectural Forum* 33 (July 1920), pp. 7–16.

42. *Domestic Architecture of Harrie T. Lindeberg*, with an introduction by Royal Cortissoz (New York: William Helburn, Inc., 1940). See also, C. Matlack Price, "The New Spirit in Country House Design as Expressed by the Work of Harrie T. Lindeberg," *House Beautiful* 57 (February 1925), p. 128. In this context, it is interesting to observe the relationships between Goodhue's and Lindeberg's houses of this period with George Howe's "High Hollow." See Robert A. M. Stern, *George Howe: Toward a Modern American Architecture* (New Haven: Yale University Press, 1975), pp. 25–29.

43. BGG to C. Peake Anderson, November 12, 1918, Goodhue Papers.

44. "La Cabaña residence at Montecito, California," *Architectural Record* 48 (October 1920), pp. 313–16.

45. "Detail of the interior, Congregational Church, Montclair, New Jersey," *Architectural Record* 60 (October 1926), plate; "First Congregational Church, Montclair, N.J." *Architecture* 33 (June 1916), plate 91.

46. "Parish House of St. Peter's Church, Morristown, New Jersey," *Architectural Record* 51 (May 1922), pp. 410–12; Elliott Lindsley, *A History of Saint Peter's Church* (Morristown, New

Jersey: Saint Peter's Church, 1952).

47. "Grolier Club, 47 East 60th Street, New York City," *Architecture* 37 (June 1918), plates 101–102.

48. "Competitive Plans, City Hall, Waterbury, Conn.," *Architecture* 28 (December 15, 1913), pp. 286–88.

49. BGG to Edward E. Goodhue, October 13, 1914, Goodhue Papers.

50. BGG to John T. Comes, September 25, 1917, Goodhue Papers.

51. BGG to Ruth Baldwin Pierson, August 30, 1916, Goodhue Papers.

52. BGG to Ruth Baldwin Pierson, November 6, 1916, Goodhue Papers.

53. BGG to Edward E. Goodhue, November 19, 1913, Goodhue Papers.

54. Among Goodhue's extracurricular activities, he was a member of the Board of Visitors to the Columbia University School of Architecture from 1915 to 1921. In 1916, he was the chairman of the committee to judge the competition entries for the LeBrun Travelling Scholarship. The program that year was for the town center of a mining community in the American Southwest, a program similar to Goodhue's commission at Tyrone. The winner of the scholarship was Austin Whittlesey, who worked in Goodhue's office at the time, and who submitted a bold, picturesque grouping of buildings composed of stripped masses adorned with Saracenic ornament and portrayed principally in a watercolor perspective. Because of World War I, Whittlesey used his scholarship to travel to Spain and North Africa. See "The LeBrun Travelling Scholarship," *Architecture* 34 (December 1916), pp. 256–61. See also: BGG to Maurice Leon, November 21, 1916, Goodhue Papers; Austin Whittlesey, *The Minor Ecclesiastical, Domestic, and Garden Architecture of Southern Spain*, preface by Bertram Grosvenor Goodhue (New York: Architectural Book Publishing Co., 1917).

55. Interview with Hugh G. B. Goodhue by the Author, October 19, 1979; BGG to Percy E. Nobbs, March 10, 1910, Goodhue Papers.

56. "Monographs on Architectural Renderers: III. The Work of E. Donald Robb," *Brickbuilder* 23 (March 1914), pp. 55–57; "Monographs of Architectural Renderers: X. The Work of Birch Burdette Long," *Brickbuilder* 23 (November 1914), pp. 274–76.

57. BGG to Percy E. Nobbs, October 13, 1915, Goodhue Papers. Goodhue fired his employee, Raymond Hood, allegedly after learning that the younger man had attended the Ecole des Beaux Arts; see Francis S. Swales, "Draftsmanship and Architecture as Exemplified by the Work of Raymond M. Hood," *Pencil Points* 9 (May 1928), pp. 258–69.

58. "Twelfth Night in Mr. Goodhue's Office," *Pencil Points* 3 (February 1922), pp. 21–26. See also, BGG to the Editor of *Pencil Points*, March 10, 1924, Goodhue Papers, for his attitude toward his office as well as its organization. The letter is printed in full here:

> I have received a request from you for an expression of opinion as to the "human element in the architect's organization." I am not quite clear in my mind as to just what is meant by this phrase. At any rate, I have no knowledge of, and no dealings with, any inhuman element, though your very question would seem to suggest that there were offices in which the inhuman element predominated—which may very well be true.
>
> My mail is made up about as follows: advertisements destined for, and promptly received by, the waste paper basket—85%; requests for information of all sorts and kinds, of

270

which yours is one—10%. The disposition to see these follow the first lot is strong, but often cannot be humoured. There remains 5% of bona fide correspondence, and of this 5%, once in a while, there is one from a client and a new commission comes in—the saving leaven in the whole lot. Feeling better, I now go on to answer your question.

The practice of architecture is always, first and foremost, a profession, which means that the architect does not "go after" work. What would you think of a lawyer, or a doctor, who tried to increase his clientele or number of patients by getting such away from other practitioners? Yet the belief that this is tolerable behavior is strongly held in certain quarters, and seems to be constantly increasing. The "human element" begins right here, I think. If you mean the treatment accorded those who aid and abet me, then let me say that, whatever is in store for humanity after death, the belief of this office, which we try to carry out in practice, is, as I think I have said before in your columns, that everybody is entitled to life, liberty and—not the pursuit of happiness—but the actual possession of happiness itself as far as this can be provided. To this end, I have no time clock. In fact on the rare occasions when I, myself, keep office hours, have found that some trifling advantage of the absence of this useful instrument so beloved by the efficiency experts, has been taken. Nevertheless, the men do fill out time sheets, and though being largely of the artistic temperament and somewhat irregular as to the hours they keep, do keep them, for the thirty-nine hours of the working week are all on their time sheets. It is the custom in many offices to specialize the men. That is again *great* from the standpoint of the efficiency expert, and is the practice in vogue of every large factory. The temptation is strong to practice it here; but it doesn't seem just that because a man does a thing well he should do that and nothing else even though he does it in less time and with more profit to his employer. Certainly routine of any kind is not conducive to happiness, and certainly a variety of interests and pursuits is.

I had almost forgotten to state that there is a filing system and a clerical force here, and that while I realize that some of the "made by the foot and sold by the mile" architects offices have very much more capable organizations in this direction, the young men and women who compose it here are about as satisfactory as could be expected. To be sure, we often have an awful time finding some drawing that has got into the wrong file, in which case we speak harshly to the filing clerk; and once in a while an office boy puts the wrong letter into an envelope, but humanity is frail and I am sure that if I were out in the system trying to file drawings and mail letters instead of sitting here idling and writing letters to you, I should do even worse.

59. "The New Offices of Cram, Goodhue & Ferguson, New York," *Architecture* 27 (May 1913), pp. 95–100, 115–16.

60. BGG to Percy Nobbs, August 17, 1915, Goodhue Papers; interview with Hugh G. B. Goodhue by the Author, October 19, 1981; interview with Frances Goodhue Satterlee by the Author, November 28, 1977.

61. BGG to Edward E. Goodhue, October 4, 1921; BGG to Samuel S. Drury, February 8, 1922, Goodhue Papers.

62. Interview with Cleveland Dodge by the Author, May 21, 1980. In general, Goodhue was not a club man in New York, although he often was seen at lunch at the corner dining table at the Century Association, where he was fondly remembered for "his lazy smile and his whimsical view of the common things of life" (*Century Association: Report of the Board of Management*, p. 11, Century Association Archives). He tended to avoid organizations that were overtly associated with the dominant American classicism, like the National Academy of Design, to

which he was elected an Associate in 1917 and an Academician in 1923 (BGG to the National Academy of Design, April 28, 1923, NAD Archives). His reticence to socialize with his classicist peers was based on a mixture of awe and disdain, the on-going dilemma of the self-educated outsider who was uncomfortable with the New York circle of Beaux Arts architects. He preferred his membership in the Meno Keosawa Club in Ontario, Canada, where he would go in the autumn to hunt moose with fellow architects Cass Gilbert, Percy Nobbs, and Louis Ayres (BGG to Percy E. Nobbs, December 30, 1915, Goodhue Papers).

CHAPTER SEVEN

1. Henry-Russell Hitchcock and William Seale, *Temples of Democracy, The State Capitols of the USA* (New York: Harcourt, Brace, Jovanovich, 1976), pp. 272–80.

2. *Annual Report of the National Academy of Sciences, 1923–24*, p. 1, National Academy of Sciences Archives, Washington, D.C. (hereafter NAS Archives).

3. Bertram G. Goodhue, "Notes on Proposed Building for the National Academy of Sciences," April 7, 1920, NAS Archives (hereafter Project Notes), p. 1.

4. Project Notes, p. 1, NAS Archives. It was most likely one of these sketches that Hale presented informally to the Commission of Fine Arts in Washington, D.C., on December 21, 1917. The Commission felt the design was inappropriate for the Mall, suggesting instead one "along classic or semi-classic lines" (Minutes, Commission of Fine Arts, December 21, 1917). The idea of a building for the Academy on the Mall was informally discussed by the Commission as early as 1914 (Minutes, Commission of Fine Arts, May 8, 1914).

5. Project Notes, p. 1, NAS Archives.

6. Charles Moore, ed., *The Improvement of the Park System of the District of Columbia* (Washington, D.C.: Government Printing Office, 1902). See also: Charles Moore, *The Life and Times of Charles Follen McKim* (Boston: 1929); Charles Moore, *Daniel H. Burnham, Architect, Planner of Cities* (Boston: 1921); Thomas S. Hines, *Burnham of Chicago, Architect and Planner* (New York: Oxford University Press, 1974); John W. Reps, *Monumental Washington, The Planning and Development of the Capital Center* (Princeton, New Jersey: Princeton University Press, 1967), pp. 111–40; *The American Renaissance, 1876–1917* (New York: The Brooklyn Museum, 1979).

7. See *The American Renaissance 1876–1917*, pp. 74–109. Henry Bacon, who had been trained in the office of McKim, Mead & White, was appointed architect of the Lincoln Memorial, in part at the strong urging of Daniel Burnham, one of the framers of the McMillan Plan. For John Russell Pope's scheme, see *Brickbuilder* 23 (January 1914), p. 7. See also, Minutes, Commission of Fine Arts, July 31, 1911; March 22, 1912; and June 21, 1912.

8. Ninth Report of the Commission of Fine Arts, 1923–1924.

9. Project Notes, p. 2, NAS Archives.

10. Goodhue was concerned about the role of the Fine Arts Commission from the moment of its inception. In 1909, he wrote to the critic Oswald G. Villard, in reference to the latter's editorial on what was then called the President's Art Commission:

    . . . official art has always been a very terrible thing, and none of the great art epochs of the world have owed their impetus to anything other than an instinct in the public, quite a different thing from a statute. Furthermore, as the world of art here is constituted to-day such a board would necessarily be, and indeed evidently is, made up with an overwhelming preponderance of sympathizers with the modern French Beaux Arts sort of thing, killing in this way any healthy initiative from without. Furthermore, art by statute invariably is the art of the most definite set of rules. In classic work these rules are clearly codified, well understood, and readily followed, though it must be confessed there is a great difference in the quality of the work produced under their guidance. All rules in architecture save absolutely basic ones are outside the subject, and the "five orders" are entitled to no more veneration than all other good constructive form (BGG to Oswald G. Villard, January 23, 1909, Goodhue Papers).

11. BGG to John D. Moore, February 6, 1919, Goodhue Papers.

12. BGG to Dr. James R. Angell, November 7, 1919, NAS Archives. See also: BGG to George Ellery Hale, December 19, 1919; *Annual Report*, p. 4, NAS Archives. There was some confusion as to the budget of the proposed building which, of course, affected the design. Goodhue noted that when the project was first discussed with Hale, $4 million had been budgeted, but that by the summer of 1919, the actual figure available was $900,000. This conflicts with an annual report of 1923–1924 which lists an amount of $1,450,000.

13. Project Notes, p. 2, NAS Archives.

14. Ibid., p. 2.

15. Charles Moore to Senator Elihu Root, January 21, 1920, National Archives.

16. Project Notes, pp. 2–3, NAS Archives.

17. BGG to Dr. James R. Angell, November 7, 1919, NAS Archives.

18. Angell to BGG, November 15, 1919, NAS Archives.

19. Minutes, Commission of Fine Arts, March 26, 1920. See also, Memorandum: James R. Angell to H. A. Bumstead, June 26, 1920, NAS Archives.

20. Project Notes, p. 4, NAS Archives.

21. Charles Moore to BGG, June 28, 1920, National Archives.

22. Ibid.

23. Charles Moore to Charles Walcott, December 16, 1920, National Archives.

24. Minutes, Commission of Fine Arts, May 12, 1921. See also the Ninth Report of the Commission of Fine Arts, 1923–1924, p. 86. For a discussion of the completed building, see Wallace K. Harrison, "The Building of the National Academy of Sciences and the National Research Council," *Architecture* 50 (October 1924), pp. 329–32. See also, George Edgell, *The American Architecture of Today* (London: Charles Scribner's Sons, 1928), pp. 255–58.

25. *Who was Who in America*, vol. 4, p. 650.

26. Whitaker, *Bertram Grosvenor Goodhue* (reprint, New York: Da Capo Press, 1976), Introduction by Paul Goldberger, p. 2.

27. *Report of Nebraska State Capitol Commission to the Fiftieth Session of the Nebraska State Legislature* (hereafter *NSCC Report;* January 1, 1935), Nebraska State Historical Society Archives (hereafter State Archives). For a general discussion of the competition and the com-

pleted building, see Eric Scott McCready, "The Nebraska State Capitol: Its Design, Background, and Influence," *Nebraska History* 55 (Fall, 1974), pp. 324–461.

28. Thomas R. Kimball to William E. Hardy (Commission member), September 15, 1919, State Archives. Kimball listed his personal choice of the seven architects to be invited to participate in the competition: Bliss & Faville, San Francisco; McKim, Mead & White, New York City; H. Van Buren Magonigle, New York City; Perkins, Fellows & Hamilton, Chicago; John Russell Pope, New York City; Tracy & Swartwout, New York City; and Zantzinger, Borie & Medary, Philadelphia. To this group, he added twenty-five names he thought worthy of consideration. From New York City were: Henry Bacon; William Adams Delano; Cass Gilbert; Bertram G. Goodhue; Thomas Hastings; Robert Kohn; Kenneth M. Murchison; Charles A. Platt; George B. Post & Sons; James Gamble Rogers; and York & Sawyer. From Boston were: C. H. Blackall; Coolidge & Carlson; Ralph Adams Cram; Guy Lowell; Arthur Wallace Rice; and R. Clipston Sturgis. From Philadelphia were: Paul Cret; Day & Klauder; and Rankin, Kellogg & Crane. From Washington, D.C., were: E. W. Donn, Jr.; and Waddy B. Wood. Also listed were: Hewitt & Brown, Minneapolis; George S. Mills, Toledo; and Eames & Young, St. Louis.

29. *NSCC Report*, p. 6, State Archives.

30. "Program: Final Stage of Competition for the Selection of an Architect to design and supervise the construction of a Capitol for the State of Nebraska, January 16, 1920" (hereafter Competition Program), State Archives. The Program is reprinted; see Eric Scott McCready, "The Nebraska State Capitol," Appendix II, pp. 431–46.

31. Ibid.

32. Ibid.

33. Ibid.

34. Report of the Jury to the Nebraska State Capitol Commission, June 26, 1920, State Archives.

35. As quoted in Harry F. Cunningham, *The Capitol, Lincoln, Nebraska, An Architectural Masterpiece* (Lincoln: Johnson Publishing Co., 1954). A year before Goodhue's tower was accepted, a Nebraska citizen, S. L. Geisthardt, proposed a skyscraper Capitol in a naive sketch sent to the State Library. Paradoxically, it was ridiculed in a newspaper article. See *[Lincoln] Sunday Star Journal*, March 3, 1919, p. C-7.

36. "Nebraska Capitol Competition," *American Institute of Architects' Journal* 8 (1920), pp. 299–306. See also, Robert Imlay, "The Proposed Nebraska State Capitol," *Architectural Record* 48 (July 1920), pp. 75–78. Nine of the ten schemes were published in the summer of 1920. See: "Nebraska State Capitol Competition," *American Architect* 118 (July 21, 1920), pp. 79–80, plates; (July 28, 1920), plates; C. Howard Walker, "The Winning Design in the Nebraska Capitol Competition," *Architectural Review (Boston)* 11 (September 1920), pp. 81–87. The elevations of all the schemes were published; see "Nebraska State Capitol," *Western Architect* 29 (July 1920), pp. 66–67. See also, Whitaker, *Bertram Grosvenor Goodhue*, plates 214–25.

37. "Nebraska State Capitol Competition," *American Architect* 118 (July 21, July 28, 1920), plates.

38. "Architectural Derring-Do," *The New York Times*, July 16, 1920, p. 10:4.

39. Ibid.

40. "New Capitoline Architecture, Prairie Style," *The New York Times*, July 25, 1920, Magazine.

41. "Prairie Architecture," *The New York Times*, July 25, 1920, p. 2:2. Goodhue's reaction to the many published reviews was expressed in a letter of August 16, 1920, to Lee Lawrie:

> Nebraska has certainly succeeded in stirring up some row. I am distinctly shocked at the inference that seems to be everywhere made that it's so new in style to be absolutely "out of the void." Have I got to live up to this impression of the design [as quoted in the Lincoln *Sunday Journal and Star*, July 17, 1932]?

42. C. Matlack Price, *The Lincoln Star*, September 1, 1921.

43. Charles Herbert Reilly, *Representative British Architects of the Present Day* (Freeport, New York: 1931), pp. 142–56.

44. BGG to Edward E. Goodhue, July 15, 1920, Goodhue Papers.

45. Henry-Russell Hitchcock, "Frank Lloyd Wright and the 'Academic Tradition' of the early eighteen-nineties," *Journal of the Warburg and Courtauld Institutes* 7 (1944), pp. 46–63.

46. Lawrence Weaver, *Houses and Gardens by E. L. Lutyens* (London: Country Life, 1914); A.S.G. Butler, *The Architecture of Sir Edwin Lutyens* (London: Country Life, 1950); Arts Council of Great Britain, *Lutyens* (London: 1982); Henry-Russell Hitchcock, *In the Nature of Materials* (New York: Hawthorn Books, Inc., 1942; reissued, New York: Da Capo Press, 1975); Hitchcock, *Architecture: Nineteenth and Twentieth Centuries* (New York: Penguin, 1958), chapters 19, 24.

47. Peter Collins, *Concrete: the vision of a new architecture; a study of Auguste Perret and his precursors* (London: 1959); Esther McCoy, *Five California Architects* (New York: Reinhold Publishing Co., 1960), pp. 59–102; Hitchcock, *Architecture: Nineteenth and Twentieth Centuries*, chapters 18,19.

48. Albert Christ-Janer, *Eliel Saarinen* (Chicago: University of Chicago Press, 1948); Hitchcock, *Architecture: Nineteenth and Twentieth Centuries*, chapter 21.

49. Robert Grant Irving, *Indian Summer: Lutyens, Baker and Imperial Delhi* (New Haven: Yale University Press, 1982); Irving, "Architecture for Empire's Sake: Lutyens's Palace for Delhi," *Perspecta 18* (Cambridge, Mass.: M.I.T. Press, 1982), pp. 7–23.

50. *Lincoln Evening Journal*, May 13, 1921. In his article, Eric McCready incorrectly states that the Capitol Commission tried to rotate the building 90 degrees but that Goodhue was able to convince them not to. This view presumes that the current orientation was Goodhue's choice from the beginning. But the competition drawings and Goodhue's thesis both show that 15th Street, which is a north-south street, went under the proposed building to provide a protected vehicle entrance. Thus, the Capitol was originally proposed by Goodhue to face west. See McCready, "The Nebraska State Capitol," pp. 368–69.

51. BGG to William E. Hardy, July 9, 1921, State Archives.

52. *NSCC Report*, p. 7.

53. The complete charges filed by Johnson, together with Goodhue's defense, are these:

> 1. Replacement of reinforced concrete floor construction with a steel system. Goodhue preferred the better quality control of a steel system, even though it was somewhat more

expensive.

2. The drawing of the plumbing specifications for the building as a whole. Goodhue felt that only one contractor should be responsible for the quality of the work, not several contractors, and that the cost would be less if let as a unit.

3. Fifty or more changes required in the architect's plans. Goodhue noted that he could not discuss changes which he had not authorized and of which he had not been informed.

4. An acoustic specification which permitted only one bidder. Goodhue noted that Rumford acoustic tile and Akoustilith were made by only one company, and that the only alternative was heavy felt, which he thought unsuitable for a monumental building.

5. The use of screw nipples on the heating radiators. Goodhue argued that screw nipples were more costly but provided better performance.

6. Window specifications. Again, Goodhue defended a tightly drawn specification on the need for quality in a monumental building.

7. The use of an allowance clause to cover the large columns in the north vestibule. Goodhue noted that an allowance clause is a customary way to cover an item of particular artistic importance to a building that may not be firmly envisioned at the time of letting contracts, and that the marble columns constituted such an item.

8. The sculptural carving contract. Goodhue argued that the sculptor, Lawrie, should have his choice of firms to do the actual carving—in this case, Edward Ardolino—in order to truly embody the ideas and the spirit of the sculptor's work, and noted that if the Commission was so interested in economy, it seemed hardly worthwhile to employ a sculptor of Lawrie's known ability.

9. The hardware specification. Goodhue argued that his tightly drawn specification did not preclude competitive bidding, and submitted the same to two manufacturers for a confirming opinion.

10. The quality of the stone.

54. BGG to Alderson Horne, June 28, 1923, Goodhue Papers. See also, BGG to Edward E. Goodhue, March 17 and April 16, 1923, Goodhue Papers.

55. "New York Architect Vindicated," *The New York Times*, March 25, 1923, p. 21:4; "Capitol Board Members Give Johnson Warm Time," *Omaha World-Herald*, March 24, 1923, p. 1:2. See also: "Minutes of the Capitol Building Commission," February 23, 1923—June 28, 1923, Nebraska Archives; BGG to Edward E. Goodhue, March 17, April 16, June 13, 1923, Goodhue Papers.

56. BGG to Alderson B. Horne, June 28, 1923, Goodhue Papers.

57. For a complete discussion of the Capitol sculpture, see: Orville H. Zabel, "History in Stone: The Story in Sculpture on the Exterior of the Nebraska Capitol," *Nebraska History* 62 (Fall, 1981), pp. 285–367; *The Nebraska Capitol* (Lincoln: Nebraska State Capitol Commission, 1926); Charles Harris Whitaker and Hartley Burr Alexander, *The Architectural Sculpture of the State Capitol in Lincoln, Nebraska* (New York: Press of the American Institute of Architects, 1926); Thomas Rogers Kimball, "Review of *The Architectural Sculpture of the State Capitol in Lincoln, Nebraska*," *Western Architect* 36 (June 1927), pp. 89–92.

58. Hitchcock, *Architecture: Nineteenth and Twentieth Centuries*, p. 400. For discussion of the ideas and forms comprising current notions of "free-style classicism," see: Gavin Stamp, ed., "London 1900," *Architectural Design* 48 (1978), pp. 303–83; Charles Jencks, ed., "Post-Modern Classicism," *Architectural Design* 50 (1980), pp. 5–17; Jencks, ed., "Free-Style Classicism," *Architectural Design* 52 (1982), pp. 5–21; Demetri Porphyrios, ed., "Classicism is not a

Style," *Architectural Design* 52 (1982).

59. Albert Christ-Janer, *Eliel Saarinen*. The Helsinki Railroad Station and Lars Sonck's Kallio Church in Helsinki have been cited as influences on the Capitol by Hitchcock. Another possible influence, closer to home, is Price & McLanahan's Pennsylvania Freight Terminal in Chicago, a broad, low mass with a tall, sculpted tower; see Irving Pond, "An Appreciation of the Pennsylvania Freight Terminal Station, Chicago," *Western Architect* 28 (July 1919). George Edgell claimed that Goodhue's Capitol possessed a degree of refinement absent in contemporary German and Scandinavian work (*The American Architecture of Today*, p. 235).

60. See McCready, "The Nebraska State Capitol," pp. 375–91, for a discussion of Lawrie's career and his development of a new "archaistic" sculpture for the Capitol. See also: "Lawrie's Creed," *Art Digest* 6 (September 1, 1932), p. 29; "Lee Lawrie's Sculpture for the Nebraska State Capitol," *American Magazine of Art* 19 (January 1928), pp. 13–16; Walter R. Agard, *The New Architectural Sculpture* (New York: Oxford University Press, 1935); Hartley Burr Alexander, "The Sculpture of Lee Lawrie," *Architectural Forum* 54 (May 1931), pp. 587–600.

61. Zabel, "History in Stone," pp. 285–367. See also: Hartley Burr Alexander, "Nebraska's Monumental Capitol at Lincoln," *Western Architect* 32 (October 1923), pp. 113–16; McCready, "The Nebraska State Capitol," Appendix V, pp. 451–54; B. G. Goodhue, "Nebraska State Capitol," *American Architect* 121 (May 10, 1922), pp. 375–81.

62. See McCready, "The Nebraska State Capitol," pp. 393–403, Appendix VI, pp. 454–58. See also: Anne Lee, "Hildreth Meiere: Mural Painter," *Architectural Record* 62 (August 1927), pp. 103–12; Hartley B. Alexander, "Hildreth Meiere's work for Nebraska," *Architecture* 63 (June 1931), pp. 321–28; Hildreth Meiere, "The Question of Decoration," *Architectural Forum* 57 (July 1932), pp. 1–8; *Augustus Vincent Tack: 1870–1949* (Exhibition catalogue: The Hilson Gallery, Deerfield, Mass., 1968).

63. *American Architect* 145 (October 1934). The entire issue is devoted to the Capitol.

64. William Ward Watkin, "Impressions of Modern Architecture, Part 3, The New Manner in America," *Pencil Points* 12 (July 1931), pp. 521–30. See also: Watkin, "Part 1, The Search for a Direct Manner in Design," *Pencil Points* 12 (May 1931), pp. 355–62; and "Part 2, The New Manner in France and Northern Europe," *Pencil Points* 12 (June 1931), pp. 421–29.

65. "Louisiana State Capitol," *Architectural Forum* 57 (December 1932), pp. 519–34; Vincent Kubly, *The Louisiana Capitol, Its Art and Architecture* (Gretna, Louisiana: Pelican Publishing Co., 1977); "The New City Hall, Los Angeles, California," *American Architect* 131 (April 20, 1927), pp. 497–508; "American Insurance Union Citadel, Columbus, Ohio," *Architect* 11 (February 1929), pp. 525–31; "Bullock's Wilshire Department Store, Los Angeles," *Architectural Record* 67 (January 1930), pp. 51–64.

66. Raymond Hood, "The American Radiator Building," *American Architect* 126 (November 19, 1924), p. 472. See also, Harvey Wiley Corbett, "The American Radiator Building, New York," *Architectural Record* 55 (May 1924), pp. 473–77.

67. Hugh Ferriss, *The Metropolis of Tomorrow* (New York: Ives Washburn, 1929). See also, Clarence S. Stein, "The Art Museum of Tomorrow," *Architectural Record* 67 (January 1930), pp. 5–12.

68. Alan Balfour, *Rockefeller Center, Architecture as Theatre* (New York: McGraw-Hill, Inc., 1978); Carol Herselle Krinsky, *Rockefeller Center* (New York: Oxford University Press, 1978).

69. For the English publication of the Capitol, see: "Nebraska State Capitol Competition," *Architects' Journal* 52 (August 11, 1920), pp. 147–48; "The Nebraska State Capitol," *Architects' Journal* 55 (June 21, 1922), pp. 876–80. For the Cambridge University Library, see: "The University Library, Cambridge," *Architect & Building News* (London) 140 (October 12, 1934), pp. 38–43; (October 19, 1934), pp. 75–79; "University Library, Cambridge," *Architects' Journal* 80 (October 18, 1934), pp. 559–68; "University Library," *Architectural Review* (London) 76 (November 1934), pp. 168–72, plates 2–7. See also, Gavin Stamp, "Giles Gilbert Scott, The Problem of Modernism," *AD Profiles 24: Britain in the Thirties* (London: Architectural Design, 1979), p. 77.

70. The ambiguous formal quality of the Capitol allowed Vincent Scully to relate its design to the rise of fascist architecture in Europe. It should be recalled in this connection that in the 1930s stripped classicism was used for public buildings in both totalitarian and democratic societies. See Scully, *American Architecture and Urbanism* (New York: Frederick A. Praeger, 1969), p. 139.

CHAPTER EIGHT

1. "The Thirty-sixth Annual Exhibition of The Architectural League of New York," *Architectural Review* (Boston) 12 (April 1921), pp. 97–104. See also, "The 35th Annual Chicago Architectural Exhibition," *Western Architect* 31 (April 1922), pp. 49–50, which observed that Goodhue's perspective drawing "dominated the room in which it was hung, and, of course, was the 'wonderful drawing' of the Exhibit."

2. "No Limit in Sight for Future Skyscrapers," *The New York Times*, July 22, 1923. Wright's proposed "Mile High Tower" for Chicago was likewise intended to be the tallest building in the world, and it, too, was portrayed in an atmospheric and poetic drawing.

3. Irving Pond, "Zoning and the Architecture of High Buildings," *Architectural Forum* 25 (October 1921), pp. 131–33; Aymar Embury II, "New York's New Architecture: The effect of the Zoning Law on high buildings," *Architectural Forum* 25 (October 1921), pp. 119–24; Harvey W. Corbett, "Zoning and the Envelope of the Building," *Pencil Points* 4 (April 1923), pp. 15–18; Arnold Lehman, *The New York Skyscraper: A History of its Development, 1870–1939* (Ph.D. diss., Yale University, 1974); Rosemarie Haag Bletter and Cervin Robinson, *Skyscraper Style: Art Deco New York* (New York: Oxford University Press, 1975); Paul Goldberger, *The Skyscraper* (New York: Alfred Knopf, 1981).

4. BGG to Henry Lanier, July 13, 1914, Goodhue Papers. In the letter, Goodhue shows an understanding of the problems of the tall building:

> As you know I have, unfortunately for my pocket book, built no skyscrapers, though I have made one or two attempts to do so, feeling that in this class of work it would be possible to effect a very great betterment. Curiously enough, here the businessman seems to look on the matter in a very superficial fashion, and in the few cases with which I have had to do, to consider only the value of the real estate, the number and rentable area of the floors, and the amount of natural illumination provided, plus, of course, the rate per foot obtaining in the neighborhood in which the building is to be built, the percentage of possible vacancies, rates of interest and the like; this without at all considering the fact that a well planned and attractively designed building would be sure to decrease the percentage of vacancies, and that a building where economy of construction was joined to art would be certain to be built for less per cubic foot than the usual run of such things.
>
> As it is, the tall buildings seem to be divided into two classes, the extremely gorgeous and elaborately carried out ones, such as, for instance, the Blair Building, the Bankers' Trust and the new Equitable . . . and the type that is just the reverse where everything is "skinned" to the uttermost minimum.

For the only known early Goodhue design of an office building, see Montgomery Schuyler, "The

Works of Cram, Goodhue & Ferguson," *Architectural Record* 29 (January 1911), pp. 24, 54, 55.

5. Watkin, "Impressions of Modern Architecture, Part 3, The New Manner in America," *Pencil Points* 12 (July 1931), p. 527. George Edgell likewise praised the Convocation Tower as "new, daring, aspiring, and refined, symbolizing the boldness and the taste of American architecture today"; see Edgell, *The American Architecture of Today* (London: Charles Scribner's Sons, 1928), p. 369.

6. "The Competition for a Memorial for Kansas City," *Western Architect* 30 (July 1921), pp. 69–71. Plates and commentary are in *Western Architect* 30 (August 1921), plates 1–10. See also: Charles H. Whitaker, *Bertram Grosvenor Goodhue* (New York: American Institute of Architects Press, 1925), plates 226–29; Oliver Reagan, *American Architecture in the 20th Century* (New York: Architectural Book Publishing Co., 1929).

7. "The Competition for a Memorial for Kansas City," p. 69.

8. Ibid., p. 71.

9. Ibid., p. 69–70.

10. Ibid., p. 69. In addition to Goodhue, the four nonlocal competitors invited to enter were: Bliss & Faville, San Francisco; Paul P. Cret and Zantzinger, Borie & Medary, Philadelphia; H. Van Buren Magonigle, New York; and York & Sawyer, New York (the latter did not finally submit). Ten local competitors took part, three of whom withdrew before the deadline. Those remaining were Brostrom & Drotts; Edward Delk; Greenebaum, Hardy & Schumacher; Hoit, Price, & Barnes; Keene & Simpson; Selby Kurfiss; and Wight & Wight.

11. Ibid., p. 69. Goodhue indicated the fervor of his involvement in the competition in a letter of June 14, 1921, to W. E. Hardy, in Lincoln:

> To begin with, it was only last Friday that we sent off the set of competitive drawings for the Kansas City War Memorial. This thing has been nearly killing me and was really what sent me off to Cuba. Such of my architect friends that have seen it tell me it's the finest set of drawings ever made, but this doesn't necessarily win the competition. Personally, I am stuck on it, indeed I think it's altogether too good to be successful. . . .

12. "The Competition for the Liberty Memorial at Kansas City, Missouri," *Architecture* 44 (August 1921), p. 235.

13. Talbot Hamlin, *The American Spirit in Architecture* (New Haven: Yale University Press, 1926), p. 229. See also, *Architecture* 58 (November 1928), pp. 289–94, for Magonigle's World War Memorial in New Britain, Connecticut.

14. "The Competition for the Liberty Memorial," p. 238. For a review of other work by Cret, see "Paul Cret—Master of Design," *Pencil Points* 19 (October 1938), pp. 608–38.

15. "The Competition for the Liberty Memorial," p. 238.

16. The scheme is portrayed in a perspective by the famous English etcher and watercolorist, William Walcot, who did his best work on grand and romantic classical designs, and who often worked for Lutyens, especially in New Delhi. See Gavin Stamp, *The Great Perspectivists* (New York: Rizzoli International Publications, Inc., 1982), p. 139. The Walcot rendering of the Kansas City Competition entry is in the care of Hugh Goodhue.

17. "The Competition for the Liberty Memorial," pp. 235–38.

18. Hamlin, "Bertram Grosvenor Goodhue," *The Nation* 120 (June 10, 1925), p. 661.

19. *The International Competition for a New Administration Building for The Chicago Tribune* (Chicago: The Tribune Company, 1923); Irving Pond, "High Buildings and Beauty, Part I," *Architectural Forum* 38 (February 1923), p. 42.

20. Colin Rowe, "Chicago Frame, Chicago's Place in the modern movement," *Architectural Review* (London) 120 (November 1956), pp. 285–89.

21. *The International Competition.*

22. Ibid.

23. Ibid.

24. Irving Pond, "High Buildings and Beauty, Part I," *Architectural Forum* 38 (February 1923), p. 42.

25. Pond, "High Buildings and Beauty, Part II," *Architectural Forum* 38 (April 1923), p. 181.

26. John Mead Howells and Raymond Hood, "The Tribune Tower, Chicago," *Architectural Forum* 43 (October 1925), pp. 185–90.

27. Pond, "High Buildings, II," p. 180. Winners and honorable mentions published in *Western Architect* 32 (January 1923), frontispiece and plates 1–7. See also, "Designs Awarded Honorable Mention—Chicago Tribune Competition," *American Architect* 123 (January 3, 1923), pp. 23–25.

28. Thomas Tallmadge, "A Critique of the Chicago Tribune Building Competition," *Western Architect* 32 (January 1923), pp. 7–8.

29. Louis H. Sullivan, "The Chicago Tribune Competition," *Architectural Record* 53 (February 1923), pp. 151–57. See also, Walter L. Creese, "Saarinen's Tribune Design," *Journal of the Society of Architectural Historians* 6 (July–December 1947), pp. 1–5.

30. Hamlin, *The American Spirit in Architecture*, p. 198.

31. Tallmadge, p. 8.

32. Pond, "High Buildings, I," p. 42.

33. Pond, "High Buildings, II," p. 180.

34. Tallmadge, p. 8.

35. BGG to Giles Gilbert Scott, January 7, 1924, Goodhue Papers.

36. William Goodyear, "The Memorial Quadrangle and the Harkness Memorial Tower at Yale," *American Architect* 120 (October 26, 1921), pp. 299–314; Susan Ryan, "The Architecture of James Gamble Rogers at Yale University," *Perspecta 18* (Cambridge, Mass.: M.I.T. Press, 1982), pp. 24–41. See also the architect's own comments on the project: James Gamble Rogers, "The Memorial Quadrangle, Yale University, New Haven, Connecticut," *American Architect* 120 (November 9, 1921), pp. 333–42.

37. John Russell Pope, *Yale University, A Plan for its Future Building* (New Haven: 1919).

38. Ibid.

39. Ibid.

40. BGG to William Lethaby, March 7, 1924, Goodhue Papers.

41. Carleton Winslow, "The Los Angeles Public Library," *Western Architect* 36 (February 1926), pp. 21–22, frontispiece, plates 19–26, 29, 30. Another design for the library, completed by Siegfried Goetze in a Viennese Secessionist style, which may have been an unsolicited scheme, is published in *Architect and Engineer of California* 50 (July 1917).

42. Winslow, "The Los Angeles Public Library."

43. H. B. Alexander, "The Sculpture and Inscriptions on the Los Angeles Public Library," *Western Architect* 36 (February 1927), pp. 19–21. See the *Handbook of the Central Building, Los Angeles Public Library* (1927) for a more complete discussion of the program of art and symbolism in the building.

44. Henry-Russell Hitchcock, *Architecture: Nineteenth and Twentieth Centuries* (New York: Penguin, 1958), p. 400. Hitchcock likened it to a "project by Tony Garnier."

45. Merrill Gage, "The Art of the Los Angeles Public Library," *Artland* (August 1926).

46. Lewis Mumford, "American Architecture Today," *Architecture* 58 (October 1928), p. 190.

47. Ibid., p. 189.

48. Ibid., p. 190.

49. Henry-Russell Hitchcock, *Modern Architecture: Romanticism and Reintegration* (New York: Payson & Clark, 1929).

50. Fiske Kimball, "Goodhue's Architecture: A Critical Estimate," *Architectural Record* 62 (December 1927), pp. 537–39. See also Review of Whitaker, *Bertram Grosvenor Goodhue* in *The Christian Science Monitor*, October 8, 1925.

51. Howell Lewis Shay, "Modern Architecture and Tradition," *T-Square Club Journal* 1 (January 1931), p. 14. See also, Hamlin, "Bertram Grosvenor Goodhue," pp. 660–61.

52. The copy of *The Glorious Mystery* containing the sketch is in the care of Hugh G. B. Goodhue.

53. BGG to Whitaker, June 21, 1922, Goodhue Papers.

54. BGG to Marie Bachman Whittlesey, January 10, 1924, Goodhue Papers. See also, BGG to Alderson B. Horne, December 15, 1922, Goodhue Papers. In regard to Goodhue's health, see: BGG to Edward E. Goodhue, April 18 and April 21, 1921, Goodhue Papers; BGG to Constance Alexander, March 19, 1924, Goodhue Papers; BGG to George Ellery Hale, January 25, 1923, NAS Archives.

    The church in Cleveland was the Epworth-Euclid Church. The self-conducted walking tour notes for the building state that

    . . . surveying the land and noting its lovely command of the nearby lagoon and University circle, Mr. Goodhue worked out his first concept of its design on the back of a menu in the nearby Clark's Coffee Shop. He visualized an edifice reminiscent of the famous French church, Mont Saint Michel.

    Thus, in one of his last works, Goodhue returned again to the romantic image that inspired him in his youth; see Whitaker, *Bertram Grosvenor Goodhue*, plate 194.

55. The almost total eclipse of Goodhue's reputation in the late 1920s and 1930s has parallels in

the career of Wright, as Hitchcock has so poignantly made clear. During the same years, Wright was similarly forgotten, only to resume his career in 1936 with the remarkable Kaufmann House and the Johnson Administration Building.

56. Death Certificate, Department of Health, City of New York. See *The New York Times*, April 26, 1924, p. 14:3 (Editorial Tribute). The details of Goodhue's death were provided by Hugh G. B. Goodhue and Frances Goodhue Satterlee: on the evening of April 23, 1924, Goodhue and his wife, Lydia, attended a dinner in honor of Dr. Howard Carter, the famed discoverer of the tomb of Tutankhamen. From dinner, the party moved on to the theater. At intermission, Goodhue complained of discomfort and returned home to rest. Lydia Goodhue returned home later, and there she found her husband in the living room of their apartment where he had died of a heart attack, attended by the "house" doctor.

        In 1925, Goodhue was posthumously awarded the Gold Medal by the American Institute of Architects. It was presented to Lydia Goodhue at a dinner at the Metropolitan Museum of Art, when the 1924 Gold Medal was presented to Edwin Lutyens. For transcripts of speeches related to both award presentations, see "Fifty-Eighth Annual Convention, A.I.A.; Presentation of Gold Medals and Fourth Day's Proceedings," *American Architect* 127 (May 20, 1925), pp. 439–43.

57. George S. Koyl, ed., *American Architects Directory* (New York: 1955), pp. 373, 397, 433. For the late churches, see: "Study, St. John's Church, Buffalo, New York," *Architect* 6 (1926), p. 696; "St. John's Episcopal Church, Buffalo, N.Y.," *American Architect* 133 (March 20, 1928), p. 403; "Sanctuary, Christ Church, Bronxville, New York," *Architect* 6 (1926), p. 694; "Christ Church," *Architect* 7 (1926–27), pp. 599–601; "Trinity Lutheran Church, Fort Wayne, Indiana," *Architect* 7 (1926–27), plates 39–41; "Christ Church, Cranbrook, Michigan," *American Magazine of Art* 20 (June 1929), pp. 219–25; "Church of the Heavenly Rest," *Yearbook, Architectural League of New York*, 1930 (no pagination). See also, "Residence of Harold Castle, Esq., Kailua, Oahu, T. H.," *Yearbook, Architectural League of New York*, 1930 (no pagination).

58. Giles Gilbert Scott, *Architectural Association Journal* 41 (April 1926), pp. 205–6.

59. Ibid. See also: Francis S. Swales, "Bertram Grosvenor Goodhue, Architect, Designer, and Draftsman, 1869–1924," *Pencil Points* 5 (June 1924), pp. 42–56; H. F. Cunningham, "Mr. Goodhue, the First True Modern," *American Institute of Architects' Journal* 16 (1928), pp. 246–48; Donn Barber, "Bertram G. Goodhue, FAIA, an Appreciation," *American Architect* 125 (May 21, 1924), pp. 477–78; Lawrence F. Abbott, "Bertram Goodhue," *American Architect* 125 (May 21, 1924), p. 478; "Bertram Grosvenor Goodhue," *Architectural Record* 55 (May 1924), p. 469; "Bertram Grosvenor Goodhue," *American Institute of Architects' Journal* 15 (May 1925), p. 155; L. B. Budden, "Bertram Grosvenor Goodhue: An Appreciation," *Architects' Journal* 59 (May 21, 1924), pp. 857–58.

60. "Tomb of Bertram Grosvenor Goodhue (from the completed model)," *Architecture* 57 (1928), pp. 205–6; "Bertram Grosvenor Goodhue Memorial," *Pencil Points* 9 (August 1928), p. 323.

LIST OF BUILDINGS AND PROJECTS

Abbreviations: BGG: Bertram Grosvenor Goodhue
                 CWG: Cram, Wentworth & Goodhue
                 CGF: Cram, Goodhue & Ferguson
                 CGF/NY: New York office of Cram, Goodhue & Ferguson
                 MMP: Bertram Grosvenor Goodhue Associates; later
                             evolved to Mayers, Murray & Phillip

1889   Competitive design for Cathedral of Saint John the Divine, New York City (BGG)

1890   Winning competitive design for Cathedral of Saint Matthew, Dallas, Texas (BGG)

1891–1892   Proposed Cathedral of Saint Matthew, Dallas, Texas (CWG)

1891–1895   All Saints' Church, Ashmont, Massachusetts (CWG); reredos, 1899 (CGF)

1892   Church of Saint John the Evangelist, St. Paul, Minnesota (CWG)

1892–1893   Saint Paul's Church, Brockton, Massachusetts (CWG)

1893   Competitive design for City Hall, New York City (CWG)

1893   Walter Phelps Dodge House, Simsbury, Connecticut (CWG)

1893–1894   Christ Church, Hyde Park, Massachusetts (CWG)

1893–1894   Church of the Open Word, Newtonville, Massachusetts (CWG)

1894   Knapp House, Fall River, Massachusetts (CWG)

1894   Merrill House, Little Boars Head, New Hampshire (CWG)

1894   First Congregational Church, Plymouth, Massachusetts (CWG)

1894   Proposed Unitarian Church, Somerville, Massachusetts (CWG)

1894–1899   All Saints' Church, Brookline, Massachusetts (CWG)

1894–1904   Saint Andrew's Church, Detroit, Michigan (CWG & CGF)

1895–1896   Second Congregational Church, Exeter, New Hampshire (CWG)

1895–1898   Newton Corner Methodist Episcopal Church, Newton Corner, Massachusetts (CWG)

1895–1900   Church of SS. Peter and Paul, Fall River, Massachusetts (CWG & CGF)

1896   "Church of Saint Kavin, Traumburg, Bohemia" (BGG)

1896   Proposed Saint Paul's Church, Rochester, New York (CWG)

LIST OF BUILDINGS AND PROJECTS

1896	Christ Church, Waltham, Massachusetts (CWG)
1896	The Phillips Church, Exeter, New Hampshire (CWG)
1896–1899	Public Library, Fall River, Massachusetts (CWG & CGF)
1897	"The Villa Fosca and its Garden, Italy" (BGG)
1897–1898	Church of Our Savior, Middleborough, Massachusetts (CGF)
1897–1910	Saint Stephen's Church, Fall River, Massachusetts (CWG & CGF)
1898	Proposed First Parish Meeting House, Cambridge, Massachusetts (CGF)
1898–1902	Deborah Cook Sayles Public Library, Pawtucket, Rhode Island (CGF)
1899	"Monteventoso, Italy" (BGG)
1899	Competitive design for a memorial monument, Dorchester Heights, Massachusetts (CGF)
1899	Proposed Carnegie Library, Atlanta, Georgia (CGF)
1899	Proposed Chickamauga Memorial Arch (CGF)
1899	Proposed house in Athens, Ohio (CGF)
1899	Richmond Court apartment house, Boston, Massachusetts (CGF)
1899	Saint Luke's Hospital (altar and reredos), Roxbury, Massachusetts (CGF)
1899–1906	Saint Stephen's Church, Cohasset, Massachusetts (CGF)
1900–1902	Emmanuel Church, Newport, Rhode Island (CGF)
1901	Public Library, Nashua, New Hampshire (CGF)
1902	Saint Mary's Church, Walkersville, Ontario, Canada (CGF)
1902	Mortuary Chapel for Lewis Day, Norwood, Massachusetts (CGF)
1902	*El Fureidis*, James Waldron Gillespie House, Montecito, California (CGF)
1902	Campus plan for Sweet Briar Institute, Sweet Briar, Virginia (CGF)
1903–1910	Campus plan and additions to the United States Military Academy, West Point, New York, including the chapel, post headquarters, riding hall, and many lesser buildings, including stables, cadet barracks, and officer housing (CGF)
1904	Competitive design for Cathedral of Saint John in the Wilderness, Denver, Colorado (CGF)
1904–1906	Hibbard Memorial Chapel, Grace Church, Chicago, Illinois (CGF/NY)
1904	Proposed house for E. H. Harriman, Arden, New York (CGF/NY)
1905	*La Santisima Trinidad* pro-cathedral of Havana, Cuba (CGF/NY)
1905–1913	Saint Thomas's Church, New York City (CGF); reredos, 1914–1920 (BGG)
1906	Saint James's Church, South Pasadena, California (CGF/NY); chancel, 1914 (BGG); tower, 1924 (BGG)
1907	All Saints' Cathedral, Halifax, Nova Scotia, Canada (CGF/NY)
1907	Proposed "House of Studies," Washington, D.C. (CGF/NY)
1907	Proposed "Community House for the Paulist Fathers," New York City (CGF/NY)

1907–1909	Saint John's Church, West Hartford, Connecticut (CGF/NY)
1908	Christ Church, West Haven, Connecticut (CGF/NY)
1908	Goodhue House renovation, New York City (CGF/NY)
1908–1913	Taft School, Watertown, Connecticut (CGF/NY)
1909	Saint Mark's Church, Mt. Kisco, New York (CGF/NY); tower, 1920 (BGG)
1909	Russell Sage Memorial Presbyterian Church, Far Rockaway, New York (CGF/NY)
1909–1910	Dutch Reformed Church ("South Church"), New York City (CGF/NY)
1909	Campus plan for the Rice Institute, Houston, Texas (CGF); individual buildings by Cram & Ferguson
1909–1912	First Baptist Church, Pittsburgh, Pennsylvania (CGF/NY)
1910	Saint Paul's Church, New Haven, Connecticut (CGF/NY)
1910	Proposed cathedral and hospital, Los Angeles, California (CGF/NY)
1910	Saint John's Church, Newport, Rhode Island (CGF/NY)
1910	Second Presbyterian Church, Lexington, Kentucky (CGF/NY)
1910	Trinity Church, Durham, North Carolina (CGF/NY)
1910	Trinity Chapel, Trinity Church, Buffalo, New York (CGF/NY)
1910–1913	Kitchi Gammi Club, Duluth, Minnesota (CGF/NY)
1910–1915	Saint Paul's Church, Duluth, Minnesota (CGF/NY)
1910	G. G. Hartley office building, Duluth, Minnesota (CGF/NY)
1910	Cavour Hartley House, Duluth, Minnesota (CGF/NY)
1910–1914	Chapel of the Intercession, New York City (CGF/NY)
1911	Competitive design for Northwestern University, Evanston, Illinois (CGF/NY)
1911	Washington Hotel, Colón, Panama Canal Zone (CGF/NY)
1911–1915	Panama-California Exposition, San Diego, California: Consulting Architect (BGG); individual buildings (CGF/NY)
1911–1924	Proposed Cathedral of the Incarnation, Baltimore, Maryland (CGF/NY & BGG)
1913	Competitive design for a city hall, Waterbury, Connecticut (CGF/NY)
1913	New York office of Cram, Goodhue & Ferguson (CGF/NY)
1913–1915	Parish House of Saint Peter's Church, Morristown, New Jersey (CGF/NY & BGG)
1913–1916	Campus plan and buildings for the Virginia Military Institute, Lexington, Virginia (CGF/NY & BGG)
1913–1918	J. E. Aldred House, Locust Valley, New York (CGF/NY & BGG)
1914–1916	Congregational Church, Montclair, New Jersey (BGG)
1914–1918	Church of Saint Vincent Ferrer, New York City (BGG)
1914–1918	Company town plan and individual buildings, Tyrone, New Mexico (BGG)

LIST OF BUILDINGS AND PROJECTS

1914–1919	Saint Bartholomew's Church, New York City (BGG); dome and community house, 1930 (MMP)
1915	Proposed house for Frederick Peterson, Westchester County, New York (BGG)
1915–1916	Herbert Coppell House, Pasadena, California (BGG)
1915–1917	Campus plan for the California Institute of Technology (BGG)

> Gates Chemistry Building, 1916 (BGG); Annex, 1927 (MMP)
> Bridge Physics Laboratory, 1922 (BGG); First Annex, 1924 (BGG); Second Annex, 1925 (BGG & MMP)
> Culbertson Hall, 1922 (BGG)
> High Potential Research Laboratory, 1923 (BGG)
> Dabney Hall, 1928 (MMP)
> Kerckhoff Biology Laboratory, 1928 (MMP); Annex, 1939 (MMP)
> Robinson Astrophysics Laboratory, 1932 (MMP)
> Arms Geology Laboratory, 1938 (MMP)
> Mudd Geology Laboratory, 1938 (MMP)

1915–1918	Henry Dater House, Montecito, California (BGG)
1916–1917	Grolier Club, New York City (BGG)
1916–1917	Montecito Country Club, Santa Barbara, California (BGG)
1917	Campus plans for Oahu College and Kamehameha School, Honolulu, Hawaii (BGG)
1918	United States Marine Corps base, San Diego, California (BGG)
1918	United States Naval Air Station, San Diego, California (BGG)
1918	Philip Henry House, Scarborough, New York (BGG)
1918	Walter Douglas House, Scarborough, New York (BGG)
1918	Proposed Goodhue House, Montecito, California (BGG)
1918–1928	Rockefeller Chapel, University of Chicago, Chicago, Illinois (BGG & MMP)
1919–1924	National Academy of Sciences Building, Washington, D.C. (BGG)
1920	*La Cabaña*, Goodhue House, Montecito, California (BGG)
1920–1924	Proposed Sterling Memorial Library, Yale University, New Haven, Connecticut (BGG)
1920–1932	Nebraska State Capitol, Lincoln (BGG & MMP)
1921	Proposed Convocational Building, New York City (BGG)
1921	Competitive design for the Liberty Memorial, Kansas City, Missouri (BGG)
1921	Proposed church in Watertown, Connecticut (BGG)
1922	Competitive design for the Tribune Building, Chicago, Illinois (BGG)
1921–1926	Public Library, Los Angeles, California (BGG, MMP; Carleton Winslow, associated architect)
1922–1927	Honolulu Academy of Arts, Hawaii (BGG & MMP)
1923–1924	Wolfshead Society Building, Yale University, New Haven, Connecticut (BGG)
1924–1926	Christ Church, Bronxville, New York (BGG & MMP)
1924–1926	Trinity Lutheran Church, Fort Wayne, Indiana (BGG & MMP)
1924–1928	Epworth-Euclid Church, Cleveland, Ohio (BGG, MMP, and Walker & Weeks)

INDEX

SOURCES OF ILLUSTRATIONS

Photographs

American Architect 118, July 21, 1920: 129; July 28, 1920: 130

American Architect & Building News 30, November 29, 1890 (courtesy of Richard Longstreth): 5; 52, May 9, 1896: 11, 12; 50, October 26, 1895 (courtesy of Richard Longstreth): 13

American Churches: 38, 52, 59

American Country Homes of Today: 28

Architectural Forum 26, January 1917: 66, 26, March 1917: 68, 69

Architectural Record 29, January 1911: 33, 70, 71, 78

Architectural Review (Boston) 1 August 1, 1892: 9, 10; 4, 1897: 20; 5, 1898: 23; 18, August 1911: 89

L'Architecture aux Etats-Unis (courtesy of the Cooper-Hewitt Museum): 72, 73, 74

Architecture 27, May 1913: 119;44, August 1921: 149

Courtesy of R. O. Blechman: 120

A Book of Architectural and Decorative Drawings by Bertram Grosvenor Goodhue: 17, 18, 19, 21, 22, 24, 25, 26, 48

Building 7, September 3, 1887: 1; July 23, 1887: 2

California Institute of Technology: 107, 108

Cathedral of Saint John the Divine, New York, New York: 3, 4

Commission of Fine Arts Archives: 121, 122

G. Condra (courtesy of the Nebraska State Historical Society): 141

Dick Fowler (courtesy of Saint Mark's Church): 50, 51

Bertram Grosvenor Goodhue, Architect and Master of Many Arts: 31, 39, 49, 53, 57, 58, 79, 87, 98, 105, 106, 109, 114, 116, 127, 147, 148, 151, 152

Samuel Gottscho: 131, 133, 135, 142, 144, 146

Lockwood Hoehl: 54, 55, 56

The Honolulu Academy of Arts: 111, 112, 113

SOURCES OF ILLUSTRATIONS

House & Garden 4, September 1903: 27

Courtesy of Hoyle, Doran & Berry, Architects: 8

Richard Hufnagle, Elinore Brown Collection (courtesy of the Nebraska State Historical Society): 134, 136, 138, 139, 140, 143, 145

The International Competition for a New Administration Building for the Chicago Tribune: 150

Wayne McCall: 29, 115

Masterpieces of Architecture in the United States: 94

The Museum of the City of New York, Wurts Collection: 40, 41, 42, 43, 44, 46, 60, 61, 62, 63, 64, 65, 90, 96, 97, 101, 118, 160

National Academy of Sciences: 123, 124, 126

Nebraska State Historical Society: 132

Richard Oliver: 100

Marvin Rand: 154, 155, 156, 157

Rice University Woodson Research Center Fondren Library: 75, 76, 77

Saint Bartholomew's Church Archives: 103, 104

Saint Thomas's Church Archives (courtesy of Gerald Allen): 45

San Diego Historical Society, Title Insurance and Trust Collection: 80, 83, 84, 85, 86

Courtesy of Frances Goodhue Satterlee: Frontispiece

The Deborah Cook Sayles Public Library: 15, 16

Security Pacific National Bank Photograph Collection/Los Angeles Public Library: 158

Taft School Archives: 67

United States Military Academy Archives: 30, 32, 34, 35, 36, 37

The Works of Cram & Ferguson: 7

Drawings

Chris Cullen (courtesy of the *American Institute of Architects' Journal*): 110

Bertram Goodhue (courtesy of John Rivers): 6, 14, 47, 88, 93, 99; (courtesy of Hugh G. B. Goodhue): 117, 137, 159

Diane Neff: 102, 125

Richard Oliver: 81, 82, 128, 153

The typeface used in this book is Cheltenham Wide,
designed by Bertram Grosvenor Goodhue in 1904.